Contents

Acknowledgements

The authors and publisher would like to thank the following for permission to reproduce copyright material: John Murray (Publishing) Ltd, London, UK, for tables 3.1 and 3.2; Shell Centre for Mathematical Education/Joint Matriculation Board, University of Nottingham, UK, for examples 3.6–3.10 and 3.16–3.18; Shell Centre for Mathematical Education, for example 3.14; Shell Centre for Mathematical Education/Joint Matriculation Board, for examples 4.2 and 4.3, published by Longman UK Limited; Australian Bureau of Statistics, ACT, for example 5.2; News Limited, NSW, for example 5.3; the Attorney General, Western Australia, for example 5.7; WestEd Media, Ministry of Education, WA, for example 5.8; Editorial Board of *Education Research and Perspectives* (formerly *The Educand* 1950–60 and *The Australian Journal of Higher Education* 1961–73), The University of Western Australia, WA, for example 5.13; Wadsworth Publishing Company for example 5.14 © 1973; Aldine de Gruyter, A division of Walter de Gruyter, Inc, Scholarly and Scientific Publishers, for example 5.15 © 1984; WestEd Media, Ministry of Education, WA, for example 7.3; Curriculum Development Centre, ACT, for examples 8.1 and 8.2, and figure 8.2.

Every effort has been made to contact the copyright owners of the table in example 5.6, but without success. We would be grateful to hear from anyone able to provide relevant information.

Preface

To be numerate is to function effectively mathematically in one's daily life, at home and at work. And 'being numerate' is one of the major intended outcomes of schooling in Australia, now as it has been in the past and will be for the forseeable future. The kinds of mathematical ideas and skills needed by people in order to function effectively in daily life are changing, however, and are likely to continue to change. The need for certain mathematical skills, particularly arithmetic and algebraic computation, is decreasing due to the ready availability and portability of calculators and computers. At the same time, other mathematical ideas, for example those associated with probability, statistics, orders of magnitude and estimation are assuming increasing importance, as is the need to understand the assumptions upon which a prediction or procedure is based. These are essential aspects of being numerate — permeating the media as they do — and are required for all levels of personal decision-making from relatively routine choices of car insurance to more complex decisions which may be necessary in court cases or in developing a viewpoint on the most appropriate balance between development and the environment.

It is disconcerting, therefore, to note that the core of mathematics taught in many Australian schools is surprisingly similar in content, and often also in pedagogy, to much of the mathematics taught early in this century. Changes brought about by such movements as 'new maths' in the 1960s and early 1970s and 'problem solving' in the 1970s and 1980s appear to have had only a superficial effect on mathematics curriculum in practice, as has the advent of inexpensive hand-held calculators and the extensive use of computing technology in the workplace. The school mathematics curriculum in many ways still reflects the demands and priorities of economies based on industry and agriculture, where a majority of people are prepared for jobs in factories or on farms and an elite minority are prepared to enter professional careers.

We hear a great deal in the media about the growing importance of mathematics in the new 'information era', and about what are regarded as inadequate levels of preparation in mathematics by school-leavers. Less often do we hear serious questions asked about what kind of mathematical preparation is needed. 'Raising standards' of achievement with a mathematics curriculum has become increasingly irrelevant, is not useful and may even be impossible. Our lives are changing and mathematics and its applications are changing, but it sometimes seems that the very groups most critical of levels of attainments in school mathematics are also the most resistant to the view that numeracy demands are also changing.

Certainly it is difficult to envisage the changes which may come about in the lifetimes of children now entering school. New technological developments, however, mean that these children will experience society differently than we have and may need an education, and in particular a mathematics education, quite unlike our own. As we enter the last decade of this century schools and the broader community must together ask what 'being numerate' really means: what kinds of mathematical outcomes are most important for daily life now and what are likely to be important in the future, what ideas, attitudes and skills really count. It is essential that we rethink what is taught in Australian mathematics classrooms in the name of numeracy, how it is taught and how it is assessed. Finally, and importantly, we must address ourselves to the question of what kind of conditions are most likely to facilitate changes in school mathematics curriculum and pedagogy.

This collection aims to contribute to this process. Each of the authors was asked to contribute his or her thoughts and research to the process of reconceptualizing what numeracy is, and what kind of educational practice might best bring it about. The collection was written for all who are concerned with these questions.

Sue Willis
December 1989

1 Numeracy and society: the shifting ground

SUE WILLIS

INTRODUCTION

I begin this chapter with three tales of mathematics in use.

Example 1.1 An extract from Part 4, section 34(5) of the *Social Security Act 1947*

> The factor to be ascertained for the purposes of Subsection (4) in relation to a relevant period —
> (a) is the number, calculated to 3 decimal places, ascertained by dividing . . .; or
> (b) if the number so ascertained would, if it were calculated to 4 decimal places, end in a number greater than 4 — is the number so ascertained increased by 0.001.

Example 1.2 Tale from an excellent paper entitled 'Mathematics as Propaganda'

> The occasion was an interview with Paul Ehrlich, author of *The Population Bomb* and popularizer of population control as a solution to the world's problems. At that time the ecology movement had just started to capture the attention of the public, and Mr Ehrlich was arguing that the solution, as always, was in population control.
>   Johnny Carson [of the 'Tonight Show' in the USA] was in top form, but the show could have bogged down if the guest had delved into subtleties or overly serious discussion. However, Ehrlich had the perfect solution. He took a piece of postboard and wrote in large letters for the TV audience: $D = N \times I$.
>   'In this equation,' he explained, 'D stands for damage to the environment, N stands for the number of people, and I stands for the impact of each person in the environment. This equation shows that the more people the more pollution. We cannot control pollution without controlling the number of people'.

> Johnny Carson looked at the equation, scratched his head, made a remark about never having been good at math, and commented that it all looked quite impressive. (Koblitz 1981, p. 111)

Example 1.3 The third tale is a personal anecdote

> The boy was just 7 years of age. We were playing a game in which each of us received a score each round. At the end of the first round I wrote down my score, and the child's, and repeated this for the second round. Immediately he interrupted me, 'No, no, you don't do it that way. You've got to do running totals'.
>
> 'What are running totals?' I asked, and he replied, 'The last time you got 54 and this time you got 27 so you have to put those both together and you just put the running total down each time'. He then proceeded to add my scores for the two games and then his own. From his nodding and his lip movements he appeared to be 'saying' 54, 64, 74, 81. He continued to add the scores mentally (and correctly) with final scores of 500 to 600. I asked how he knew to do that and he replied, 'Well, I just know it, I just worked it out'.
>
> Later the same evening I glanced through some work he had brought home from school and noticed pages of 'add-ups' (set out in the traditional vertical form) including a series like '54 + 27' which involved carrying from the units to the tens column. Every exercise which did not involve carrying was answered correctly while every one involving carrying was answered incorrectly. A while later I suggested that we pretend to play a game, I would make up subscores for him to do the running totals. He obviously thought it was a fairly peculiar request. Why would you do mathematics in isolation, it serves no purpose? Nonetheless, he did it. Of course I chose for my subtotals ones that matched his incorrectly completed written exercises. When he completed them correctly mentally I exclaimed with exaggerated surprise, 'That's funny, how come you got something different here?', and pointed to the written exercise. His reply: 'No', he said, 'they're not running totals, they're add-ups and this is the way you do it. Our teacher told me that this is the way you do it'.

Each of these tales reveals something of our everyday experiences of mathematics and each tells us something about numeracy. The first was brought to the notice of readers of the *Australian Mathematics Teacher* by John Truran, who asked:

> After all these years, have we been so unsuccessful in teaching a precise meaning for 'rounded to three decimal places' that our parliamentary draftsmen feel obliged to resort to this imprecise verbosity to express a simple, and common, idea. (Truran 1989, p. 23)

I, as any mathematics teacher would, shared his dismay. Does this just happen to be a piece of clumsy writing? Does the writer believe it is less ambiguous than referring to 'rounding'? Does it reflect ignorance on the part of the writer(s)? Or a belief that those who will have to read the text may not know what rounding means? What might we expect to be the response of the average reader trying to interpret this passage? Would she or he recognize that the writing left something to be desired, that the difficulty was with the writer and not with the reader? Would this be just one more piece of evidence that 'I never could do mathematics' and would it persuade the reader to place his or her faith in someone else's interpretation?

In the second tale, how many people in the audience of 'The Tonight Show' would have had the confidence and the competence to challenge the equation? Is Ehrlich suggesting that the I for the owners of the Exxon company responsible for the 1989 Alaskan oil spill is the same as the I for you and me. Or that the I for a suburban Australian is the same as the I for an Aboriginal Australian living a traditional lifestyle? Clearly preposterous! Johnny Carson responded quite typically to this use of mathematics — the words were 'I was never very good at mathematics' but the reality was a disownment of the mathematics in such a way that his capacity to make a judgement was inhibited. Many viewers would be sufficiently intimidated by the psuedo-equation to suspend their common sense temporarily. Who can argue with mathematics?

In the third tale, the child happened to be wrong about the way that you 'do it'. Presumably, he'd misremembered the teacher's rule, but he could equally well have remembered correctly. In neither case would he have had any access to the meaning for the 'add-up' tasks; indeed, he had no idea that they related to running totals at all. Furthermore, all the power was in the teacher's hands. The child only knew whether the exercise was correct when he got ticks. He didn't have access to a way of checking whether the answer made sense because the task had no meaning for him — it was his teacher's task and his teacher's rule, not his.

WHAT IS NUMERACY?

Surprising as it may seem, the notion of numeracy is a fairly recent one. The Crowther Report (UK, 1959) originally introduced the concept of numeracy, and the word itself, defining numeracy as:

> . . . a word to represent the mirror image of literacy . . . On the one hand an understanding of the scientific approach to the study of phenomena — observation, hypothesis, experiment, verification. On the other hand . . . the need in the modern world to think quantitatively, to realize how far our problems are problems of degree even when they appear to be problems of kind. Statistical ignorance and statistical fallacies are quite as widespread and quite as dangerous as the logical fallacies that come under the heading of illiteracy. (quoted in Cockcroft 1982, para. 36)

The word 'numeracy' has rapidly become part of the Australian vernacular. A brief analysis of the use of the term in education policy documents in Western Australia, however, shows that the meaning ascribed by Crowther has not withstood the pressures of the coincident importation from the USA of the 'back-to-basics' movement. In 1977, the Education Department of

Western Australia published a policy on literacy and numeracy which stated:

> The term 'numerate' is understood to mean mathematical literacy . . . A person is considered to be literate and numerate when he has acquired the skills and concepts which enable him to function effectively in his group and community, and when his attainment in reading, writing and mathematics make it possible for him to continue to use these skills to further his own and his community's development. (Education Department of Western Australia 1977)

The policy document then elaborated, indicating that for numeracy this meant:

1. Mastery of basic number facts (tables).
2. Competence in operations (+ , − , × , +) with whole numbers, fractions, decimals, percentages, money and measurements.
3. Skills in estimation in relation to these operations, and the habit of making estimates.
4. Sound spatial concepts, including competence with the basic concept of mensuration.
5. Skill in interpreting graphs.
6. Sound proportion concepts.
7. Statistical literacy based on experiences with the chance processes.

(Education Department of Western Australia 1977)

Seven years later, the Beazley Committee of Inquiry into Education in Western Australia (Beazley 1984) adopted the more general part of this definition but supported the use of two different lists to elaborate their description of numeracy. The first was taken from the College Board of United States' list of the mathematical competencies needed by all students entering tertiary studies (as quoted in Beazley 1984). The second list was developed by the Cockcroft Committee of Inquiry into the Teaching of Mathematics in England and Wales to describe:

> a 'foundation list' of mathematical topics which . . . should form part of the mathematics syllabus for all pupils [and] the greater part of the syllabus of those pupils in about the lowest 40 per cent of the range in attainment in mathematics. (Cockcroft 1982, para. 455)

Thus, we have two lists offered as descriptions of numeracy, neither developed for that purpose, one presenting a mathematical foundation for higher education and the other a mathematical foundation for all students, but with the needs of lower attainers particularly in mind. That they were imported lists is not surprising since very little attention has been given in Australia to investigating the mathematical needs of adults at home or at work (for exceptions see chapter 6). In this respect, the Cockcroft Committee expended considerable effort and money, in the form of commissioned research studies, in order to find at least partial answers to the question of the mathematical needs of adult life. These studies used the traditional strategy of asking employers' organizations and tertiary institutions what they wanted of school-leavers, but they placed greater emphasis on developing a large number of case studies of adolescents and adults at home and at work in all the major occupational and educational groups. This is in stark contrast with the more typical approach of determining the meaning of numeracy by committees that are usually informed by little more than tradition and, occasionally, by responses to questionnaires in which the questions are formulated from a traditional viewpoint. Numeracy requirements developed by the latter strategies tend to be more content oriented but also more low-level skill oriented than are requirements determined from evidence of how people who cope mathematically do so. This is probably due, in part, to the evidence that there is really very little formal mathematical *content* needed by the bulk of the population at home or at work (see, for example, the Cockcroft Report, chapters 2 and 3).

The College Board recommendation is useless as a statement of policy since it does not indicate *how* the computations are to be performed, at what degree of difficulty, level of accuracy or speed. We have, as the first in the list of mathematical requirements published by the College Board (USA), 'The ability to perform with reasonable accuracy the computations of addition, subtraction, multiplication and division using natural numbers, fractions, decimals and integers' (quoted in Beazley 1984, p. 126). On the other hand, from the studies commissioned by the Cockcroft Committee:

> . . . the methods which are used when at work to carry out calculations are frequently not those which are traditionally taught in the classroom. Employees use a variety of idiosyncratic and 'back of envelope' methods, especially for long multiplication and division . . . The methods which are used depend very much on the user's confidence in his own mathematical ability. (Cockcroft 1982, para. 71)

Many people, however, would interpret the College Board as recommending the mastery of standard computational algorithms to a traditionally required high degree of accuracy and speed, in direct conflict with the evidence that those who are mathematically effective in daily life use these traditional methods very rarely.

The third recommendation from the College Board was, 'Use effectively the mathematics of: integers, fractions, and decimals; ratios, proportions, and percentages; roots and powers; algebra; geometry' (quoted in Beazley 1984, p. 126). 'Integers' refers to the extension of natural numbers to include the negatives. The vast majority of people, including those who are tertiary bound, would never need to compute with negative numbers. Comparing temperatures is probably the single use of negative numbers most people ever make. Even bank accounts are rarely expressed in the abstract terms of negative and positive. Similarly, 'to use effectively the mathematics of . . . algebra' is a nonsense — how much is enough and of what kind? Do they mean 'use' algebra to interpret graphs in the daily newspaper, transpose formulae arising in a trade, manipulate trigonometric expressions, investigate group structures or to understand the nature and power of algebraic models of the world. Perhaps those who prepared the list knew very little algebra, or perhaps they were ignorant of the disagreements about what comprises 'useful' algebra for the majority of people and of the debate about the relative emphasis we should place on manipulative algebra compared with modelling with functions and graphs. Differences in knowledge of algebra are not just a matter of how far you get through an established sequence. They are differences in kind, not in degree.

The Beazley Inquiry provides us with a perfect example of too few people, with too little time and too large a brief trying to deal with numeracy alongside many other competing concerns. They were required to consider the content and structure of the whole school curriculum, K–12, and were forced, by the time-limit of one year and a limited budget, to rely heavily on voluntary submissions and on the reports of overseas committees with vaguely similar briefs. Ironically, we often have little access to the process by which these overseas committees come to their conclusions and, as a consequence, must judge them at face value. We have had our fingers burnt by 'face validity' and it is an inappropriate means for determining the numeracy needs of a community.

The Beazley Report acknowledged that the College Board list was 'meant for students intending to pursue tertiary studies [and] the mathematical or numeracy skills . . . may not be as appropriate for all students', and they suggested that, 'knowledge of algebra or of probability and statistics, may not be relevant for all students' (Beazley 1984, p. 127). Thus they supported the College Board list with algebra, probability and statistics removed for some students. The result was a list considerably more sterile than the WA Policy statement of 1977 and bore no relationship to the Crowther definition. What were we left with? The mathematical diet *they* had at school: computation, some measurement and (possibly inadvertently) geometry, with no reference to estimation, chance processes or graphing as such. All students to receive essentially the curriculum their parents did, with the 'less able' doing a watered-down version of the curriculum set for the 'more able'.

The Cockcroft Report equates numeracy with, firstly, 'an "at-homeness" with numbers and an ability to cope confidently with the mathematical demands of everyday life', and secondly, 'an appreciation and understanding of information which is presented in mathematical terms, for instance in graphs, charts or tables or by reference to percentage increase or decrease' (Cockcroft 1982, para. 39). To the extent that skills with graphs, charts or tables are developed at all in school mathematics, they are within the parts of the curriculum labelled 'algebra' and 'probability and statistics'. Thus, the Cockcroft Committee, on the basis of extensive studies of the mathematical needs of everyday life, employment and education, emphasized just the areas that the Beazley Committee so blithely dismissed. Clearly the two areas identified by the Cockcroft Report are central aspects of numeracy and several of the papers in this collection elaborate on them.

The list of foundational topics provided in the Cockcroft Report is well-informed and realistic regarding the mathematical *content* everyone needs for daily life. Nonetheless, it is not at all clear that mastery of the topics in the Cockcroft foundation list produces numerate people, and the

Cockcroft Committee has not claimed that it does. Nor is it clear that people would be numerate to an extent commensurate with their acquisition of that mathematical content. What the list does not address is the contexts in which people are expected to act, and the processes and qualities that are necessary if one is to function mathematically in those contexts. Choosing and using mathematical ideas to understand, to explain and to solve is what numeracy is about, and it is involved at every level of mathematical sophistication.

The Beazley Committee began with a broad definition of numeracy as the mathematics for effective functioning in one's group and community, and the capacity to continue to use these skills to further one's own development and that of one's community. They ended up with a subset of a traditional mathematics curriculum. This kind of thinking is not peculiar to the Beazley Committee: the recent emphasis on students learning to be numerate appears to have been equated generally with acquisition of what are called the 'basic skills'. Even the terms 'problem solving' and 'application' are distorted to mean the practice of procedures for a fairly restricted range of oversimplified and often unlikely 'everyday uses of mathematics'.

This distortion results from dual beliefs. The first, usually explicit, is that school mathematics is useful, and the second, usually implicit, is that for the majority of students 'getting' mathematical skills automatically leads to their choosing and using them. Each of these beliefs is questionable. There is general agreement that mathematics is useful, but whether that makes school mathematics useful, or at least useful for numeracy, is another matter. Furthermore, it is not at all clear that numeracy can be achieved through the acquisition of skills and standard problem solutions.

IS SCHOOL MATHEMATICS USEFUL?

It seems almost heretical to suggest that school mathematics may not be useful or at least not in quite the way many people assume. Nonetheless, it does seem that many people become numerate almost in spite of school mathematics rather than because of it.

The technique-oriented curriculum

The school mathematics curriculum K–12, with all the developments of recent decades, is still essentially technique-oriented, based around procedures, methods, skills, rules and algorithms (Bishop 1988). Bishop suggests, 'the technique curriculum is based on the expectation of the pupil becoming a user' (Bishop 1988, p. 8). The metaphor which is extended is that of a tool-kit which equips the users to deal with the situations they are likely to confront in their future at work and home. While a small minority of people will become mathematicians, or enter fields in which mathematics is central, the vast majority will not. Many will enter occupations which use some mathematical techniques but, as John Foyster shows in chapter 6, the evidence is that the techniques used both within and across occupations are very diverse and are also quite specific to occupations. No mathematics curriculum could possibly prepare young people for all the specific mathematical procedures that they might need in the future.

But perhaps daily life is where school mathematics comes into its own. Recently I had a week's duty for the tea club at work. I visited the supermarket to buy coffee and found that a 'special' was available on the brand I prefer. I could buy a 200 g can with an attached smaller can of 50 g for $5.48. The size I normally bought was 375 g for $11.65. Which was the better deal? This is one of the types of situation that people who are numerate are supposed to be able to deal with comfortably and textbooks abound with problems such as this:

> Coffee is 250 g for $5.48 or 375 g for $11.65. Which is the better buy?

A typical response amongst conscientious and successful students would be to calculate and compare unit prices, that is, calculate $5.48 ÷ 250 and $11.65 ÷ 375 and compare the results. Is this useful maths? Is this numeracy? How would you do it?

What I did was double, respectively, 250 and $5.50 (close enough to $5.48), to get 500 g for roughly $11. Clearly a better buy than 375 g for $11.65. You may have used a different strategy but if you bothered at all to do a price comparison you probably thought about it quickly and chose from amongst several possible computations the one which made the least demands upon your arithmetic. You almost certainly did it mentally and then interpreted the results of the computation in the context. Had the price of the 250 g jar been $6.48, you would have found that 500 g cost about $13 and the decision would have been a little harder. You may have decided that the smaller units would stay fresh longer and, as they seemed no more expensive, the smaller jars would be your choice. Or you might have performed another computation: if 375 g costs $11.65 then an extra 125 g would cost another third which is between $3 and $4, so 500 g would cost more than $14. You would have made judgements, you would have performed mental arithmetic, you almost certainly would not have carried out an accurate unit pricing; if you did, I suspect it would be because you carry a small calculator.

Why do so many of our students perform the mathematical equivalent of cracking nuts with a sledge hammer? In this case, the problem would almost certainly have first appeared in the context of unit pricing, possibly even on a page headed 'Unit pricing' and immediately after exercises of the following kind:

> If soft drink costs $2.20 for 1.25 litres, how much does it cost per litre?

The students will have been 'motivated' to learn how to calculate rates such as cost per gram or cost per litre by being told that it will enable them to compare prices when they shop in supermarkets (after all this is 'relevant' maths). From the teachers' point of view the task is to practise the techniques associated with calculating unit prices and the students will be in little doubt about this. From the students' points of view the eventual task is to perform in order to obtain positive judgements and avoid negative judgements from the teacher or examiner, certainly not to improve their shopping strategies. The feeling of security and control, albeit of a precarious kind, one can get from getting right answers can be irresistible. But, while the pleasure of ticks may be quite justifiable, it isn't numeracy.

Some students resist the pressure to conform in this way in school or out; others conform in school but develop more efficient strategies to use elsewhere. These students will become numerate in spite of school mathematics. Still others will stick with the 'unit pricing' strategy — some will use it correctly, if not necessarily sensibly, probably using an approximation or a calculator, while others will half remember it and become completely confused. Many will not attempt to deal with such situations mathematically at all.

What is needed by a shopper who wishes to make such a price comparison? The particular computation I used here was a simple rounding of $5.48 to $5.50 which I then mentally doubled, others may have performed a different computation. Being able to double money amounts such as $5.50, is not sufficient, however, to enable this problem to be solved and being able to perform tedious long divisions such as $11.65 ÷ 375 is not even necessary. The attitude that mathematics may help and that good use of mathematics is about being lazy and choosing the easiest way to the right answer is necessary, as is confidence in one's ability to find and execute an appropriate and reliable strategy. Effective computation, in this situation as in all others, requires that the shopper decide how accurate the result needs to be, decide what operations to perform, select a means of carrying out the operation, perform the operation, and make sense of the answer.

One of the important outcomes of mathematics education is the capacity to deal with commonly occurring (familiar) situations readily and almost automatically. The practice of some routine procedures for standard situations may be appropriate for this purpose, but *not* at the expense of common sense. Interpreting unit prices *is* useful when shopping and, to do so, the shopper has to understand what unit prices are. This may be learned in school by exploration of the relationship between unit costs and overall price, and for this a calculator is the natural tool. To suggest, however, that *calculating* unit prices is an important part of the shopper's 'tool-kit' is not common sense, but mathematics classrooms and textbooks abound with such 'applications'.

The development of numeracy is a service; it should enable students to deal with other aspects of their lives, at home, at work and across the curriculum. We may teach mathematics for many different reasons, but it seems ludicrous that we should try to justify numeracy on grounds other than its usefulness in practical situations. For school mathematics to be useful one would expect it to at least reflect the arithmetic techniques in regular adult use. But quite clearly it does not.

Choosing and using mathematics

Most lists of numeracy requirements are based on the view that the acquisition of standard techniques is what numeracy is about and little serious attention is paid to the skills that need to be developed in choosing and using mathematics in appropriate ways. Indeed, the tool-kit metaphor is an apt one because our typical approach to numeracy is analogous to giving an apprentice carpenter a bag of tools and expecting her, as an immediate result, to be a carpenter.

While some of these techniques are in fact quite helpful, they are usually decontextualized with the view that if students first learn the necessary skills we can later pay some attention to their uses in everyday life or elsewhere. This view is mistaken in at least two ways. Firstly, many students learn mathematical skills in isolation for the whole of their schooling and never experience mathematics as useful. Secondly, unless students see the relationship between mathematics and its uses as they proceed they may never develop a view of mathematics as making sense in *their* world and as having relevance to the solution of *their* problems.

Students need experience of the use of mathematical concepts and skills in a range of contexts and with tasks which vary from the relatively familiar to the unfamiliar, from the structured to the unstructured, so that they come to see that part of the power of mathematics lies in the potential for particular ideas to be used in many different situations. I would take this a step further, however, and argue it is insufficient to provide practical problems for students to solve where the purpose clearly is to practise quite specific techniques. There is nothing wrong with practising techniques as long as both teachers and students acknowledge that that is what is going on, and that it is not the key to the development of numeracy. The real problem is that too often students '. . . never get a sense of [mathematical] ''skill-using'' to achieve a purpose that itself is more important than the practise of a particular mathematical skill' (Open University 1980, Unit 1, p. 22).

Students should learn to recognize when mathematics might be useful and what is the most appropriate mathematics in the given circumstances. Therefore, from the earliest years, they need experiences which enable them to use mathematics in solving 'real-world' problems of immediate and practical interest to themselves. Some activities may be explicitly mathematical such as calculating the cost of lunch. Others, such as designing a book, may not be overtly mathematical. In the latter situations students should have opportunities to decide for themselves whether or not mathematics might be helpful and, if so, to choose the mathematics to use and to evaluate its effectiveness in the situation. Only through such experiences is it likely that the majority will come to understand when to use mathematics, what mathematics to use, how to do mathematics, and how to use the results provided by the mathematics (Open University 1980, Unit 14, pp. 23–4).

School mathematics is, however, only rarely like this. Because the mathematics curriculum tends to be defined in terms of techniques, teachers feel compelled to ensure that students have acquired them. Students who, for example, do not practise the procedure for calculating unit prices because they can 'just tell' which is the cheaper way to buy coffee are not playing the school mathematics game. The teacher is in quite a dilemma. While the broad goals of the curriculum (or the broad definition of numeracy) may talk of the practical use of mathematics, the specifications talk of the techniques for unit pricing — and that is what will be assessed. I am appalled to recall exhorting any of my students who had developed 'easier' methods and not 'shown their working', that *my* way was better because it always worked — even for more awkward numbers. I explained to them that if they didn't show their working I wouldn't be able to help them see where they'd gone wrong. And in case that wasn't convincing enough, if they showed their working and had the right idea, but made an error, they would be able to get partial marks. No working, no part marks. The oppression of school mathematics was such that, in those early days of teaching, I felt obliged to overlook the fact that my methods often increased tenfold the likelihood of error and of making the wrong choices and that I would never use the strategies I was teaching outside the walls of a classroom. I felt obliged to suspend my common sense and to ask my students to do likewise.

As Alan Bishop has argued, the technique curriculum cannot educate because it:

> . . . cannot help understanding, cannot develop meaning, cannot enable the learner to develop a critical stance either inside or outside mathematics. . . For the successful child it is at best a training, for the unsuccessful child it is a disaster. (Bishop 1988, pp. 8–9)

Nonetheless, in mathematics classrooms students spend many hundreds of hours drilling decontextualized procedures. The development of mathematical competence in this form is *not* cost-effective, too much time being needed for too few useful outcomes. It is a major and real inefficiency in school mathematics and a luxury we cannot afford. Why do we do it? Christine Keital offers the following possibilities:

> . . . the maintenance of extensive arithmetical learning in mathematics education is either beyond justification ('you simply must know how to . . .'), or founded in nostalgia ('at least once in one's life one should have done . . .'), or merely a relic in the syllabuses, or a formative enrichment like art and music which at best feeds into leisure time occupations. Is this usefulness? (Keital 1989, p.11)

To repeat her question: Is this usefulness? Perhaps we have to look beyond usefulness to the reason for school mathematics.

WHAT IS SCHOOL MATHEMATICS FOR?

David Wheeler has remarked, 'People know, mostly by hearsay, that mathematics has contributed powerfully to technological advances, and it is said to be "important" for society', but he adds, 'their personal experience of it may only be of routine numerical calculation or of struggling through the mysteries of algebra or the formal proof of a geometrical theorem. *What is mathematics ''for''?'* (Wheeler 1986, p. 60, italics added)

Nostalgia or relic?

Although the word 'numeracy' was coined quite recently, the context in which numeracy is supposed to be achieved, that is, the school mathematics curriculum, is a relic of an earlier time. For children entering school now, a typical lifetime after school will span the period from about the year 2000 until 2050 or more. To get some idea of the changes that we can expect, we need only to think back a corresponding time to the late 1920s. We can expect at least as many, most would predict more, changes in the sixty-year period between 1990 and 2050 as we have experienced between 1930 and 1990. It would be quite ludicrous to expect the same basic ideas in science or geography that were taught sixty years ago to be taught now but it seems many people do not consider this to be true of mathematics.

The basic substance or content of the mathematics curriculum in the primary and lower secondary years remains remarkably constant. There are fashions in language and style, and topics are added, but few are removed. Large chunks of the curriculum are there because they have always been there. With a few notable exceptions, and with some relatively minor adjustments, the 'basic skills' part of the mathematics curriculum has remained unchanged for decades. Curriculum documents which, in their introduction, argue convincingly for a de-emphasis on standard written computation, continue to place it at the heart of the curriculum while everything else, even mental arithmetic, is considered a 'value-added' extra.

The International Commission on Mathematics Instruction (ICMI), which met in Kuwait in 1986 to discuss school mathematics in the 1990s, used the expression 'the canonical mathematics curriculum' (Howson & Kahane 1986, p. 20) to highlight the unfortunate perception of school mathematics as one of the unchanging things in a world of change. It certainly is the case that many mathematical ideas and even techniques are durable and versatile — fundamental mathematical ideas which are recognizably the same as those of thousands of years ago are used in everyday life by the majority of people and also in modern mathematics, science, economics and design. Thus, while many of the fundamental ideas which underpin the school mathematics curriculum are 'old', they are not necessarily 'old-fashioned' or 'out-of-date'.

Mathematics, however, is rapidly growing in both quality and quantity. This growth is a result both of new conceptual tools in mathematics and of the use of sophisticated computing technology. Mathematics is the basis of all modern technology, but also the technology is driving a new revolution in mathematics (Steen 1988). Computing technology has changed the way mathematics is produced and also the way it is applied at *all* levels of mathematical sophistication. Some things will now be done differently than they were in the past, some things will be done that previously were not possible or at least not practicable, and some things done in the past may no longer be necessary. This is as true of everyday arithmetic as it is true of the mathematics of tradespeople, technicians, and technologists; shop assistants, accountants and economists; social, physical and biological scientists; and professional mathematicians.

Many of these newer developments in mathematics and its applications raise questions about what are the basic mathematical ideas and perspectives students should develop in school. However, suggestions that the traditional basics may no longer be basic are often greeted with anger and scorn. The use, or lack of use, of calculators in primary schools provides an excellent example of this. Four-function and scientific calculators are cheap, readily available and natural tools with which to carry out arithmetical operations and, as David Wheeler has remarked, 'it is impossible to believe that [calculators] can have a harmful effect on mathematics teaching even in situations where their full potential is neglected' (Wheeler 1986, p. 56). Yet there is considerable resistance to their widespread use in classrooms. The following extract appeared in a recent newspaper editorial following the release, by the Ministry of Education in Western Australia, of curriculum guidelines which assume primary school children should use calculators:

> Plans for the push-button mathematics syllabus to be introduced in 1991 flies in the face of repeated complaints by employer groups about a worrying decline in basic literacy and numeracy skills amongst prospective employees. (*West Australian* 11 Aug. 1989, p. 10, editorial)

We use technology every day and, as the use of a new technology becomes more widespread, old skills are lost and new skills are developed. Paper-and-pencil algorithms have no intrinsic merit, they are a means of performing tasks rather than an end in themselves. Furthermore, they were developed to make use of the technology of paper-and-pencil (or chalk-and-board) and were limited to what was achievable with those media. Restricting ourselves to these practices seems rather ludicrous, analogous to insisting that children learn to use the quipu for counting, the abacus for addition or Napier's bones for multiplication, or, indeed, having them learn to make fire by rubbing sticks together.

Laurie Buxton (1981) has suggested that part of the anger some parts of the community express about what they consider to be a lowering in standards of computational skill is the suggestion that the things they learned, possibly painfully, may no longer be as necessary as they once were. They feel de-skilled, and as Buxton suggests, 'a part of themselves is under attack' (Buxton 1981, p. 118). Some support for this notion is provided from recent Australian research which surveyed community attitudes to school mathematics. Galbraith & Chant inferred that 'those calling loudly for the "basics" are unlikely to be among the more mathematically literate themselves' (Galbraith & Chant, forthcoming).

Many who demand that the mathematics curriculum emphasize the skills they learned at school, do not regard as essential, or even particularly useful, mathematical concepts and skills they did *not* learn at school. For example, it is difficult to think of a person being numerate who does not have a good sense of chance processes but, because *we* didn't develop ideas about chance during the early years of schooling, our children need not. Ridiculous statistical distortions appear in the newspapers every day with no such outcry about standards — presumably because many members of the media are insufficiently numerate themselves to understand the basic principles of questionnaire design and sampling and, in any case, often are the perpetrators of the distortion. A few days after the editorial quoted earlier, the following note appeared in the same newspaper without comment:

> Of 429 callers to the West Hotline at the weekend there were 371 no votes and 58 yes votes to the question: Should calculators replace the traditional method of teaching maths in primary schools? (*West Australian* 15 Aug. 1989, p. 10, editorial note in letters to the editor)

The editor clearly thought this supported his point of view. This is interesting because I think it supports mine.

The nostalgia for the past seems ironic given the widespread alienation people feel towards mathematics. Traditional school mathematics may not have been a comfortable experience for many adults but it is comfortably familiar to teachers, parents and employers alike — we all recognize it well. The ICMI symposium even suggested that people would be disappointed if mathematics wasn't difficult:

> More perversely, however, there is a widespread popular feeling in some countries that school mathematics *should* be difficult, a feeling perhaps associated with a vague belief that it has a role in character training. . . It is a belief that must be countered by every means possible, and it underlies, for example, the extraordinary reluctance of many teachers, even whole school systems, to allow calculators into schools within societies where they are readily available outside schools to all who have need of them. (Howson & Kahane 1986, p. 13)

The real problem for schools, however, is that the nostalgia for the past is often accompanied by a conflicting and contradictory demand for more 'relevant' and 'marketable' skills. On the one hand, schools are told that we need better problem solvers:

> The Business Council of Australia in its Education and Training Council had called for improved analytical and problem-solving skills. . . Industry no longer needed students to act as substitute calculators; they needed students who could think mathematically to solve problems. Teachers will need to develop new ways of teaching mathematics . . . (Dawson 1988)

On the other hand, three weeks later:

> . . . a private sector think tank funded by more than a thousand Australian companies, will use the policy unit to highlight what they see as the need for a more traditional and basic education. (Millar 1988)

Industry, commerce and the community (as represented in the media), can not reach a consensus about whether the problem with school mathematics is that students *are* still learning the things their parents learned or whether the problem is that they *aren't*!

School mathematics and selection

Trite as it may seem, it is still necessary to point out that the mathematics curriculum for the compulsory years of schooling is designed as a preparation for school mathematics in the post-compulsory years and as a filter to educational and occupational opportunities. Almost any Australian secondary student can tell you how mathematics is used:

> [Int]: Do you need maths?
> Boy 2: Yeah. Yeah. But . . .
> Girl 1: You need basic maths — but you don't really need to know [algebra] . . .
> [Int]: Saul. Do you reckon you'll need this sort of maths?
> Saul: You only do it because they use it to see if you understand and if your brain knows how to do it.
> [Int]: And do you think it's important that your brain knows how to do it? Will you need to know how to do it for your later life?
> B3: Yeah, you need to know how to do it. That's why we do it. To make sure we know how to do it. (The other students laugh.)
> Int: That sounds great. But where in your later [life], do you need to do pyramids?
> B3: Oh they just use it to see how fast you can work out things and that, how you catch on, and you understand them.
> Int: Oh, how you catch on?
> B3: And you can work them out.
> G2: They just want to see if you don't understand it.
> (Holland quoted in Willis 1989, p. 29)

As these year 8 students are only too aware, a major use of mathematics is selection. Helen Bannister cites Clarice Ballendon as arguing that 'the preparatory and selective functions of tertiary course preparation are often confused' (Bannister 1987, p. 19). This confusion is not peculiar, however, to the tertiary sector as demonstrated by the following personal experience:

> Recently, a psychologist asked me to assist him to check whether the existing mathematics test for applicant prison officers was consistent with the Year 10 mathematics curriculum. Since the test used only imperial units, I could have answered the question fairly quickly. Instead, I suggested that, rather than preparing a new set of textbook exercises based on the school curriculum, the prisons department identify the kinds of problems and situations (mathematical or otherwise) a prison officer would be likely to confront, and design their battery of tests around those. Not too surprisingly, my suggestion met considerable resistance. My offhand comment that, since applicant prison officers must be several years removed from Year 10, there would always be a time lag in using the school curriculum as a basis for selection was received somewhat more warmly than my argument that entrance tests should relate to the nature of the future position. I was told, essentially, that what I suggested was neither necessary nor desirable. 'We just use the maths test to pick the most intelligent people. You do think [*rather accusingly*] that prison officers should be intelligent, and more intelligent ones must be better than less intelligent ones.' (Willis 1989, p. 35)

The capacity to use mathematics in ways that contribute to 'on the job' performance was irrelevant. School mathematics was being used as a *de facto* measure of intelligence. It does an excellent job of this and its use in this way is an international phenomenon. Not surprisingly it manages to select much the same people as did the now widely discredited IQ tests. People who do mathematics are simply brighter and better, in every way that counts, than those who don't!

In countries throughout the world mathematics occupies a central place in the school curriculum. Indeed, it is the only subject taught in practically every school in the world. Not only does it maintain a privileged position in schools everywhere, but, as the ICMI symposium concluded, there is:

> . . . an astonishing uniformity of school mathematics curricula world-wide . . . [and] faced with a standard school mathematics textbook from an unspecified country, even internationally experienced mathematics educators find it almost impossible to say what part of the world it comes from without resource to . . . clues of language and of placenames. (Howson & Kahane 1986, p. 8)

But surely the whole world can't be wrong! Surely this provides ample evidence of the universal usefulness of school mathematics. Or does it? Mathematics does have a great many uses, but can the *same* school mathematics curriculum offer 'useful' knowledge to people in all circumstances all over the world? The ICMI symposium argued not:

> Its justification as usually stated is to a large extent its 'usefulness', in employment and the future daily lives of students as citizens. Seen in this light, such uniformity is strange. Employment opportunities vary widely, making very different demands on both the nature and levels of mathematical skills and understanding, while the societies concerned span the range from subsistence living to high technology urban life. (Howson & Kahane 1986, p. 8)

All over the world, desirability of mathematics curricula has been sacrificed to comparability of mathematics curricula — comparability between students within schools, schools within systems, systems within countries and between countries. I remarked earlier that students who perform well in mathematics are regarded as better than those who don't, it seems that countries who performed well on SIMS (the Second International Mathematics Study carried out in 1978) are also better than those that didn't. General acknowledgement of the desirability of mathematics curricula which prepare students to meet the various demands of their future lives cannot compete with the compulsion to compare and to rank.

We are told that mathematics is powerful, and we believe that learning mathematics will give us power. But most people's experience of the power of mathematics is not of personal power, indeed, many feel quite powerless in the presence of mathematics. We saw in the introduction of this paper three tales of the use of mathematics. In the first, mathematics was used in ways which are likely to obscure, mystify and, possibly, intimidate, but not empower. In the second tale, the use of mathematics is extremely powerful; it produced a spurious impression of precision and profundity, and of certainty. In the third tale, we saw how it all begins. In the case of the running totals the child had used mathematical thinking to make sense, for control and power. He owned that mathematics, he understood it and could use it. But there was apparently no link with school mathematics, which was 'other-owned'. All the power lay elsewhere. Importantly, both he and his teacher would, the next day, conclude that the child couldn't yet 'do' addition with regrouping and so too would the statewide test of the 'basics' a few weeks later. And the long-term effects of 'getting them wrong' in school can be crippling, emotionally and economically. Mathematics is powerful and it is useful, but for whom?

Many people do feel quite powerless in the presence of mathematical ideas and this kind of powerlessness has been systematically reinforced in our culture which sees mathematics as accessible to a talented few. Easley & Easley (1982) have argued that elitist attitudes about mathematics, and acute inequities in mathematics learning, have become part of what oppresses many groups who are educationally disadvantaged on the basis of their gender, class or race. Mathematics is powerful, but much of the power of school mathematics resides not in the mathematics but in the myth of mathematics, in the meritocratic prestige of mathematics as an intellectual discipline. Knowledge is power, particularly when that knowledge has high cultural value and is exclusive. The following quotation from Mary Harris illustrates the point quite well, one simply needs to replace 'weaving' by mathematics, and the African names with European ones:

> In cultures where men do the weaving the educational aspect of weaving is admitted under the equation weaving = knowledge = power. Alier Saine, one of several weavers recently interviewed in The Gambia, where only men weave, remarked, 'Weaving is a very good occupation where individuals can develop their talents and abilities'. Another, Nyde Jangne, 'Weaving is an art, just like any other branch of knowledge and you cannot finish learning it'. N'jagga Jhene, 'Weaving is a very important and progressive occupation'. Belal Fye, 'Weaving is a continuous business, the more skills you have the more patterns you can create' and Momodou Njie, 'The ginnies gave me the power of weaving . . . you see knowledge is very powerful'. (Harris 1987, p. 43)

There is a fundamental contradiction between the desire to broaden the access of students to mathematics — to increase their mathematical power — and at the same time to maintain the prestige and privilege which is credited to the mathematical elite. I will not elaborate here the contradictions and conflicts (see Willis 1988/9; 1989), but simply remark that, while comparison and selection is a major use of school mathematics, it is hardly numeracy.

In Australian schools, maintaining comparability of mathematics curricula quite clearly takes precedence over desirability. Certain kinds of life chances are rationed and school mathematics is one of the means by which the rationing process happens, justifying predictable inequalities of outcomes. Even those most concerned with the social justice aspects of school mathematics have tended, until quite recently, to focus on exclusion as the problem. Richard Johnson (1983) has argued that this is also true of views about access to schooling generally. He suggests that the problem of access is typically considered to be 'to get it rather than change it' (Johnson 1983, p. 15). As a result it is only relatively recently that attempts have been made to change the school curriculum in significant ways. There have been changes in school mathematics over recent years, but it is difficult to believe that these changes have had the effect of empowering those who have traditionally been excluded from school mathematics and from the range of options that come in its wake. Children from groups who historically have been disadvantaged by school mathematics continue to be.

Invidiously, students are compared on mathematical skills and concepts which were developed to serve the priorities of a different time, are decontextualized and are quite often irrelevant and useless by any sensible criteria. They are, for example, still drilled on long division for several years even though this skill is of practically no use in everyday situations and may only be useful in a preparatory sense to the minority of students who may later wish to factorize polynomials (and for which they will probably, in any case, use symbol-manipulating calculators). Failure to develop such skills may, nonetheless, be sufficient to ensure that you are not given the opportunity to benefit from a 'proper' mathematics education. Proper mathematics — empowering mathematics — often is 'saved' for later and sometimes never.

The sequencing and structure of mathematics in the compulsory years often means that those students who do not continue with mathematics beyond the compulsory years never gain access to the 'useful' mathematics. It is true that across Australia systems and schools are developing courses in mathematics which try to focus on practical mathematics. They tend to be called 'Mathematics for living' or 'Mathematics in society' or 'Applicable mathematics' and the irony of the names seems lost on most. What is the rest of the mathematics about and for? Commonly, these courses occur in the post-compulsory years, although increasingly they are offered in lower secondary school. In either case they are for students who have not succeeded with 'real' mathematics. In either case, they tend to close off future mathematical options. In Australian schools, the choice is simple, you can have valuable mathematics or valued mathematics, but not both. Through such courses students may gain access to useful mathematics but only as long as they are prepared to define themselves as out of the real race altogether. Such is the invidious nature of this approach to numeracy in school mathematics.

This may not be the rhetoric of alternative mathematics courses which are 'useful', but it is the reality. I believe that at least a partial solution lies in making these alternative courses the mainstream courses! By this I simply mean that the content and pedagogy for the mainstream (that is, the optimal) mathematics curriculum during the compulsory years should be based on the mathematics that everyone needs. Numeracy is about the mathematics that everyone needs and what it comprises requires careful and insightful analysis, unhampered by the habits of the past.

WHAT DOES EVERYONE NEED?

School mathematics is in the somewhat peculiar position that, with the advent of electronic computation, many of the traditional demands met by it are no longer required. On the other hand, as the flood of information available to every person rises, the need to understand more general mathematical concepts and processes is increasing.

Earlier, I described the contention of the Cockcroft Committee that numeracy involves 'an "at-homeness" with numbers and an ability to cope confidently with the mathematical demands of everyday life', and 'an appreciation and understanding of information which is presented in mathematical terms, for instance in graphs, charts or tables or by reference to percentage increase or decrease' (Cockcroft 1982, para. 39). I have also argued that a technique-oriented curriculum cannot produce numeracy and that 'choosing' and 'using' skills are neglected to the disadvantage of many students. Several papers in this collection provide elaboration on what numeracy may mean, some demonstrate that a technique-oriented curriculum does not provide the conceptual apparatus necessary for numeracy. The authors of these papers have provided alternatives, while others describe the executive or problem solving skills which form an essential component of numeracy, and consider how pedagogy and assessment practices should change to support their development. Still others consider professional development strategies to support needed changes in pedagogy. The various papers move towards a reconceptualization of numeracy in these ways and I will not elaborate on them further. However, before concluding, I wish to consider an aspect of 'being numerate' which is implicit in what I have said so far, and in several of the papers which follow, but which has not been made explicit.

It has been suggested that a great part of the usefulness of mathematics lies in its provision of 'a means of communication which is powerful, concise and unambiguous . . . [and that] . . . the principal reason for teaching mathematics to all children' is its communicative power — 'to represent, to explain and to predict' (Cockcroft 1982, paras. 3, 8). This is somewhat ironic given that for a great many people the expression of ideas in a mathematical form actually may prevent communication. However, the capacity to access ideas and arguments which involve mathematical concepts, or are presented in mathematical forms, and to access them critically, are essential for full participation in society. Neal Koblitz asks, 'How can we impart the analytical abilities and the qualities of skepticism and sophistication needed to be able to deal intelligently with quantitative arguments about social and psychological phenomena?' (Koblitz 1981, p. 119). A tall order? Perhaps. But presently the development of such interpretative skills is ignored almost completely in school mathematics and totally in assessments.

In order to develop these analytic and interpretative skills students need to understand something of the nature of mathematical arguments, and the relationship between mathematics and its applications. For example, the general ideas associated with the mathematical modelling process seem essential for all students. Mathematics does not have the potential to prove or decide anything with respect to the real world. Mathematics *applied* involves making assumptions and setting up models of the economy, of population growth, of the weather, and so on, but many people do not appear to understand the relationship between assumptions and conclusions and, as a consequence, are vulnerable to all sorts of manipulation. The basic ideas are accessible to most students, as is the basic distinction between deterministic and probabilistic models of our physical and social world, but traditionally very few have developed them in school.

But what of content? Perhaps one example will suffice. As society's use of information in a variety of forms increases, all people need to understand strategies for handling and interpreting data, the nature of chance processes, and the assumptions that underlie predictions and procedures. The process of drawing conclusions or making predictions based on data and principles of chance underlie such diverse matters as weather prediction, economic indicators, forensic analysis, risk insurance and gambling. For most people, for the majority of time, the important skills are those involved in making sense of and interpreting data which have been collected, organized, summarized and represented elsewhere. Most will only rarely need to collect and handle raw statistical data and communicate it to others. The mathematics curriculum should reflect this, placing a priority on understanding and interpreting data rather than, as is typically the case, calculating summary statistics and drawing graphs for no purpose. (This point is elaborated in chapter 5.)

In order that they not be susceptible to the kind of manipulation implied by the expression 'you can prove anything with statistics', students should develop the confidence and competence to judge the quality and appropriateness of data collection and presentation for answering the questions at hand, and to question the assumptions underlying data collection, analysis and interpretation, and the reasonableness of results and conclusions. The 'research' offered by the editor of the *West Australian* newspaper (15 Aug. 1989, p. 10) to support the contention that the 'community' overwhelmingly did not want calculators used in primary schools, provides an excellent example of the reason why *all* students need to develop critical skills regarding statistical information. Data analysis forms the basis of advertising, and of environmental, economic and social forecasting and policy development. Ultimately, it affects the lives of all people — individually and collectively. It seems, then, that the mathematics that *everyone* needs bears a strong resemblance to numeracy as described in the Crowther Report in 1959!

Recently, a colleague and I asked a group of 'community leaders' why it was important for girls to participate more in mathematics and science. Their answers varied, but a persistent and interesting feature was the emphasis placed on participation by all groups in society in social and political decisions:

> Those who have no grounding or interest in these matters lock themselves out of understanding some of the more important political issues of the time. (Richard Sweet quoted in *GEMS* 1988, p. 2)

It is important that all people, but especially members of less privileged or powerful groups, are able to understand mathematics and science sufficiently to have confidence to join in public debates, social action and decision-making on the numerous issues . . . such as taxation, computing and nuclear power. (Brian Martin quoted in *GEMS* 1988, p. 4)

There are major decisions which [every Australian person is] going to have to make which will have to be made democratically because the impact of those decisions is enormous. Those issues are to do with human life (like reproductive technology), the environment (like biosphere destruction issues), nuclear holocaust (like very major sustainability issues), and the issue of redundancy, or the planned introduction of technology. (Rhonda Galbally quoted in *GEMS* 1988, p. 5)

Science and maths are part of the language. We live in an increasingly complex society, and if we don't make an attempt to come to grips with what's going on in the world around us, the whole thing becomes more and more bewildering. (Barry Jones quoted in *GEMS* 1988, p. 8)

Vicki Webber has suggested that a mathematics curriculum designed to these purposes would look very different from the techniques curriculum described in this paper. As she suggests:

Mathematical skills for empowerment means far more than the ability to calculate. It means developing the ability to grapple with a problem until we come to a critical understanding of it. It means learning to create as well as solve problems, to ask questions, to gather and extract useful information, to criticise assumptions, and to use numbers to support or refute opinions. It means learning to cooperate and share ideas, and to place the mathematical component of a problem in a meaningful context. It means owning all aspects of the learning experience. (Webber 1987/8, p. 8)

The technique-oriented curriculum, however, encourages passivity, unthinking responses and the suspension of common sense. Like the young boy in my third tale at the beginning of this paper, we are taught in mathematics classrooms to trust completely things we do not understand. Many grow up, like Johnny Carson in my second tale, unable to distinguish valid mathematical arguments from invalid, and use from misuse. Mathematics is regarded as a collection of objective truths about the universe, rather than as a way of knowing and finding out. It is dehumanized and presented as impersonal, irrefutable and authoritative, and as socially and ethically neutral. That this is nonsense is clear (see for example, Ernest 1986; Maxwell 1985; Webber 1987/8; Abraham & Bibby 1988) but in the view of many the disassociation of mathematics from people and their decisions is almost a defining characteristic of the subject. I suspect that were schools to develop 'relevant' mathematics curricula they would be accused of the politicization of curricula as has happened recently in the United Kingdom (see Abraham & Bibby 1988; *GEMS* 1989).

Nonetheless, attempts to introduce 'relevant' mathematics curricula are occurring around Australia. Many teachers struggle to maintain their confidence in the changes while schools continue to be castigated for their inattention to 'the basics'.

CONCLUSION

The ICMI symposium on school mathematics for the 1990s argued that, as a major outcome of school mathematics:

> ... students must appreciate that with mathematical knowledge and understanding they acquire desirable power. For they must learn that mathematics can help in the solution of *their* problems and in their own decision making. (Howson & Kahane 1986, p. 22)

This is the essence of informed numeracy. Unfortunately, for the majority of students, even amongst many who apparently succeed, school mathematics still falls considerably short of this ideal.

An appropriate curriculum to develop numeracy in all students would focus on developing: the attitude that mathematics is relevant to me personally and to my community; the learning skills (listening, reading, talking and writing) and *fundamental* mathematical concepts needed to access personally new mathematical ideas; and the confidence and competence to make sense of mathematical and scientific arguments in decision-making situations (from the personal to the political, from the choice of detergent to the choice of deterrent).

For all students the development of this kind of numeracy should be a high priority, for very few students is this an easy matter, and for practically no students can it be achieved through the acquisition of even a reasonably large repertoire of standard problem solutions.

References

Abraham, J. & Bibby, N. 1988, 'Mathematics and society: Ethnomathematics and a public educator curriculum', *For the Learning of Mathematics*, **8** (2), 2–11.

Bannister, H. 1987, *Gender and Tertiary Selection: Research Paper No. 2, Participation and Equity Program*, Ministry of Education, Melbourne.

Beazley, K. 1984, *Education in Western Australia: Report of the Committee of Inquiry into Education in Western Australia*, Education Department of Western Australia, Perth, Western Australia.

Bishop, A. 1988, *Mathematical Enculturation*, Kluwer Academic Publishers, Dordrecht.

Buxton, L. 1981, *Do You Panic About Maths?* Heinemann Educational Books, London.

Cockcroft, W. H. (Chairman) 1982, *Mathematics Counts: Report of the Committee of Inquiry into the Teaching of Mathematics in Schools*, HMSO, London, UK.

Dawson, C. 1988, 'Degree value now in decline', *Australian*, 20 Jan., p. 16.

Easley, J. & Easley, E. 1982, *Math can be Natural: Kitamaeno priorities introduced to American teachers*, Committee on Culture and Cognition, University of Illinois, Urbana Champaign.

Editorial 1989, 'Miscalculation', *West Australian*, 11 Aug., p. 10.

Education Department of Western Australia 1977, *Policy from the Director General's Office*, No 6.

Ernest, P. 1986, 'Social and political values', *Mathematics Teaching*, **116**, 16–18.

Galbraith, P. & Chant, D. (forthcoming), 'Factors shaping community attitudes to school mathematics: Implications for future curriculum change', *Educational Studies in Mathematics*.

GEMS 1988, 'What the experts say', *GEMS*, **1** (1), 2–8.

GEMS 1989, 'On relevance and politics', *GEMS*, **1** (2), 13–14.

Harris, M. 1987, 'Mathematics and fabrics: Review', *Mathematics Teaching*, **120**, 43–5.

Howson, G. & Kahane, J.-P. (series ed.) 1986, *School Mathematics in the 1990s*, Cambridge University Press, Cambridge.

Johnson, R. 1983, 'Educational politics: the old and the new', in *Is there Anyone Here from Education?* eds A. Wolpe & J. Donald, Pluto Press, London.

Keital, C. 1989, 'Mathematics education and technology', *For the Learning of Mathematics*, **9** (1), 7–13.

Kobitz, N. 1981, 'Mathematics as propaganda,' in *Mathematics Tomorrow*, ed. Lyn A. Steen, Springer-Verlag, pp. 111–20.

Letters to the Editor 1989, *West Australian*, 15 Aug., p. 10.

Maxwell, J. 1985, 'Hidden messages', *Mathematics Teaching*, **11**, 18–19.

Millar, D. 1988, 'Get schools back to teaching basic skills institute urges', *Herald*, 12 Feb., p. 4.

Open University 1980, *PME Mathematics Across the Curriculum*, The Open University Press, Milton Keynes, UK.

Steen L. (ed.) 1988, *Calculus for a New Century: A pump not a filter*, MAA Notes Number 8, The Mathematical Association of America.

Truran, J. 1989, Letter to the editor, *Australian Mathematics Teacher*, **45** (2), 23.

Webber, V. 1987/8, 'Maths as a subversive activity', *Education Links*, **32**, 8–9.

Wheeler, D. 1986, 'The teaching of mathematics in primary and secondary schools', in *Innovations in science and technology education*, ed. D. Layton, Unesco, Paris.

Willis, S. 1988/9, 'Maths should be more relevant: What *do* they mean?', *Education Australia*, **4**, 14–16.

Willis. S. 1989, *'Real Girls Don't Do Maths': Gender and the construction of privilege*, Deakin University Press, Geelong, Victoria.

Becoming numerate: developing number sense

ALISTAIR McINTOSH

INTRODUCTION: THREE IMPORTANT WAYS OF CALCULATING

Recently I have discussed the question of computation in primary schools with a variety of groups of pre-service teacher education students, students (mainly primary school teachers) enrolled in Bachelor of Education courses, and groups of teachers on in-service courses. I invite them to estimate the following from their experience: 'What percentage of the time devoted to computation in primary schools is concerned with (a) written computation (b) calculator use and (c) mental computation?' There are minor variations in the responses but the basic pattern of responses is remarkably consistent: (a) 90% (b) <5% (c) 5%.

I then ask them to estimate: 'What percentage of calculations done by the majority of people in the ordinary course of life is done by (a) written computation (b) calculator use and (c) mental computation?' Again there are minor variations in the responses but the basic pattern of responses is very consistent: (a) 10% (b) 15% (c) 75%.

It is generally agreed that we spend the vast majority of classroom time on a form of computation — that is pencil-and-paper calculation — which is very little used by adults, and little time, and in some cases no time at all, on methods of computation — namely mental computation and calculators — which are frequently used by almost everyone.

It is difficult to dispute the facts given, or to suggest that the groups questioned are ignorant of the real situation or deliberately distorting the truth. As far back as 1957, research by Wandt & Brown (1957) found that 75% of adult calculations were performed mentally. The relative amount of attention given to the three methods of computation in primary schools can be confirmed by spending time in almost any primary classroom or by

24

page-counting in primary texts. In primary texts, calculators are hardly mentioned except in optimistic generalizations in the publisher's blurb and/or introductory pages. If people know specifically how to use calculators in any coordinated way they are not saying.

Mental arithmetic is scarcely taught at all, although it is often tested by short bursts of one-step low-level questions. Ask teachers how they teach mental forms of computation and, by and large, they are not even aware that there are any such methods to be taught: there is, in their view, only a collection of facts (e.g. multiplication tables, basic addition facts, number of millilitres in a litre) which children need to learn by heart. They associate mental arithmetic with facts, not with networks of relationships between numbers or with methods of computation. Methods of calculating mentally? You just do it or you can't. As for the calculator, some may allow it for checking calculations and a few for some games of making words by turning the calculator display upside down ('the children love it') but by and large it is shunned as a dangerous and potentially debilitating beast.

So there we have the picture: great amounts of time and energy dedicated to written calculation which is little used or trusted by people out of school. Little or no time devoted to improving mental computation which is used daily by everyone. Little or no time devoted to calculator use, though everyone would agree that the calculator could, indeed does, make everyone able to compute.

In what follows, I propose to take each of the three methods of computation in turn and to consider its present place and its relevance in the primary school today, particularly with regard to its contribution to children's numeracy.

THE ROLE OF WRITTEN COMPUTATION

The view of many people with regard to written computation is that it is one stable and enduring feature of a world in turmoil. However fashions may change with regard to mathematics, methods of written computation remain as they always were — fixed and immutable — the one right way of doing things.

·Of course it isn't true. Until recently in world history it was never considered necessary or practicable for more than a small percentage of the population to be able to calculate with paper and pencil. People might write down quantities, but the actual calculations would be done by some form of calculator: the soroban or some variation of it in Eastern countries, the Roman abacus and its successor the medieval 'counter' in Western civilizations. Hence the shop 'counter', on which the shopkeeper moved pebbles and calculated ('calculate' from the Latin word 'calculus' meaning 'a small pebble'). As written methods spread they evolved and changed continually — consider, for example, the 'gelosia' or 'grating' method of long multiplication in use in the middle ages or the 'crossing out' method of subtraction (which works very effectively from left to right), both shown in figure 2.1.

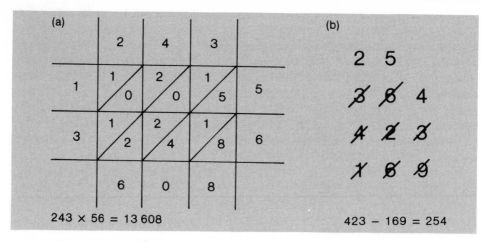

Figure 2.1 Examples of (a) gelosia multiplication and (b) subtraction by crossing out

Both methods are simple to learn and efficient, but quite different from current written algorithms. Even the written methods currently taught are scarcely traditional. In my own lifetime the method of subtraction prescribed to be taught has changed from 'decomposition' to 'equal additions' and back again to 'decomposition'. 'Borrowing and paying back' has, theoretically at least, been replaced by 'trading' or 'exchanging'. In long multiplication, debate has raged over whether to multiply by the units first or last.

There has been a fair degree of polarization over the question of whether it is necessary or even desirable to understand the various written algorithms. I recall with affectionate horror a teacher who raced to the back of her classroom where I was assessing a student teacher who was attempting to explain to a year 7 remedial group the niceties of long multiplication. 'She is not', she queried in a stentorian whisper, 'doing that "understanding" is she? It only confuses them!'. Her assumption, which is still common among primary teachers, is that what you need to know ('understand') is what to do next, not why. 'Theirs not to reason why, theirs but to multiply.' In the terms popularized by Skemp (1976), this teacher emphasized instrumental understanding ('what do I have to do?') rather than relational understanding ('how does this make sense in relation to the things I understand so far?').

You may well sympathize with this view, in which case I challenge you to appraise the subtraction algorithm in example 2.1 which seems to me to be extremely easy to operate and extremely difficult to understand. The example is 435 — 276 but you can check for yourself that it applies to any subtraction. It may not catch on, but it may serve as a reminder that current formal written methods are not the only possible ones, have changed frequently and recently, and will continue to evolve.

The subtraction algorithm described in example 2.1 raises another important and unfortunate feature of formal written computational methods which is only now being realized and commented upon: using written methods even frequently does not necessarily improve one's under-

Example 2.1 A subtraction algorithm

1. Change the subtraction sign to 'add'	435 − 276	435 + 276
2. Take each digit of the top number from 9		564 + 276
3. Add		840
4. Take each digit of the result from 9		159
5. This is the answer to 435 − 276.		

standing of how that algorithm in particular works or of how numbers in general behave. The algorithm is very easy to learn to perform and each step is simple. And yet you could use it consistently from now on without ever gaining insight about how exactly it works or how numbers behave. You would learn nothing about the algorithm, nothing about subtraction, nothing about numbers.

This is equally true of our current written methods. Many adults 'borrow and pay back' without ever having the slightest idea why. Hardly anyone who has to divide fractions would care to explain why they 'turn it upside down and multiply' — which is why they frequently invert the wrong fraction.

> The practising of traditional methods does not develop an awareness of the structure and properties of number. Contrary to this it will allow those with little understanding of place value to obtain right answers. (Jones 1988, p. 42)

Right answers are fine. But it is important to realize the dangers of not understanding why the procedure one uses works.

Those who would be inclined to disagree with me, and they would presently include the overwhelming majority of primary teachers, as well as the general public, would justify the continued emphasis on teaching written computation on one or both of two grounds: it is, in itself, an essential skill for survival and/or it provides a means whereby children acquire an understanding of number.

Hitherto neither of these reasons has been seriously questioned or considered by any but a very small number of individuals. Now that they are being raised as matters for urgent consideration by the teaching profession and the community at large, it is perfectly conceivable (some would say that it is perfectly obvious) that neither of these two justifications for the concentration of attention on written algorithms stands up to scrutiny at the present time.

Let me draw an analogy. There was a time not so long ago when a significant proportion of the educated population in the UK had to learn Latin. It had always been so. Not only was it perceived to be important in itself as forming an essential part of the fabric of our past (I speak as an Anglo-Scot), but moreover it provided a means of acquiring a true understanding of the structures and possibilities of English, and, even further, it provided an unmatched means of training the brain to think.

It was patently obvious to me as a Latin teacher that Latin was, in reality, important to few students, and an impediment to thought to the vast majority. To the few who appreciated it and accepted the challenge it was worthwhile — though no more worthwhile than many other disciplines. The teaching profession, always a conservative force, was very slow to see the daily evidence of their own eyes. When finally their consciousness was raised, they saw, in effect, that this particular emperor had no clothes. Today few study it. This does not mean that Latin is unimportant: it means that it is not of sufficiently significant importance for most to study it.

We would be rash to dismiss the parallel between the place of Latin in our schools thirty years ago and the place of written arithmetic today. Latin then, as written arithmetic now, was seen to have both practical importance in itself and also to offer a gateway to the understanding of wider issues. On analysis it was seen not to fulfill those goals in the case of the majority of students who studied it. The goals, in so far as they were important, could be more effectively achieved by other means.

It may be so today with written arithmetic. The ability to obtain the correct answer to calculations in a variety of situations is clearly still a vital skill. It is by no means so obvious that this ability is best achieved through the present concentration on written computation:

> It is becoming increasingly unusual for standard written algorithms to be used anywhere except in the mathematics classroom. (French 1987, p. 39)

> It may well be the case that a combination of reliable mental methods and the ability to use a calculator are sufficient for all practical purposes. (Brown 1981, p. 47)

Maier (1980) points to the discrepancy between what goes on in mathematics classrooms and the mathematics that people use in the real world. 'School mathematics', Maier says, 'ought to emulate folk mathematics', which he describes as the 'mathematics that folk do' (Maier 1980, p. 21). He continues:

> Some of the general differences between school maths and folk maths are clear. One is that school maths is largely pencil-and-paper mathematics, while folk maths is not. Folk mathematicians rely more on mental computations and estimates and on algorithms that lend themselves to mental use. When computations become too difficult or complicated to perform mentally, more and more folk mathematicians are turning to calculators and computers. In folk maths, paper and pencil are a last resort. Yet they are the mainstay of school maths. (Maier 1980, p. 22)

Clearly then, it is hard to sustain the first justification offered for the continued emphasis on teaching written computation, namely that written arithmetic is an essential tool for survival.

To turn to the second justification, it is often suggested that written computation provides a means through which children acquire an understanding of number. A general familiarity with numbers and the way they behave, the ability to think and to assimilate information presented in quantitative terms (in other words having a general number sense) may *not* be best accomplished by an excessive concentration on written forms of calculating. As I have said, there is a growing agreement that it is not. This was expressed briefly and forcefully ten years ago by Michael Girling:

> At a time when a cheap calculator can be bought for the price of two good cabbages, we need to redefine our aims for numeracy. I suggest the following definition. 'Basic numeracy is the ability to use a four-function electronic calculator *sensibly.*' (Girling 1977, p. 4)

Later in his article Girling suggests the effect of this point of view on written algorithms:

> I am not going to suggest that paper and pencil algorithms should not be taught, but that they should *only* be taught as part of the armoury of techniques that we have to help in an understanding of number *and not because they are useful*. This is not just a slight difference in emphasis but, I believe, has quite dramatic consequences:-
> (a) The concentration is now unequivocally on understanding the process involved.
> (b) There is a very clear advantage in studying as many different algorithms as can be manufactured; for example all possible methods of subtraction should be used!
> (c) The most refined methods of long division, for instance, which may be the least illuminating, need not be taught — at least not to everyone.
> (d) There is no need for anyone to be stopped in their progress in mathematics through being unable to perform the useless algorithms we now require.
> (Girling 1977, p. 5)

A further weakness in our present stress on formal written methods is considered in detail by Ginsburg:

> A good deal of elementary school education is devoted to addition, subtraction, multiplication and division with whole numbers. Children first add and subtract with small numbers and then they repeat the operations with larger ones and then larger still. They are taught standard methods of computation. These algorithms, developed and codified over the course of centuries, are guaranteed to achieve the correct result; applied properly, they always work. So formal education tries to make available to children some powerful procedures. But what use do children make of their cultural legacy? We shall see that they often ignore the standard procedures and instead rely on methods of their own invention. (Ginsburg 1977, pp. 90–1)

Ginsburg goes on to describe in detail a variety of informal methods clearly devised by the children themselves. One of the most remarkable was that developed by Kye, an 8-year-old.

Example 2.2 An informal method for subtraction

Kye's teacher had written on the board:

$$64 \\ -28$$

and she was explaining that 'you can't take 8 from 4, so you have to regroup the 64 as . . .' At this point Kye interrupted. Kye said, 'Oh, yes you can. 4 minus 8 is negative 4.'

He wrote:

$$
\begin{array}{r}
64 \\
-28 \\
\hline
-4
\end{array}
$$

'And 40 and negative 4 give you 36 ... the answer is 36.'
He wrote:

$$
\begin{array}{r}
64 \\
-28 \\
\hline
-4 \\
40 \\
\hline
36
\end{array}
$$

In brief, Kye subtracted 8 from 4, getting negative 4; he subtracted 20 from 60 getting 40; and then he added negative 4 to the 40, getting 36, which is the correct answer. (Ginsburg 1977, p. 105)

Strangely enough, a 9-year-old child in Canada revealed to me that she was, quite independently, using the same strategy herself. She had discovered it for herself, found that it never let her down, so used it. Her teacher had no idea that she was using this subversive method, since there was no outward or visible sign. Her form of words was: '4 from 8 is 4, 4 from 40 is 36', which she wrote as the answer. She admitted to me that she hadn't considered telling her teacher as 'It isn't the way she wants'.

I have documented (McIntosh 1978, 1979) a variety of informal methods of subtraction and multiplication used by individual children in different classrooms and schools. These methods were only unearthed by their teachers as a result of a small piece of action research described in the articles. What was significant was that none of the teachers had had any idea that the written calculations being marked correct in their classrooms had often been computed by methods quite different from those taught by them to the children. Similar findings by Jones are reported in Plunkett:

One of the most remarkable things about these methods [standard written algorithms] is that they are used so little. In some research directed to quite other ends, D. A. Jones investigated the methods used by each of 80 11-year-olds to calculate 67 + 38, 83 − 26, 17 × 6 and 116 ÷ 4. The questions were written in this form, and the children were free to use written or mental methods. Over half of the 320 calculations were successfully completed by non-standard methods, e.g. 83 − 26: 83, 73, 63, 60, 57; 17 × 6: 12 × 6 = 72, 72 + 30 = 102. Thus despite the heavy teaching of standard algorithms, they are not necessarily chosen for calculations of this order of difficulty. (Plunkett 1979, p. 3)

I remember Ruth Rees, a researcher at Keele University, describing research she was conducting into the numeracy standards of apprentices in England. She was watching them as they underwent a written test of mixed calculations when, quite unintentionally, she found herself distracted by the strange scribbles many of them were making on 'rough paper'. After the test she collected these and discovered a rich world of idiosyncratic, informal methods of calculating. Whatever methods these 16-year-olds had been taught in school over the previous ten years, many of them had clearly abandoned them in favour of more rough and homespun, but undoubtedly more tried and trusted procedures of their own.

- Written methods may not be essential for survival.
- They may not help us to acquire a good sense of number.
- They may not be trusted by many who have learned them.
- Finally, in many cases they are patently less efficient than other methods.

Two instances of the last will suffice. Anyone who, in order to calculate
1000 − 1, writes this down as:

$$\begin{array}{r} 1000 \\ -\ 1 \\ \hline \end{array}$$

and then proceeds to hunt along the row of zeroes for something to decompose is manifestly innumerate. That might be acceptable for a machine, but not for a thinking being. And yet many children come to believe, because of the emphasis given in schools to written methods, that that is really the *correct* way, and that mentally counting back one from one thousand is somehow underhand or downright cheating. In reality it is of course both more efficient and more mathematical, since an essential feature of real mathematics is its predilection for the simple, neat and lazy way of doing things.

As a second, and somewhat less simplistic example, how would you calculate 24 × 25? You might set it out as:

$$\begin{array}{r} 24 \\ \times\ 25 \\ \hline \end{array}$$

and multiply 24 by 5 and then 2 (or 20) and add the 120 and 480 to reach the correct answer of 600. This is the correct formal written method. But how much neater, and quicker, to note the 25 and for that to register immediately as one-quarter of 100, to note that 6 × 4 = 24, and hence to compute the result as 600.

Eighty years ago that would not have been an appropriate reaction. Those who were taught arithmetic were taught it so that some of them could perform simple computations of a repetitive nature for small reward, working as clerks. They were not required to think, or rather, they were required *not* to think. But we no longer have employment for unthinking human computers. We have inhuman ones which are in the long run much cheaper, much quicker and much more reliable for arithmetical drudgery. What we still need, in fact what we all need to become, are thinking calculators with an ability to adapt and improvise methods and to test quickly the reliability of results produced by machines. And we need, now more than ever in this calculator age, a well-developed and flexible sense of number.

THE ROLE OF THE CALCULATOR

And what of the calculator? It might be thought that possession of a calculator brings with it the ability to perform any ordinary calculation. Far from it. Effective use of a calculator requires an understanding of numbers.

Ten years ago I worked on a project involving the use of calculators in primary schools (see Bell *et al.* 1978). On numerous occasions I spoke to groups of parents who doubted the good of introducing calculators to their children at an age when the children had not yet learned to calculate without calculators. One worry was that children would become lazy and turn mindlessly to the calculator to do their work for them. It is worth noting from the project report that:

> Children have been encouraged, when doing paper and pencil computation, to check their answers on the calculator — This has not however led them to use the calculator instead of paper and pencil methods since they were perfectly clear that it was the latter which they were trying to improve. (Bell *et al.* 1978, p. 31)

I used to find it helpful to start the evening by providing each parent with a calculator and asking them to use it to calculate the sum of $1.37 and 13 cents. I found that I could rely on between one-third and one-half of the parents telling me that the answer was $14.37. Many of the remainder told me that the answer was 1.5. It was then much easier to discuss the mathematical demands made on children by the use of a calculator both in feeding data into the calculator and in interpreting the results.

Even checking written calculations by means of the calculator is not always a trivial task. I remember watching a child who had reached $2.50 as the result of a written addition. The calculator, when used to check the answer, produced 2.5. Did this confirm or contradict her result? She wasn't sure.

Again any attempt to check with the calculator that 97 divided by 13 gives a remainder of 6 is frustrated by the calculator's insistence that the answer is 7.461 538. It requires a good understanding of the effect of division, the status of a remainder, and the significance of the display to persuade the calculator to divulge what that remainder is.

There have been several attempts to list the basic number skills needed to ensure efficient use of the calculator. Girling (1977, pp. 13–14) includes the following in his list of number skills necessary for sensible use of the calculator:

1. The need to be able to check whether we or the calculator have made a mistake and given the wrong result. This checking may take several forms including:
   (a) asking whether the answer makes sense;
   (b) repeating the calculation using a different operation or procedure;
   (c) making a very rough approximation; and
   (d) using pattern (for example checking the units digit).
2. The need to understand the relative size of numbers.
3. The need to be able to perform mental calculations for speed, for convenience and so as to be able to hold our own in the commercial and industrial world. Girling considers that minimum requirements here are:
   (a) the ability to give and receive change by 'counting on';
   (b) multiplying and dividing by 10;
   (c) addition facts to 20 (quick recall);
   (d) doubling and halving; and
   (e) multiplication facts to 10×10.

Each of us might want to modify this list in some way but there would, I believe, be general agreement with the conclusion reached by Bell:

From the work so far, three basic computational skills seem essential when the calculator is used freely:
(a) facility in single-digit arithmetic
(b) a good understanding of place value, including decimals
(c) ability to estimate and check.
(Bell *et al.* 1978, p.31)

To these we would have to add a clear understanding of the various operations and their purposes, and an ability to see in real-life situations what calculation is necessary, and to translate the calculator result back into its setting. In passing it is worth mentioning that our present classroom practice is not noticeably efficient in passing on the majority of these basic skills. Even in the calculator age there is still plenty to do.

This is not the place to argue the case for *some* use of the calculator in primary schools. The most recent comprehensive analysis of findings on the effects of calculators on student achievement and attitude (Hembree & Dessart, 1986) integrated the results of 79 research reports. Among its conclusions were:

1. In Grades K–12 (except Grade 4) students who use calculators in concert with traditional instruction maintain their pencil-and-paper skills without apparent harm. Indeed, a use of calculators can *improve* the average student's basic skills with paper and pencil, both in basic operations and in problem-solving . . .
4. Students using calculators possess a better attitude toward mathematics and an especially better self-concept in mathematics than noncalculator students. This applies across all grades and ability levels.
(Hembree & Dessart 1986, p. 96)

They conclude: 'It no longer seems a question of *whether* calculators should be used along with basic skills instruction, but *how*' (Hembree & Dessart 1986, p. 97). And, in spite of the unexplained hiccup at Grade 4 (which would seem plausible since this is the stage at which traditionally children really begin to be hit with full formal written computation), the authors' principal recommendation is that 'calculators should be used in all mathematics classes of Grades K–12' (Hembree & Dessart 1986, p. 97). This recommendation is endorsed by every major report and study I have seen. As they say, not whether, but how.

Most of the research has focused on the possibility that the use of calculators will harm basic skills. Little effort has been given to the enhancement of students' achievement through a systematic use of calculators. (Hembree & Dessart 1986, p. 91)

There is general agreement that there are two essentially different purposes for which a calculator can and should be used in the classroom. The first, and most obvious, is as a number-cruncher to deal with computations which are awkward, complex, tedious, or whose performance by paper-and-pencil methods would interfere with the main purpose of the particular lesson: it might be to check whether a number pattern continues with large numbers, to work out distances for a scale model, to enhance understanding of large numbers by estimating and then calculating the meaning of a million seconds (amazingly only eleven and a half days), or any of a number of stimulating and educationally beneficial mathematical investigations which are available to most students only in the presence of a calculator. This use of a calculator to assist with awkward calculations is an obvious and natural use, unlikely to cause dissent, and readily acceptable to anyone who considers that mathematics should not only be seen to be useful but actually be used in the classroom.

There is, however, another quite different role for the calculator in the classroom, which is less obvious but which appears to have equal, though as yet barely explored, potential. Planned activities with the calculator can help children with the acquisition and reinforcement of many mathematical concepts, skills and processes. In effect, the calculator is the latest in the long list of aids for mathematical learning — it joins counters, Unifix cubes, Cuisenaire rods, Multibase Arithmetic Blocks (MAB) and the rest as an instructional aid in the classroom. A few examples of the use of the calculator in this role may help to clarify the idea.

A child is exploring its grasp of place value with whole numbers: 'Put 7483 in your calculator display. Change the 4 to 0. What did you do? Change the 7 to 1. What did you do?' In order to perform the task the child has to understand that the 4 stands for 400 and that the 7 stands for 7000. In other words, in order to perform the task the child has to display an understanding of place value at this level. Of course, this concept can and should also be developed by experiences other than calculator use. The calculator simply provides an enlarged range of activities which may prove helpful for some children. Moreover it has two considerable advantages over many materials. Firstly, its use is highly motivational for children. This is not simply a classroom object like Unifix or MAB. Few adults of their acquaintance go round with pockets full of blocks, flats, longs and units in case they meet a calculation beyond the scope of their mental powers. But children will see many adults, including those in their family, reach for a calculator, so when they themselves use it in the classroom it is giving them a powerful and positive message about the relevance of their school experiences to the world outside.

A second advantage of the calculator is that it provides immediate and neutral feedback. You may think you should subtract four thousand (instead of four hundred) in the example above and, instead of merely writing this down and finding out your error later when the teacher has time to give you some attention, and when you have consequently already reinforced your incorrect assumption by several more wrong answers, the calculator provides the opportunity for you to test your answer immediately without any embarrassment or loss of self-respect or any sign of exasperation, annoyance or derision from others. You can then try to rectify the situation and to learn and profit from your mistake. No wonder Hembree & Dessart report that 'students using calculators possess a better attitude toward mathematics and an especially better self-concept in mathematics than noncalculator students' (Hembree & Dessart 1986; see also Hembree 1986).

Here are two more examples of how the calculator can be used as an instructional aid. The constant function for addition and subtraction provides a very simple and flexible means for children to practise counting on and back efficiently and with immediate feedback. Counting on from zero in sevens for example gives useful reinforcement to the seven times table. Counting back in eights from one hundred helps add speed and confidence to mental arithmetic.

Again, children find great difficulty in reaching, if they ever do reach, a full understanding of what fractions are. Using an equivalence between ¼ and 1 ÷ 4, children can convert the following list of fractions into decimals and look for relationships: ½, ²/₂, ¼, ²/₄, ¾, ⁴/₄, ³/₆, ²/₈, ⁴/₈, ⁶/₈. This activity when structured in with parallel experiences, and if accompanied by discussion, will help, for some at least, to throw light on an area which by all accounts is not effectively taught at present.

There is a great need for curriculum development in this area and for bringing together the experimental activities of individual teachers and projects into a coherent form which can provide an easily usable resource for the majority of teachers. The Curriculum Development Centre (CDC) and the Australian Association of Mathematics Teachers (AAMT), in cooperation, have provided excellent leadership with the publication of their National Statement on the Use of Calculators for Mathematics in Australian Schools — a statement which has been publicly endorsed by every Department and Ministry of Education in Australia. The essence of its contents is as follows:

> It is recommended that, as far as resources allow, teachers should:
> 1. Ensure that all students use calculators at all year levels (K–12);
> 2. Ensure that the calculator is used both as an instructional aid and a computational tool in the learning process;
> 3. Be actively involved in the curriculum change in content and methods arising from calculator use;
> 4. Take full advantage of calculators for mathematics within the total curriculum;
> 5. Initiate discussion locally regarding the role of calculators in the school and society.

(AAMT & CDC 1987, p. 1)

THE ROLE OF MENTAL ARITHMETIC

There is considerable dialogue concerning the place of calculators in schools: the role of mental arithmetic seems scarcely to be considered at all with any seriousness. The Cockcroft Report (1982, p. 92) is fairly bland on the subject: 'There has been a decrease in the use of mental mathematics in recent years and we believe that this trend should be reversed'. In fact, its importance appears to have fluctuated widely during this century according to the prevailing perceptions of its function:

> One movement towards a deemphasis on mental computation began early in the twentieth century as a strong, negative reaction to the theory of mental discipline that prevailed during the latter part of the nineteenth century. This theory viewed mental computation as a perfect technique for developing the faculties of the mind. Mental arithmetic was revived in the

> 1930s and 1940s when the social utility of mathematics was emphasised. A third swing of the pendulum began in the late 1950s and early 1960s, when mathematics instruction began to focus on structural properties of the mathematical systems taught in schools. This deemphasis was ironic, because most proponents of mental computation have ... cited better understanding and use of structural relationships with numbers as a benefit of mental computation. In the 1980s the pendulum appears to be swinging toward increased attention to mental computation. This attention partly results from the back-to-basics movement, but it is primarily caused by the growing availability of technology and a recognition of the important role mental computation plays in the efficient use of technology. Although some attention is currently being given to mental computation, it is typically sporadic ... (Reys 1984, p. 549).

None of these pendulum shifts, however, have suggested other than that mental computation is the bridesmaid of written computation. It is true that an occasional isolated voice has queried this assumption. For example, as far back as 1908, Benchara Branford, Divisional Inspector to the London County Council, formerly Lecturer in Mathematics in the Victoria University, argued:

> It is certainly true that mental arithmetic is often advocated and, to a small extent, taught; but only in conjunction with ordinary or written arithmetic. Its preeminent office appears to have been much misunderstood. At present, written arithmetic is the standing dish, while mental arithmetic is a mere sauce, palatable or otherwise — which may therefore be taken or left. Exactly the contrary, it seems to me, should be the case in education: mental arithmetic should come first and form the solid food: written arithmetic should be the luxury, given where and when it can be appreciated. (Branford 1908, p. 90)

This suggested reversal of the relative roles and status of mental and written computation has a powerful ally in Edith Biggs, HMI in the United Kingdom:

> When children can give an immediate answer to questions like 68 + 6 they need further experience with pairs of two-figure numbers such as 68 + 26, 38 + 46, and so on until these, too, can be performed mentally by an efficient method (that is, without counting on in ones at any stage). For example to add 68 and 26, some may add the tens first, 80, the units next, 14, and give the answer: 94. Others may add the units first and tens second. Some add 68 and 20, 88, and then add 6: 94. Now, if at the last step they count on in ones from 88, this is not an efficient method and it usually means that the child is not yet ready to benefit from practice in two-figure additions (tens and units). This then is a crucial test of readiness for practice in written computation with tens and units: the ability to add two 2-digit numbers mentally by an efficient method ... (Biggs 1965, p. 27)

Quoting the above passage, Ewbank comments:

> At first sight this sounds like putting the cart before the horse. But on reflection I feel it makes good sense. You see, the [written] algorithm for doing 37 + 25 is a procedure that can be extended to numbers of any size,

numbers well beyond the mental computational abilities of all save a few calculating prodigies. So when you write down 37 + 25 to work it out, fragmenting it into 5 plus 7, and 30 plus 30 [sic] (or some such scheme), you are writing down what you already understand in your mind. The opposite of this — which I contend is what most children do — is to write down the procedure without understanding. (Ewbank 1977, p. 29)

Reys (1984) lists this relationship between mental and written methods as the first of five reasons (which he believes are widely accepted) for teaching mental computation. These are:

1. it is a prerequisite for successful development of all written arithmetic algorithms;
2. it promotes greater understanding of the structure of numbers and their properties;
3. it promotes creative and independent thinking and encourages students to create ingenious ways of handling numbers;
4. it contributes to the development of better problem-solving skills; and
5. it is a basis for developing computational estimation skills.

(Reys 1984, p. 549)

CONSEQUENCES FOR THE PRIMARY SCHOOL

Enough is enough. For the rest of this chapter I am going to assume that the argument is convincing and to explore the even more thorny problem of what the consequences are and what we might do about it.

Let me repeat the conclusions first so as to avoid any possibility of misunderstanding where I have reached.

1. The importance of people's ability to handle numbers and to compute with numbers has not diminished.
2. Mental computation is the foremost computational skill used in society, and is also the mechanism most readily available for the understanding of how numbers behave in general; as a consequence mental arithmetic, which includes estimation, should be at the forefront of computational work in schools.
3. Calculator usage should complement mental computation in the classroom to handle those calculations for which mental computation is inappropriate.
4. Written forms of computation should continue to have a place in the classroom provided they meet one at least of the following criteria:
   • they help to illuminate the way numbers behave;
   • they provide a source of intrinsic interest (to the students!) in their own right;
   • they are being developed as informal methods to extend and support the use of mental methods; or
   • their development is being used as a problem solving exercise.

If all this is accepted, then the consequences, for the primary school curriculum at least, appear formidable. For most schools over half of what fills the mathematics lesson at present becomes redundant. A whole generation of teachers needs to rethink their intentions when teaching number.

They need the support of programmes of instruction containing broad aims, detailed syllabus goals, developed teaching sequences, instructional methods and ideas for individual lessons, not to mention forms of assessment, none of which are conspicuously available at present.

However, the scene is not nearly as bleak as this. To begin with there is already a ground-swell of dissatisfaction with present practices and a willingness to find a more natural approach to number work. Moreover, many teachers and others have been questioning the rationale for teaching computation. As long ago as 1967, the Association of Teachers of Mathematics (UK), always known and respected for its radical approach to mathematics education, suggested a fundamentally altered approach to computation, and one which has much to offer at the present time:

> We reject an exclusive concentration on the acquisition of computational skills. We also reject the separation of computation from other mathematical activity and the attempt to deal with it as though it were learnt differently. This distinction has no reality for us (or for children, as far as we can see). One characteristic mathematical activity is the generation of algorithms and routine procedures. The choices that are made in the creation, selection and operation of these procedures are important mathematical decisions and an integral part of mathematical strategy. It is not that children now need to know less about numbers and how to compute with numbers. On the contrary they should know much more about number relationships and the operations that can be performed with numbers. Through games with numbers, play with patterns of numbers and free compositions with numbers, children can learn, without drill, to deal empirically with situations involving numbers, and develop a flexible set of procedures for handling such routine as is necessary. (Wheeler 1967, p. 6)

They elaborated on this theme a decade later in *Notes on Mathematics with Children*:

> The ability to compute quickly and accurately is clearly a useful skill to possess when it is likely that tasks will be met which require its use . . . Not long ago children spent part of every day of most of their school lives working towards this pattern of skill to the exclusion of all else in mathematics . . . The assumption was that it would take them many years to achieve good standards of arithmetical skill. We take the view that such a skill can be acquired by the time it is needed with relative ease, virtually as a by-product of some important mathematical activity that should be taking place in the earlier years. The mathematics we have in mind, as the sections so far have indicated, is associated with number and the operations on number which take us 'behind the scenes' of the conventional procedures and reveal the underlying transformations.
>
> The need is to make the construction of arithmetical procedures a problem [problem-solving] area for children. Telling them how to do their sums, or so to structure their learning that they are inevitably led to a set of algorithms of which the teacher approves, short-circuits a rich field of mathematical experience. Decision-making, creating problem-solving strategies, and the refining of home-made algorithms, are integral parts of mathematics and it is precisely in these areas that children will gain experience if they are allowed to generate their own computational procedures. (Wheeler 1977, p. 94)

I recall an example of this some years ago when a 7-year-old girl tugged my sleeve as I was standing by the blackboard in her classroom: 'I've got to add 47 and 26 and I don't know how. Can you help me?' At the time I was influenced by a section in *Notes on Mathematics with Children* which suggested the point of view that all computations were really 'transformations' — in the case of addition you were trying to change or transform two (or more) numbers into one number under certain conditions. She agreed that we wanted to end up with one number instead of two. I asked her to write the two numbers on the board a distance apart.

'Do you know anything about 47?'

'It's 40 and 7.'

'Rub out 47 and put 40 and 7. Now we have three numbers, 40, 7 and 26.' Then 26 was replaced by 20 and 6 giving four numbers! It appeared to be getting worse.

'Is there anything there you can add?'

'40 and 20 is 60, that's easy.'

In rapid succession 40 and 20 were replaced by 60, 7 and 6 by 13, 13 by 10 and 3, 60 and 10 by 70 and finally with great excitement 70 and 3 by 73.

This is only a simple example, and that really is the point: once developing an algorithm is seen not as a set sequence of rules to be taught by the teacher but a creative challenge for children calling into play their own powers and perceptions, and directed by their own probing and experimentation, it can become a fresh and free area for exploration and one which builds up the problem solving abilities and the self-confidence of children, instead of being an isolated area of mathematics which has to be 'learnt differently'. Here at least is one positive view of how written computation could take up a different and yet significant and integrated role within the whole field of computation.

With regard to calculator use, after a hiatus of several years during which everybody seemed to turn their technological attention to computers and tag the words 'and calculators' on to the end as though they were simply miniature versions of big brother, productive work is now being done in looking seriously at the implications of living in a calculator age and in producing more central calculator-based material for primary schools. However, it is still true that almost all the published material for calculators provides isolated activities, often trivial or peripheral, which may provide material for a 'calculator lesson' but do not help integrate the calculator as a normal feature of the primary mathematics classroom. An unresolved problem is how deeply to embed calculator activities into commercial mathematics series. If you entrench them centrally and consistently as a *sine qua non* then as a publisher you run the horrendous risk of being ahead of your potential customers — educationally admirable but financially disastrous.

With regard to mental computation there are a number of signs that things are progressing beyond the general invective of change and moving towards analysis of how to translate the ideals into practicable classroom practice. For example there is a chapter by Paul Trafton entitled 'Estimation and Mental Arithmetic' in *Developing Computational Skills*, the 1978 National Council of Teachers of Mathematics (NCTM) Yearbook, which contains a useful and usable analysis of some procedures for performing computations mentally. He lists four alternatives to the standard (written) algorithm for addition with the comment that 'these algorithms are as systematic as the conventional ones; yet their front-end nature permits easier remembering of partial answers and more meaningful interpretation of the numbers themselves' (Trafton 1978, pp. 207–8). Two alternatives for mentally computing 48 + 35 are given in example 2.3.

Example 2.3 Two methods of mental computation

1. Add the tens	*40 and 30 is 70*
2. Add the ones	*8 and 5 is 13*
3. Add the two sums	*70 and 13 is 83*
OR	
1. Add a number to one addend to make it a multiple of ten	*48 and 2 is 50*
2. Subtract the same number from the other addend	*35 − 2 is 33*
3. Add the two numbers	*50 + 33 = 83*

The reader will no doubt be conscious of having used such procedures: but it is highly doubtful that he or she will have any recollection of having been taught them. There is no doubt that many such procedures exist and are in constant use. Much work needs to be done in documenting and analysing them so that methods of systematically incorporating them into learning programmes can be explored.

Trafton and others are clear that such algorithms should be explicitly and methodically taught in the same manner as instruction of thinking strategies for learning basic facts advocated by Rathmell and others (Rathmell 1978). Others believe that it is preferable to give children encouragement to calculate mentally as they wish, and then by discussion draw out the different methods they have used. (The same difference of opinion exists over the best way of 'teaching' problem solving strategies to children.) It is not clear whether one or the other method, or a blend of both, is most effective. What is clear is that systematic analysis of these mental methods is urgently needed, so that they become as familiar to teachers as are the current written methods and so that they acquire status as 'respectable' means of calculation. In the two previously cited articles (McIntosh 1978, 1979), I have documented some of the methods used by primary children for subtraction and multiplication — some of them highly efficient and some highly complex; often children were reluctant to reveal them and were almost ashamed to admit that they had used other than what they had been led to believe was the 'right' way.

A key necessity is to alter the present model of what are misnamed 'mental arithmetic sessions' but which are in reality a series of short, low-level unrelated questions to which answers are to be calculated instantaneously and the answers written down at speed. Typically such sessions are then marked quickly with little or no discussion before the teacher moves on to the main purpose of the lesson. This model is wholly inappropriate as a means of developing powers of mental computation, and for a variety of reasons, not the least of which is that it has been shown even on its own terms to be ineffective. Biggs, in *Mathematics and the Conditions of Learning* (1967), used data from a survey of about 5000 children to draw conclusions about the various outcomes of different approaches to the teaching of arithmetic in the primary school. The data include the number of minutes devoted to mental arithmetic per day in 69 classes employing a variety of approaches to mathematics teaching. The approach categorized as traditional had as one of its characteristics 'a great deal of "mental" arithmetic in which speed of response is encouraged'. In all types of classrooms the number of minutes per day devoted to mental arithmetic varied from nil to '11 and over'. Among the conclusions of the study are:

> [Number anxiety] tends to increase slightly with more time devoted to mental arithmetic. The general conclusion then is that mental arithmetic is probably not a pleasant exercise for the children. . .
> Allocation of time to mental arithmetic bore no relation at all to attainment. (Biggs 1967, pp. 211, 220)

There are further reasons for altering the current form of mental arithmetic sessions in classrooms: the present form of short, sharp, question-and-answer sessions is designed not to teach but to test. There is no opportunity to learn anything other than that the teacher considers the matter important and that you were, for each question, either right or wrong. The questions are almost always low-level, one-step calculations or word problems. The range of situations for which we require and use mental computation is barely touched. There is rarely discussion of how answers were arrived at. There is little discussion of anything by the teacher and none on the part of the children. There is no means of involving or acknowledging the full range of abilities present in the class. Only occasionally is there a coherence or planned progression within or between sessions as is recognized to be essential in the remainder of mathematics lessons. I have recently produced (McIntosh 1988) a package of formats for mental arithmetic sessions to provide alternative practical ways of better meeting some of these objectives. These suggestions are a more detailed account of some ideas which were trialled by teachers as a result of in-service courses that formed the basis of an earlier article (McIntosh 1980).

For instance, the teacher writes a number on the board, 17 for example, and children initially offer calculations to which this is the answer. The class monitors the correctness of the suggestions, while the teacher writes them in a structured format on the board. All suggestions are accepted equally. From then on the teacher directs the session in any of a number of directions: 'Give me more like this one; How many more like this do you think there are?; No more of this kind; Give me some using four numbers, . . . using a × and a + sign; and so on. This one starting point would usually take up the whole session with a mixture of challenges, discussion and calls for children to spot, continue, explain or justify observations or assertions.

Another format simply requires the teacher to give a calculation within the mental powers of the class, for all to agree on the answer, and then for children to explain how they performed the computation.

In a third activity children explore estimation: they have to arrive at an estimate of a quantity or measure by negotiating upper and lower limits within which *every* child in the class agrees the answer lies.

The suggestions have been well received by teachers and children who have trialled them, but they only scratch at the surface of needed reforms and curriculum development in this area.

CONCLUSION

We appear to be at the start of a long process of considerable structural change involving the central core of the primary mathematics syllabus. The process will be slow and painful, but I and many colleagues find the prospect exhilarating. Mechanical arithmetic is now an anachronism. It is surely worth the struggle to replace it with a more relevant alternative, one in which children are enabled to increase their ability and confidence in selecting and using the most appropriate form of computation from amongst those currently available. Isn't this what it means to be numerate?

REFERENCES

Australian Association of Teachers of Mathematics & Curriculum Development Centre 1987, *National Statement on the Use of Calculators for Mathematics in Australian Schools*, CDC, Canberra, Australia.

Bell, A., Burkhardt, H., McIntosh A. J. & Moore, G. 1978, *A Calculator Experiment in a Primary School*, Shell Centre for Mathematical Education, Nottingham, UK.

Biggs, E. 1965, *Mathematics in Primary Schools*, HMSO, London, UK.

Biggs, J. B. 1967, *Mathematics and the Conditions of Learning*, NFER, Slough, UK.

Branford, B. 1908, *A Study of Mathematical Education*, Oxford University Press, UK.

Brown, M. 1981, 'Number operations', in *Children's Understanding of Mathematics*, ed. K. M. Hart, John Murray, London, UK, p. 47.

Cockcroft, W. H. (Chairman) 1982, *Mathematics Counts: Report of the Committee of Inquiry into the Teaching of Mathematics in Schools*, HMSO, London, UK.

Ewbank, W. A. 1977, 'Mental arithmetic: A neglected topic?', *Mathematics in School*, 6 (5), 28–31.

French, D. 1987, 'Mental methods in mathematics', *Mathematics in School*, 16 (2), 39–41.

Ginsburg, H. 1977, *Children's Arithmetic*, Van Nostrand, New York, USA.

Girling, M. 1977, 'Towards a definition of basic numeracy', *Mathematics Teaching*, 81, 4–5, 13–14.

Hembree, R. 1986, 'Research gives calculators a green light', *Arithmetic Teacher*, 34 (1), 18–21

Hembree, R. & Dessart, D. J. 1986, 'Effects of hand-held calculators in pre-college mathematics education: A meta-analysis', *Journal for Research in Mathematics Education*, 17 (2), 83–99.

Jones, P. 1988, 'Mental mathematics moves ahead', *Mathematics in School*, 17 (3), 42–44.

Maier, E. 1980, 'Folk mathematics', *Mathematics Teaching*, 93, 21–3.

McIntosh, A. J. 1978, 'Some subtractions: What do you think you are doing?', *Mathematics Teaching*, 83, 17–19.

McIntosh, A. J. 1979, 'Some children and some multiplications', *Mathematics Teaching*, **87**, 14–15.

McIntosh, A. J. 1980, 'Mental arithmetic — Some suggestions', *Mathematics Teaching*, **91**, 14–15.

McIntosh, A. J. 1988, 'Mental arithmetic', in *MCTP Activity Bank Volume 1*, eds C. Lovitt & D. Clarke, Curriculum Development Centre, Canberra, Australia.

Plunkett, S. 1979, 'Decomposition and all that rot', *Mathematics in School*, **8** (3), 2–5.

Rathmell, E. C. 1978, 'Using thinking strategies to teach the basic skills', in *Developing Computational Skills*, ed. M. N. Suydam, NCTM, Reston, USA.

Reys, R. 1984, 'Mental computation and estimation: Past, present and future', *The Elementary School Journal*, **84** (5), 547–57

Skemp, R. R. 1976, 'Relational understanding and instrumental understanding', *Mathematics Teaching*, 77, 20–6.

Trafton, P. 1978, 'Estimation and mental arithmetic', in *Developing Computational Skills*, ed. M. N. Suydam, NCTM, Reston, USA.

Wandt, E. & Brown, G. W. 1957, 'Non-occupational uses of mathematics: Mental and written — approximate and exact', *Arithmetic Teacher*, **4** (4), 151–4.

Wheeler, D. H. (ed.) 1967, *Notes on Mathematics in Primary School*, Cambridge University Press, UK.

Wheeler, D. H. (ed.) 1977, *Notes on Mathematics for Children*, Cambridge University Press, UK.

Becoming numerate: developing conceptual structures

MALCOLM SWAN

INTRODUCTION

In any discussion of numeracy, it is essential to pin down exactly what we mean by the word. Most people appear to equate the word 'numerate' with 'able to perform basic arithmetic calculations' (Collins Concise Dictionary). Others maintain a much broader interpretation, for example 'acquainted with the basic principles of mathematics and science' (Oxford English Dictionary). In this chapter, I would like to use the term in the sense used in the Cockcroft Report (1982) which states:

> We would wish the word 'numerate' to imply the possession of two attributes. The first is an 'at-homeness' with numbers and an ability to make use of mathematical skills which enable an individual to cope with the practical mathematical demands of his everyday life. The second is an ability to have some appreciation and understanding of information which is presented in mathematical terms, for instance in graphs, charts or tables or by reference to percentage increase or decrease. Taken together, these imply that a numerate person should be expected to be able to appreciate and understand some of the ways in which mathematics can be used as a means of communication. Our concern is that those who set out to make pupils 'numerate' should pay attention to the wider aspects of numeracy and not be content merely to develop the skills of computation. . .
>   Most important of all is the need to have sufficient confidence to make effective use of whatever mathematical skill and understanding is possessed, whether this be little or much. (Cockcroft 1982, paras. 34, 39)

The recurring emphasis is on developing understanding, appreciation and confidence in order that mathematics may be useful in the everyday lives of students. Within this context, this paper addresses the following issues:

- What should be included in a 'numeracy' course?
- How well do students understand mathematical concepts?
- What teaching strategies develop greater understanding, appreciation and confidence?

In particular, the latter two questions are addressed to the two areas emphasized by Cockcroft: the 'at-homeness' with numbers, particularly with regard to the use of a calculator, and the ability to interpret data.

WHAT SHOULD BE INCLUDED IN A NUMERACY COURSE?

In a review of research on mathematical education, Bell, Costello & Küchemann (1983) identified four components of mathematical competence: facts and skills, conceptual structures, general strategies and attitudes. These may be familiar but they do provide an excellent structure for thinking about the ingredients for a numeracy course, and set this chapter in its proper context.

Facts and skills

Facts are items of information which are essentially unconnected or arbitrary. These include notational conventions (e.g. $3\frac{1}{2}$ means $3 + \frac{1}{2}$, 32 means $(3 \times 10) + 2$, ab means $a \times b$), and names attached to concepts (e.g. equilateral triangle). Skills are very well established multistep procedures (e.g. the ability to multiply decimals). Many skills are capable of being implemented on calculators or computers.

Conceptual structures

These are richly connecting networks of concepts and relationships. They make mathematics meaningful, underpin the performance of skills, and their presence is shown by the ability to remedy memory failures and transfer or adapt procedures to fresh situations. Most common mathematical texts and teaching practices seem to be based on the implicit belief that repeated rehearsal of facts and skills somehow result in better conceptual understanding. (You understand decimals better if you learn to add them up successfully; you understand graphs better if you practise drawing them.) There is now an abundance of research evidence that refutes this view. Generally speaking, most 15-year-old students do not fully understand what a decimal means even though they can add them up successfully. Most 15-year-olds are not able to interpret a Cartesian graph, even though they have had endless practise at choosing scales, plotting points and so on. Evidence for these statements follows.

General strategies

These guide the choice of which skills are appropriate, and enable children to use mathematics to tackle unfamiliar problems. The acquisition of these strategies involves students in reflecting upon their own approaches and thought processes (e.g. Am I being systematic? Have I enough data? Shall

I use a graph?). Many lists of general strategies exist; the most recent is contained in *Mathematics for Ages 5 to 16*, the proposals for the National Curriculum for Mathematics in England:

> When they use mathematics to tackle real-life problems, pupils should be able to:
> • formulate a plan of what needs to be done, identifying any sub-tasks;
> • decide whether there is enough information — and if not, decide what they need and where to find it;
> • distinguish between important and irrelevant information;
> • see how the task is similar to, differs from earlier tasks;
> • recognise patterns, relationships/connections and/or general rules;
> • select the appropriate mathematics to create a model;
> • apply commonsense and reasoning skills;
> • select and use the most appropriate technology;
> • recognise that the best mathematical solution may not be the best real solution;
> • complete the task.
> (DES/WO 1988, p. 49)

Attitudes and qualities

We once invited a group of employers to produce a list of attitudes and qualities that they would like to see in young adults about to enter into their professions. They would like to appoint people who are:
• confident
• articulate
• creative
• outgoing
• adaptable
• cooperative
• committed
• at ease with figures
• able to plan their time and sort priorities
  − communicate clearly
  − think logically
  − take a global view
  − use resources (including other people)
  − work in a team

How can such attitudes be developed in mathematics lessons?

Our view of mathematics will govern the way we teach it. Teachers who view their task as transmitting 'facts and skills', tend to adopt an expository style, while those who desire to encourage the development of conceptual structures will include more practical work and reflective discussion. (This will form the main focus of this chapter.) The development of general strategies and positive attitudes will require the tackling of whole, practical problems in unfamiliar, real and relevant contexts. (The Shell Centre's Numeracy through Problem Solving project is designed to develop such strategies; see chapter 4.)

On the following pages some of the 'gaps' in students' current understanding of mathematical concepts are described, and teaching methods by which understanding may be developed are discussed.

UNDERSTANDING MATHEMATICAL CONCEPTS

A great deal of research has been conducted in recent years on children's understanding of mathematical concepts. Useful summaries appear in the reports of the Assessment of Performance Unit (Foxman 1980), the Concepts in Secondary Mathematics and Science (CSMS) project (Hart 1980, 1981), the Mathematics Education Group at Brunel University (Rees & Barr 1984), and in research reviews (e.g. Dickson, Brown & Gibson 1984; Bell, Costello & Küchemann 1983). In this section, the discussion is restricted to two specific areas: the concepts required to make effective use of a simple four-function electronic calculator, and the concepts required to interpret graphical data. The implications for teaching, I believe, can be generalized from these areas to many others.

Concepts involved with calculator usage

'Basic numeracy is the ability to use a four-function calculator sensibly' (Girling 1978, p. 13). This provocative definition makes us re-examine the place of pencil-and-paper algorithms. Why spend hours trying (often in vain) to equip children with a calculating power equivalent to that of a $5 calculator? Even given calculators, children need to be able to give meaning to the symbols on the buttons and the numbers on the display, they need to know when to divide (rather than how to divide) and they need methods which enable them to know whether an answer is reasonable. What does research show?

Decimal notation

> Most 15 year olds do not understand decimals: that is the lesson of the five years the Assessment of Performance Unit spent testing over 150 000 pupils.

This stunning headline appeared in the *Times Educational Supplement* in 1985 (Foxman 1985; see also Ruddock, Mason & Foxman 1984). It seems astonishing that the misconceptions unearthed recently have remained unknown to most teachers. A few of the areas of difficulty are outlined below, based on my own research (see Swan 1983), the work of the APU team and that of the CSMS team.

It appears that when children are unsure of the meaning of a decimal, then they try to change the unfamiliar into the familiar by treating the number according to what it looks like. Many seem to ignore the decimal point altogether, or treat the number as if it were two independent natural numbers, separated by a dot. Thus 5.62 may be interpreted as 'five hundred and sixty-two' or the two separate numbers, 'five and sixty-two'. Others appear to confuse the decimal point with 'separators' such as the 'r' in 9 r 2 (nine remainder two). It is worth reflecting on the number of situations in everyday life where a dot is used to separate a larger unit from a smaller one. A time may be written as 8.59 p.m. or the number of overs left in a cricket match as 6.2. Many children believe that these are decimals because 'they look like decimals'.

Frequently, the first evidence we get that children may have serious misconceptions is when they read a decimal number incorrectly. In the CSMS research, students were asked how they would say the number 0.29. Their responses are given in table 3.1.

Table 3.1 An example of the ways students read the number 0.29 (Hart 1981, p. 52)

Question: How would you say the number 0.29?				
	Age (years)			
Response	12	13	14	15
(Nought) point two nine	26	32	41	41
(Nought) point twenty-nine	25	32	30	27
Twenty-nine	19	13	8	10

The high proportion of children who answered '(nought) point twenty-nine' may be influenced by the use of decimal currency, or even other metric units. The amount $5.29 is usually read as 'five dollars twenty-nine', not as 'five point two nine dollars'. Thus the '2' is seen to represent two tens, not two tenths, and the role of the decimal point is therefore seen as 'the thing that separates the dollars from the cents'. This may also account for the large proportion of children who interpret a calculator answer of $0.9 as 'nine cents' or $0.108 as 'a hundred and eight cents.'

Comparing decimals

In most situations when people have to compare decimal quantities, the numbers are usually quoted to the same number of decimal places (for example, when deciding who won a 100 m race if the finishing times were 10.00 seconds, 9.90 seconds and 9.93 seconds). Such situations present no problems for students. When calculators are used to process data, however, trailing zeros disappear and many students cannot understand why. For example, when comparing two rates in a 'best buy' type problem: 'Which is better value 1.5 litres of drink at $2.82 or 1.25 litres at $2.24?' If students decide to calculate the cost per litre of each drink, they will need some understanding of the relative sizes of 1.88 and 1.792. Lynn Joffe, in chapter 7, describes the evidence from the APU studies for the fact that many students experience difficulty when comparing decimals of different lengths. For example, many believe that the longer the digit string after the decimal point, the smaller the number; that is, they will say that $0.625 < 0.5$ because '0.625 has more digits', or because '0.625 is in thousandths, while 0.5 is in tenths, and thousandths are smaller than tenths' (Swan 1983). Thus, 'longer decimals are smaller in value'!

One further result is that when two decimals are the same 'length', some students appear to believe that the one with the largest fractional part has the smallest value. Thus they believe that because $625 > 375$ then $0.625 < 0.375$. Several explanations for this were suggested by the APU: by analogy with fractions, where the larger the denominator for a given numerator, the smaller is the fraction; or by analogy with whole numbers — the more digits a whole number has, the larger it is, so, working in the opposite direction, it may be thought that adding digits after the decimal point decreases the value of the number.

The implications of this research are serious. Most 15-year-old students have no 'feeling' for the relative sizes of decimal numbers at all. When this fact was publicized in the *Times Educational Supplement*, the immediate reaction of one teacher was to propose that students would find it more helpful if decimals were always quoted to the same degree of approximation. Thus students are simply told to fill in with zeros until all the decimals are the same length, then compare them as if they are whole numbers. This rule (which to many will seem arbitrary and meaningless) provides correct answers, but will not help to remove any of the misconceptions. It may even perpetuate them.

Using zero as an intermediate place holder

Consider the following item from the 1980 APU survey, and try to predict all the common errors yourself, before reading on!

Example 3.1 An item from the 1980 APU survey (Foxman *et al.* 1980, p. 24)

> Write a number in the box to complete the statement
> $73.45 = 70 + 3 + 0.4 + \square$

Fifty-one per cent of 15-year-olds were successful with this item. The most common errors included 5 (16%), 0.5 or .5 (8%) and 0.41 or .41 (5%). These last responses are from students who appear to view the decimal point as separating two whole numbers.

The denseness of decimals

The current proposals for the national curriculum in England state that the average 11-year-old student should 'understand that $7 \div 3 \times 3 = 6.999\,999\,9$ may occur on a calculator' (DES/WO 1988). However, the proximity of $6.999\,999\,9$ to 7 is not well understood by many students, as by now you might expect! Very few students at any age appreciate that there exists a large, let alone an infinite, number of decimals between any two given numbers and consequently that, for any given decimal number, a second number can be found arbitrarily close to it. This is confirmed by the CSMS item in table 3.2.

Table 3.2 Students' concepts of decimals (Hart 1981, p. 55)

Questions: How many different numbers could you write down which lie between 0.41 and 0.42?

	Age (years)			
Response	12	13	14	15
infinitely many, more than you can count	7	7	16	16
lots, hundreds	5	3	5	4
8, 9, 10	22	39	36	38
1	17	8	8	9
0	9	5	4	2

Contexts for decimals

Example 3.2 attempts to see whether children can think of a suitable, realistic context in which decimals may be added and whether or not the decimal numbers can be used correctly within the chosen context.

Example 3.2

> $$5 + 2 = 7$$
>
> A story which goes with this sum is: John had 5 records. His father gave him 2 more for his birthday. So now he has 7 records altogether. Write your own story to go with this sum: 4.6 + 5.3 = 9.9

Inappropriate contexts usually involve quantities which cannot be subdivided, for example:

> James had 4.6 sweets. His best friend gave him 5.3 sweets and he has 9.9 sweets altogether.

The stories that children write often give valuable insights into their misconceptions about the decimal numbers themselves:

> John had 4 apples and 6 Quaters his mum gave him 5 apples and 3 Quater so he had 9 apples and 9 Quater

> mr Brown had 4 and a half dozen sausage rolls (4.6) and Mrs Brown brought 5 and a quarter dozens Sausage rolls (5.3) so for tea they now have 9 and three quarter dozen rolls (9.9) for their tea.

The CSMS research contained a similar item (Hart 1981, p. 56) and found that only 33 per cent of 12-year-olds, rising to 41 per cent of 15-year-olds, can produce a satisfactory story. Many of the stories were heavily influenced by artificial, stereotyped textbook questions and had little to do with the real world. These results suggest that many students would not know of situations when it would be appropriate to make use of a calculator.

Understanding the number operations

Children usually build up their understanding of the four arithmetic operations from their experiences with small, whole numbers. These operations are usually introduced by means of simple models which do not generalize to decimals, and which therefore lead to many misconceptions. For example, students who are only taught to see multiplication as repeated addition will be unable to understand or estimate the result of 0.62×0.31, and will firmly believe that 'multiplication always makes numbers bigger'. Similarly, if children only view division as a sharing operation, they will be unable to give any meaning to $12 \div 0.4$. (You cannot share 12 apples among 0.4 people!) Common misconceptions concerning division include:
- you can only divide larger numbers by smaller ones;
- you can only divide longer numbers by shorter ones;
- you can only divide by a whole number;
- $3 \div 6$ means the same as $6 \div 3$;
- $3 \div 6$ means 'how many threes go into 6?'; and
- division always makes numbers smaller.

Such misconceptions often prevent children from knowing which buttons to press when faced with a problem. The interview in example 3.3 (carried out in the United Kingdom) illustrates this rather vividly.

Example 3.3

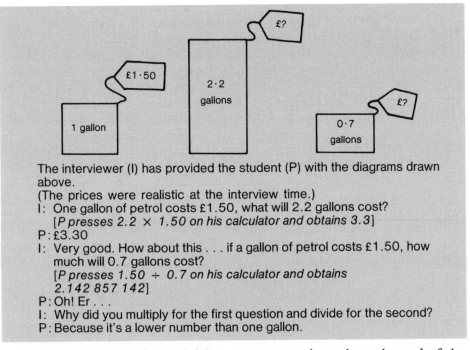

The interviewer (I) has provided the student (P) with the diagrams drawn above.
(The prices were realistic at the interview time.)
I: One gallon of petrol costs £1.50, what will 2.2 gallons cost?
  [*P presses 2.2 × 1.50 on his calculator and obtains 3.3*]
P: £3.30
I: Very good. How about this . . . if a gallon of petrol costs £1.50, how much will 0.7 gallons cost?
  [*P presses 1.50 ÷ 0.7 on his calculator and obtains 2.142 857 142*]
P: Oh! Er . . .
I: Why did you multiply for the first question and divide for the second?
P: Because it's a lower number than one gallon.

This student rejected multiplying 1.50×0.7 through to the end of the interview, because 'that would have given an answer bigger than £1.50'. For such reasons many students believe that the operation to be performed resides in the numbers rather than in the structure of the problem.

Before students can reliably choose operations to perform, and estimate the results that will be obtained, they need to have attached meanings to the four operations. Let us consider multiplication and division, by far the hardest of the four operations to understand. Both 6×4 and 6×4.3 can be interpreted as repeated addition ('6 lots of 4 or 4.3 added together'). But 4.3×6 and 4.3×6.2, on the other hand, may not. These latter multiplications are usually performed when a rate of some kind is involved (unit price $\times$ quantity, speed $\times$ time, and so on) and are much more difficult to identify. This explains, for example, why the first of the two problems shown in example 3.4 is much the easier to recognize as multiplication.

Example 3.4 Ways in which questions requiring multiplication are framed (Bell, Fischbein & Greer 1984)

> 1. In the school kitchen the cooks use 0.62 kg of flour to make one tray of doughnuts. How much flour will it take to make 27 trays?
> 2. An international cross-country runner completed a training run in 1.13 hours. He maintained an average speed of 9 miles per hour. How long was the course?

The sum $24 \div 6$ may be viewed in two ways: as a partition or sharing ('If 24 objects are shared into 6 groups, how many objects in each group?'); or as a quotition ('How many groups, each containing 6 objects, may be obtained from a collection of 24 objects?'). In the first case, the group size is unknown, while in the latter case the number of groups is unknown. These models appear to be equally easy to recognize.

The sum $6 \div 24$ may be conceived of as a fractional partition ('If 6 is shared between 24 people, how much does each person get?') but not as a quotition. However, $6 \div 0.24$ cannot be seen as a partition, but can be seen as a quotition ('How many lengths of rope, each measuring 0.24 metres, may be cut from a rope 6 metres long?'). For expressions like $0.4 \div 0.57$ to have any meaning at all the quotition concept needs to be extended to fractional quotition: 'A milk jug holds 0.4 litres. A one-pint milk bottle holds 0.57 litres. What fraction of a pint does the milk jug hold?'.

It is interesting to note that when children are asked to spontaneously suggest contexts for particular division computations with decimals, they nearly always choose partition, even when this proves a rather contrived thing to do! This is presumably due to the fact that children learn from an early age to associate the sign ' $\div$ ' with the word 'share'. Example 3.5 is one girl's story designed to embody $17 \div 4.25 = 4$.

In Brown's (1981) research on children tackling decimal number problems set in realistic contexts, she notes that less than 10 per cent of 15-year-old children were consistently successful at identifying the operation to be performed, and thus could be said to have a sound understanding of the meaning of number operations. The results for adults do not appear to be much more promising. Sewell (1981) asked fifty adults to work out the cost

Example 3.5

> We went Carol Sing We made
> 17 pounds One left early there were
> 4 of us and we gave a quarter
> to the fifth who went early
> We had 4 pounds each

of 3.4 metres of cloth at £2.54 a metre, using any method they wished, including calculators. Only four of the fifty attempted it, and the three who obtained a correct answer used informal methods rather than school taught rules of algorithms. As the researcher reported, 'This sum was widely viewed with horror and alarm' (Sewell 1981, p. 62).

Interpreting data

We are bombarded with data every day, from train timetables to graphs showing fluctuations in interest rates. Many students and adults find such data at best confusing and at worst, incomprehensible. To take one example, let us look at students' understanding of Cartesian graphs.

Existing research (see, for example, Janvier 1987; Bell, Brekke & Swan 1987a, 1987b; Kerslake 1981) supports the view that while most children are capable of learning many of the technical skills associated with point plotting and so on, few are able to interpret the meaning of global features contained in a graph, even when it is set in a familiar context.

Major areas of difficulty are illustrated in the following examples (3.6–3.10). The tasks are taken from Swan (1985) and the data from Brekke (1987), which concern a sample of 192 third-year students (a fairly representative 13–14 years age-group) from a Nottingham Comprehensive School.

Coordinating the information relating to two variables

Example 3.6 Bags of sugar (Swan 1985, p. 100; Brekke 1987, pp. 11, 44)

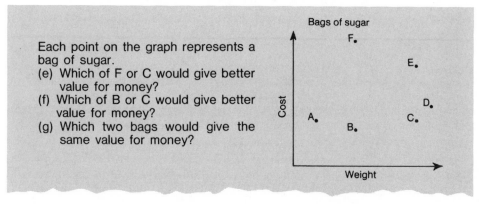

Each point on the graph represents a bag of sugar.
(e) Which of F or C would give better value for money?
(f) Which of B or C would give better value for money?
(g) Which two bags would give the same value for money?

Abby's responses:

(e) C. C is less money

(f) B. Because it is lower in price

(g) A,C. they both the same price

Overall facility levels

	Correct explanation	Wrong explanation using one variable only (like Abby)	Wrong explanation with two variables
(e)	45%	31%	8%
(f)	31%	39%	13%
(g)	7%	44%	17%

Example 3.6 requires students to compare the relative positions of the points in a qualitative way. Question (e) is the easiest, requiring only that students realize that C weighs more but costs less than F . Question (f) is more difficult, requiring that students notice that C weighs about twice as much as B but only costs a little more. Question (g) is by far the hardest, requiring a clear understanding that bags with a given cost per unit weight will be represented by points lying along a straight line which passes through the origin. As the complexity of the task increases, more students (like Abby) appear to focus entirely on one variable in their argument.

Confusing a graph with a picture of a situation

Example 3.7 Hoisting the flag (Swan 1985, p. 102; Brekke 1987, p. 9)

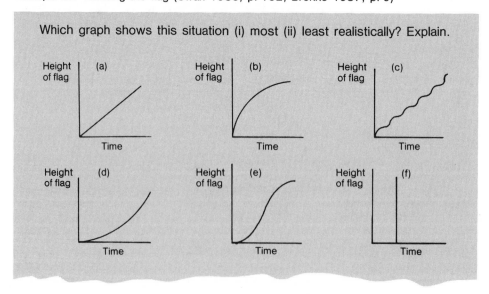

Which graph shows this situation (i) most (ii) least realistically? Explain.

Maria's responses:

(i) Most realistic:

f. This graph would mean that the flag is going in the same direction.

(ii) Least realistic:

c. This graph would mean that the pole is a funny shape.

	Overall facility levels	
	Correct explanation	Picture interpretation
(i) Most realistic	42%	41%
(ii) Least realistic	34%	38%

Many students, like Maria, interpret graphs as if they are pictures of the given situations, rather than abstract representations; that is 'If the flag goes straight up then so must the graph'. In this question, the graph that Maria rejects as being least realistic is, in fact, the most realistic if the flag is hoisted by pulling the rope arm over arm. To illustrate this further, we offered the following graph (example 3.8) to an able group of 13-year-old students and asked them to identify a sport that it could represent.

Example 3.8 Which sport? (Swan 1985, p. 74)

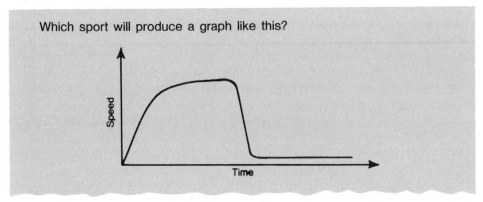

Which sport will produce a graph like this?

A selection of responses

Susan:

> (I think it is a horse - jumping. The horse canters up (jumps). Sorry
> had second thoughts
> Its a shotput the put is thrown up it travels and drops, then
> rolls It just reminded me of a shotput.

Joanne:

> I think this graph shows what a polevaulter would do
> because it shows the height of the vault and then they
> would have a sharp drop like the graph shows.

Tony:

> I think the sport is football because at the beginning of the
> game all the players are lively and not so weak but as the
> game is nearly over the player strength drops and stay at
> a steady level till the game ends.

Greg:

> I have Reasons to believe that it will be a
> Parachuties because the plane goes up and then
> along the parachuties jumps out of the plane
> and lands then he goes for a walk. Or
> a diver who climbs up a cliff and dives of and
> then starts swimming.

Interpreting intervals and gradients

Example 3.9 The motorway journey (Swan 1985, p. 215; Brekke 1987, p. 21)

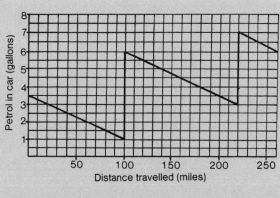

(d) Where did I have less than 2 gallons in my car?
(f) At which station did I buy the most petrol?
(h) How much petrol did I use over the entire journey?

Sean's response:

> At 220 miles because it is the highlight point on the graph

Facility levels:

(d) 20% answered correctly: the interval from 60 to 100 miles.
     54% answered 100 miles only.
      3% answered 60 miles only.
      8% answered a single number between 60 and 100 miles.
     49% answered correctly: at 100 miles.
     18% answered like Sean.

(h) 10% answered correctly: 6.5 gallons.
     11% answered 12.5 gallons (3.5 + 5 + 4).
     10% answered 16.5 gallons (3.5 + 6 + 7).
      9% answered 7 gallons (highest value).

Most students appear to find the interpretation of intervals difficult and often confuse them with values at particular points. In question (d) only 20 per cent realized that 'where' could refer to more than one place, and in question (f) 18 per cent believed that more petrol was bought at the second station because the graph goes 'higher'. In question (h), the students had to find the total of three interval lengths; 11 per cent added together the three 'rises' at 0, 100 and 220 miles, 10 per cent added the values at the three highest points and 9 per cent just gave the highest value on the graph.

Example 3.10 Growth curves (Swan 1985, p. 216)

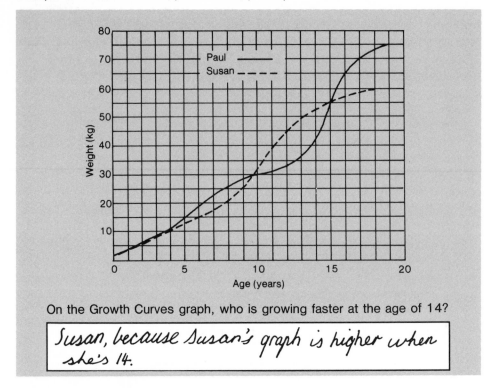

On the Growth Curves graph, who is growing faster at the age of 14?

Susan, because Susan's graph is higher when she's 14.

Example 3.10 illustrates how similar kinds of errors occur when gradients are to be interpreted. (This is similar to the problem encountered by the many adults who believe that when inflation decreases then prices should fall.)

From results such as those quoted above, it appears that less than half of the students aged 13–14 years have any depth of conceptual understanding of Cartesian graphs. We have no reason to expect these figures to improve for older students.

Some possible causes and implications

These results reveal that our priorities in teaching mathematics are misplaced. Most teachers seem to lay more emphasis on equipping students with facts and skills than on enabling them to build conceptual structures. Lessons on decimals or graphs, for example, simply involve children in carrying out sequences of routine manipulations (adding up rows of numbers or plotting points) without ever stopping to discuss or reflect on the meaning of what they are doing. Textbooks also place their main emphasis on the rehearsal and practise of facts and skills. They are written to minimize the demands on the busy teacher and their language is therefore kept as simple as possible and tasks are fragmented into small isolated steps that can be mastered one at a time. Children are kept busy, and discussion is kept to a minimum.

Frequently teachers and textbooks unintentionally encourage students to develop misconceptions and methods which are non-generalizable. For example, how often have we heard, when carrying out long division 'Sixes into three won't go'? (Fifty-one per cent of 12-year-olds, falling to 23 per cent of 15-year-olds, believe that there is no answer to 16 ÷ 20; see Hart 1981). Or, how often have we seen graphs embellished into pictures, as in example 3.11?

Example 3.11 Graphs are often embellished into pictures

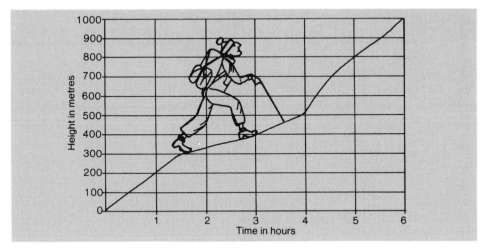

Textbook problems are usually designed to provide a vehicle for the practice of one particular technique. Students are not usually required to select from a repertoire of techniques. Consider example 3.12.

Example 3.12 Textbook problems

1. A farmer has 484 cabbages. She plants them in 4 equal rows. How many cabbages are there in each row?
2. A hotel caters for school parties of less than 30 people, and has the following rules:
   All parties must   (i)   comprise more than 20 people;
                    (ii)   include at least three adults;
                    (iii)   include not more than six adults.
   Take p to represent the number of pupils in the group and a to represent the number of adults. Write the four statements above in algebraic form and graph the information. If a school party includes 15 pupils, how many adults will there be in the party? What is the maximum number of pupils there can be in a party which includes only 4 adults?

In both cases, the techniques to be applied may be obtained from the context of the problem. The first problem is taken from a page entitled 'Division', while the second from a chapter on 'Linear programming'. The numbers are 'sanitized' to make the working easier. The first problem does not even need to be read, the numbers themselves indicate the operation to be performed. Most word problems can be solved by similar cues; for example:

- if there are more than two numbers, add them;
- if two numbers are similar in magnitude, subtract the smaller from the larger;
- if one number is relatively large compared to a second number, divide;
- if the division answer has a remainder, cross out your work and multiply.

Just for fun, you may like to try choosing the correct operation for each of the five problems in example 3.13. They are taken from different pages in a primary mathematics textbook in Chinese. (The answers are given at the end of this chapter.)

Example 3.13 A page from a Chinese mathematics textbook

1 輪船上有乘客共 2672 人 ， 其中中國籍人仕有 2098 人 ， 問該輪船上外籍乘客有多少人？

2 玩具 24 件，平均分給 8 人，每人可分得幾件？

3 李宅本季水費 105 元 ， 恰是陳宅的 3 倍，陳宅本季水費若干元？

4 被加數是 2405，加數是 7504，和是多少？

5 每週上數學課 6 節 ， 19 週共上數學課幾節？

We now have considerable research evidence to suggest that to understand a mathematical concept it is better to work through a few well chosen problems, than to work through lists of exercises. These problems must embody key concepts, and be discussed and tackled in depth, allowing alternative strategies to surface. This 'diagnostic' methodology is developed more fully, in the next section.

DIAGNOSTIC TEACHING

In this section, we will begin to look at teaching methods and materials which actively take account of the research, and which attempt to produce long-term learning. At the Shell Centre, a number of experiments have been conducted to test the effectiveness of diagnostic methods which involve the deliberate exposure and discussion of common errors and misconceptions in the classroom (e.g. Swan 1983; Bell *et al*. 1986; Onslow 1986). On the basis of these, packages of materials have been devised, some of which are now generally available to teachers (e.g. Swan 1983; 1985). Some of the main features of this work will be discussed with examples based on two of the conceptual areas we have already explored in this chapter: decimal notation, and the interpretation of Cartesian graphs.

A teaching experiment

We will now briefly describe a small-scale teaching experiment which illustrates the value of a teaching approach that focuses sharply on known misconceptions and makes these explicit to the children. (It has been more fully described in Swan 1983.) Two teaching styles were examined. The first of these, the conflict approach, was intended to involve the students in discussion and reflection of their own misconceptions and errors, thus creating an awareness that new or modified concepts and methods were needed. There was therefore, a destructive phase, in which old ideas were shown to be inaccurate or insufficient, before new concepts and methods were introduced. The second teaching style, the 'positive only' approach, made no attempt to expose and discuss errors, but tried to help students to develop a correct conceptual understanding from the start. Correct methods were then demonstrated and practised intensively. As much as possible, the same teaching material was used with both groups. The relative effectiveness of the two teaching methods was monitored by a pre-test, an immediate post-test and a delayed post-test (three months later) together with observations made during lessons.

Two parallel classes of second-year students (12–13 years old) were chosen from a suburban comprehensive school in Nottingham, UK. These classes were chosen so that their performances on the pre-test were reasonably comparable and both contained a wide spread of ability. The same teacher taught both classes for eight one-hour lessons using the two teaching approaches. The content of the lessons in both groups can be roughly divided into two areas:

- *Decimal notation* This section attempted to provide the students with a concrete model for decimal place value (the number line), and encourage the children to visualize this line when performing simple additions and subtractions. The correct verbalization of decimals was emphasized.
- *Comparing decimals* Number lines were provided to enable students to correctly compare decimal numbers containing different numbers of digits. The students were then encouraged to formulate their own rules for comparing decimals without using the number lines.

As this list makes clear, the teaching styles in both groups were essentially diagnostic and untypical in that they focused on the known areas of difficulty discovered by the pre-test, but only the conflict group were asked to examine and reflect on the misconceptions and errors exposed by that test.

The conflict teaching style

Each lesson followed a similar pattern, involving four phases.

C1. *The intuitive phase* Students were given a task which would expose their existing misconceptions. At this stage, they were asked to work individually, and the teacher made no attempt to correct any of their errors. It was hoped that once everyone had committed their ideas to paper, they would be more able to contribute to the group and class discussions which followed. For example, in one lesson, the students were asked to continue a collection of sequences, such as:

$$0.2, 0.4, 0.6, \ldots, \ldots, \ldots$$

Many, as expected, produced answers such as 0.8, 0.10, 0.12.

C2. *The conflict phase* Students were now asked to repeat the tasks, but this time they were asked to use methods suggested by the teacher. In our example, they were asked to view the sequence as bouncing along a number line (figure 3.1).

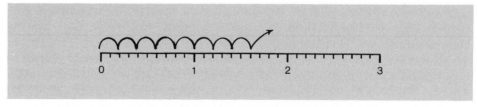

Figure 3.1 Explanation of the tasks by 'bouncing along a number line'.

They were also invited to check their sequences using a pocket calculator. Students were then encouraged to reflect on, debate, resolve and write down the reasons for any inconsistencies in their answers. This often made the students aware of their own need for new concepts.

C3. *The resolution phase* A class discussion was then held to make students aware of the errors and misconceptions exposed by the previous phase. For example, in one discussion, students stated that:

• There is no such number as nought point ten.
• Nought point ten can be exchanged for a whole number.
• Nought point one nought is the same as nought point ten.

This last comment was made by a student who had generated the sequence 0.05, 0.10, 0.15, 0.20, and then checked it on a number line and on his calculator, obtaining 0.05, 0.1, 0.15, 0.2.

By the end of this stage, most students could explicitly describe the thinking behind their own and each other's errors, as well as show that they had understood the concepts being discussed.

C4. *The consolidation phase* The correct concepts and methods were then used to solve further problems. Students were also asked to adopt the role of the teacher and mark exercises which contained mistakes (made by fictitious, though representative, students), then diagnose and correct the errors themselves.

The positive only teaching style

In these lessons, there were only two phases.

P1. *The teaching-the-concept phase* The concepts were explained and methods were taught for obtaining correct answers, based on understanding. They were the same methods as those adopted in C2 with the conflict group.

P2. *The consolidation phase* These concepts and methods were then reinforced using similar activities to those described in C4, except that students were never asked to mark work or diagnose errors. This group covered the work much more quickly than their conflict counterparts, and so more demanding, supplementary activities were provided.

Some observations

The conflict lessons made greater demands on the teacher than the positive only approach. This was mainly because of the considerable debate (and noise) that was created when students were actively encouraged to make and verbalize their errors. The positive only group worked very quickly and quietly and made few mistakes: 'It was a ''joy'' to teach them!'.

The conflict group solved each problem using at least two different methods. In contrast, the positive only group only used one, that supplied by the teacher. This group therefore covered the work much more quickly than their conflict counterparts, and so more demanding, supplementary activities were provided. A casual observer would have concluded that they were making better progress.

The test results

Each student was asked to complete a test — containing 48 items on the comprehension of decimals — immediately before the teaching programme, immediately afterwards, and again approximately three months later, after a school holiday. This test evolved by a succession of interviews and class trials from that devised by the CSMS team and reported by Hart (1980). The test was given in an uncompetitive atmosphere, with every student being given adequate time to complete it. Only the scores of those students who completed all three tests and who attended a minimum of five out of the eight lessons are included. The mean scores on each of the three tests are given in table 3.3

Table 3.3 Results of comparative Diagnostic Teaching experiment (Swan 1978)

	Pre-test	Post-test	Delayed post-test	Gain pre-test to delayed test
Conflict group (22 students)	44%	78%	80%	+36%
Positive only group (25 students)	52%	75%	76%	+24%

It can be seen that both groups made substantial gains during the teaching and that these gains were retained in the delayed post-test. The overall gain made by the conflict group was much greater (this proved statistically significant), and a more detailed analysis showed that no students in either group regressed on their pre-test performance in either of the two post-tests. This was particularly comforting since in the case of the conflict group there had been some fear that students who were already competent may have become confused when they were introduced to misconceptions that they did not themselves possess. There was also evidence that both teaching approaches did produce learning which transferred to an untaught context, but that the positive only approach is perhaps more likely to result in mechanical, rule-based learning.

Generating classroom discussions

Since this experiment, several more have been conducted on different mathematical topics and with much larger samples (e.g. Onslow 1986; Brekke 1987). These have consistently shown that more vigorous and intensive conflict discussions are associated with long-term progress. These discussions have been generated in many ways, for example via games and tasks which involve role reversals. Some methods are outlined in the following sections.

Games

Games which engaged the players in choices involving the key concepts and misconceptions are potentially very powerful learning situations. If well designed, they offer immediate feedback (either in-built or by an opponent's challenge), self-adjustment to a student's own level and repetition with variety. Experiments have shown that for a game to achieve its potential value it must be accompanied by discussions which focus on the principles to be learned or the misconceptions to be overcome, and these principles must be explicitly articulated by students as well as by the teacher. One example of a game which exposes the 'multiplication makes things bigger' misconception and which promotes a great deal of estimation is demonstrated in example 3.14.

Example 3.14 Target calculator game (Swan 1983, p. 75)

This is a calculator game for two players.

Player One enters any number onto the calculator.
Player Two then has to multiply this by another number so that the answer will be as near to the target, 100, as possible.
Player One then multiplies this new answer, trying to get nearer still to 100. The players take this in turns until one player hits the target by getting 100.**** on the calculator display.

Here is a sample game.

Player	Keys pressed	Display shows	Thoughts!
1	64	64	
2	× 1.5	96	Hmmm . . . a bit small
1	× 1.2	115.2	Oh . . . it's about 15 out
2	× 0.9	103.68	Nearly! Only 3 too big
1	× 0.9	93.312	I keep missing . . . 7 too low.
2	× 1.08	100.77696	I win!

Now try playing Target when you are only allowed to press the ÷ button.

Collaborative games or puzzles

These are games where students work together to achieve a desired result. For example, they may be given a large cardboard grid and a collection of small cards. The task is to place the cards on the grid in a particular way. The group discussions naturally focus on the correctness of the positioning

Example 3.15 A card game for provoking classroom discussion

Example	Words	÷	⌐	Answer
8 apples are shared among 2 girls. How many apples does each girl get?				
	How many ¼'s are there in 10?			

2 ÷ 8

8 divided by 2

2 apples are shared among 8 girls. How much of an apple does each girl get?

4

2)8‾

How many ¼ litre mugs can I fill from an urn containing 10 litres of tea?

8)2‾

10 ÷ ¼

¼ ÷ 10

40

and it is quite simple for students to change their minds. Example 3.15 is designed to provoke discussion about the interpretation of the various notations used for division. Students are asked to position the cards so that each row contains a consistent set of expressions.

Role reversal tasks

Usually, teachers ask the questions and students provide answers which are subsequently marked by the teacher. It is often helpful to reverse these roles, where the students are asked to generate questions from an initial situation, or where the students are asked to mark and criticize a piece of work. In example 3.16, students are asked to discuss and solve a problem collaboratively, and then go on to invent further problems of their own.

Example 3.16 Sketching graphs from pictures (Swan 1985, p. 88)

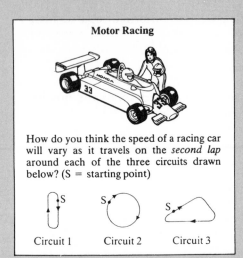

Motor Racing

How do you think the speed of a racing car will vary as it travels on the *second lap* around each of the three circuits drawn below? (S = starting point)

Circuit 1   Circuit 2   Circuit 3

Explain your answer in each case both in words and with a sketch graph. State clearly any assumptions that you make.

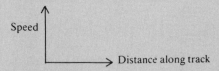

Speed

Distance along track

Compare your graphs with those produced by your neighbours. Try to produce three graphs which you all agree are correct.

The graph below shows how the speed of a racing car varies during the second lap of a race.

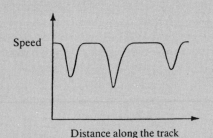

Speed

Distance along the track

Which of these circuits was it going round?

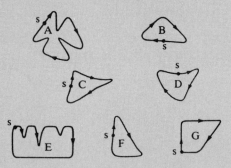

Discuss this problem with your neighbours.
Write down your reasons each time you reject a circuit.

Now invent a racing circuit of your own with, at most, four bends.

Sketch a graph *on a separate sheet of paper* to show how the speed of a car will vary as it goes around your circuit.

Pass *only* your graph to your neighbour.

Can she reconstruct the shape of the original racing circuit?

Handling classroom discussions

Children learn by talking and listening and should be given more opportunities to talk. Children talking in small groups are taking a more active part in all their work. Tentative and inexplicit talk in small groups is the bridge from partial understanding to confident meaningful statements. Present talk is future thinking. (Kerry 1981, p. 67)

Or, as one colleague put it, when asked why he had not written a paper for a conference, 'How do I know what I think until I've heard what I've got to say!'

Many mathematics teachers, unlike colleagues within other departments, are unused to handling classroom discussions. Oral work is often restricted to brief periods of questioning by the teacher followed by monosyllabic replies by students. Little opportunity is offered for students to describe and develop their ideas, and even when such opportunities arise, students are often too self-conscious, inarticulate and more concerned about the quality of their performance than the content of their contribution. The following sections illustrate some of the issues involved in handling small group and full class discussions, using an extract taken from *The Language of Functions and Graphs* (example 3.17).

Example 3.17 Are graphs just pictures? (Swan 1985, p. 74)

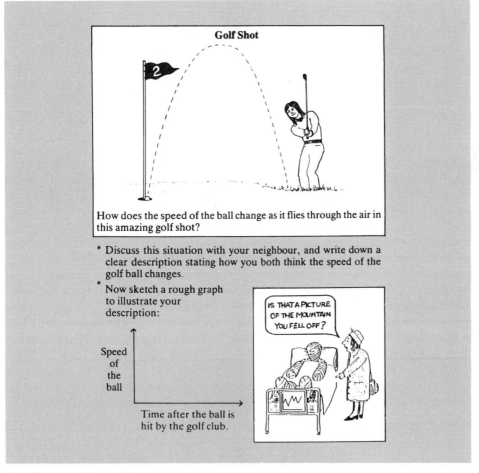

Small group discussions

After the problem has been introduced the children are usually asked to work in pairs or small groups until some kind of consensus has been reached.

At the beginning of a new task, it often takes some time to absorb all the information and ideas. The group discussions at the beginning of the task may therefore be fragmentary, using keywords, half sentences, questions and so on. This is the exploratory discussion stage. Although it often appears somewhat disjointed and poorly articulated, if the group is left to work undisturbed, it is here that organizing and reformulation of ideas can emerge. Example 3.18 shows four solutions reached during such a discussion.

Example 3.18 Types of responses that may come out of group discussions (Swan 1985, p. 76)

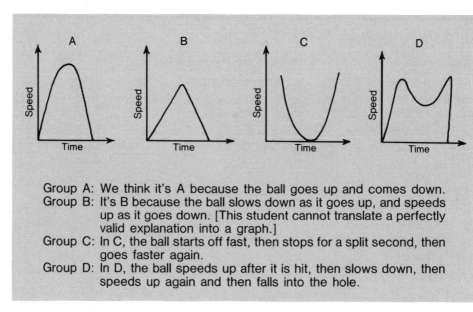

Group A: We think it's A because the ball goes up and comes down.
Group B: It's B because the ball slows down as it goes up, and speeds up as it goes down. [This student cannot translate a perfectly valid explanation into a graph.]
Group C: In C, the ball starts off fast, then stops for a split second, then goes faster again.
Group D: In D, the ball speeds up after it is hit, then slows down, then speeds up again and then falls into the hole.

During these discussions it is very difficult for a teacher to resist the urge to intervene and point out why such answers are incorrect. The danger of succumbing too quickly to this form of 'teacher-lust' has been demonstrated by Brekke (1987). He observed two teachers (among others) who had very contrasting styles. One always tried to help students in a positive way by directive teaching, explaining and correcting errors as they occurred. The other allowed the students to come to their own conclusions in discussions, and did not pre-empt the discussion by stating the correct answer. (This teacher also emphasized a strategy for working, and closed each lesson with a reflective discussion on what had been learned, drawing specific attention to the misconceptions that had been overcome.) A post-test showed that much more substantial progress and interest had been generated by this second approach.

As the nature of the audience has such a profound effect on children's thought processes, the teacher should be careful of the timing and frequency of interventions or interruptions. Eventually a group will be ready to offer its ideas to the whole class, but it will first need time and space to work out its own ideas within the group.

Whole class discussions

Asking children to present work or explain ideas to the whole class needs very sensitive handling. It is essential to try to create an atmosphere in which errors and poorly expressed ideas are welcomed and discussed rather than criticized and ridiculed. Attempts to achieve this kind of atmosphere can take on many practical forms. For example, the teacher may collect a few suggestions from students, write them on the blackboard and discuss them anonymously — thus avoiding any embarrassment. Or the teacher might ask a representative from each group to describe the consensus view obtained by the group. Solutions thus become associated with groups rather than with individuals. It is also possible to rearrange the desks or tables (in a U shape, for example) so that it becomes clear that the activity is discussion rather than exposition.

The Language of Functions and Graphs, recommends that, during a whole class discussion, a teacher's role should:

- Mainly be that of a 'chairperson' or 'facilitator' who:
  - directs the flow of the discussion and gives everyone a chance to participate   *Thanks Paul, now what do you think Susan?*
  - does not interrupt or allow others to interrupt the speaker   *Listen to what Jane is saying. How do you react to that Andrew?*
  - values everyone's opinion and does not push his or her own point of view   *Are there any other ideas?*
  - helps students to clarify their own ideas in their own terms.   *Could you repeat that please Joanne?*

- Occasionally be that of a 'questioner' or 'provoker' who:
  - introduces a new idea when the discussion is flagging   *What would happen if . . .?*
  - follows up a point of view
  - plays a devil's advocate
  - focuses in on an important concept   *What can you say about the point where the graph crosses the axis?*
  - avoids asking 'multiple', 'leading', 'rhetorical' or 'closed' questions, which only require monosyllabic answers.

- Never be that of a 'judge' or 'evaluator' who:
  - assesses every response with a 'yes', 'good' or 'interesting', etc. (This often prevents others from contributing alternative ideas, and encourages externally acceptable performances rather than exploratory dialogue.)   *That's not quite what I had in mind. You're nearly there. Yes, that's right. No, you should have said . . . rather. Can anyone see what is wrong with Jane's answer?*
  - sums up prematurely

(Swan 1985, p. 243)

This table is not intended to suggest that judging, or evaluating a student's response is always inappropriate, but rather to recognize that if the teacher operates in this way, then the nature of the discussion will change, either into a period of teacher-led exposition or into a rather inhibited period of 'answer guessing' where the emphasis is on externally acceptable performances rather than on exploratory dialogue. Typically, therefore, if judgements have to be made, then they should be made towards the end of a discussion. It is, perhaps, sometimes more helpful to leave a discussion in mid-air, so that the students leave the lesson still thinking and arguing.

CONCLUDING REMARKS

In this paper, I have attempted to show how traditional approaches to teaching mathematics have tended to divorce methods from meanings, and focus on facts and skills at the expense of developing sound conceptual structures. The facts and skills that are taught are often quickly forgotten precisely because there is no conceptual foundation. Thus, the 'spiral' curriculum has become essentially 'circular' for many, where the same ground is revisited year after year.

Diagnostic teaching, on the other hand, provides a more effective alternative. This methodology involves allowing students to discuss a few carefully chosen problems and situations in depth and examine the errors and misconceptions which surface. Research evidence seems to show that the resultant learning is much more meaningful and permanent, and thus more likely to be of use to the students. This approach, however, takes time and the 'coverage' of mathematical concepts may, in the early years, be less than we have grown accustomed to. Time spent here, however, may be saved later on, if the curriculum can become a true spiral as a result.

REFERENCES

Bell, A. W., Brekke, G. & Swan, M. 1987a, 'Diagnostic teaching 4: graphical interpretation', *Mathematics Teaching*, **119**, 56–9.

Bell, A. W., Brekke, G. & Swan, M. 1987b, 'Diagnostic teaching 5: graphical interpretation — teaching styles and their effects', *Mathematics Teaching*, **120**, 50–7.

Bell, A. W., Costello, J. & Küchemann, D. 1983, *A Review of Research on Mathematical Education Part A: Learning and teaching*, NFER/Nelson, London.

Bell, A. W., Fischbein, E. & Greer, B. 1984, 'Choice of operation in verbal arithmetic problems: the effects of number size, problem structure and content', *Educational Studies in Mathematics*, **15**, 129–47.

Bell, A. W., Swan, M., Onslow, B., Pratt, K., Purdy, D. *et al.* 1986, *Diagnostic Teaching — Teaching for long term learning*, Report of an ESRC project, Shell Centre for Mathematical Education, University of Nottingham, United Kingdom.

Brekke, G. 1987, *Graphical interpretation: a study of pupils' understanding and some teaching comparisons*, Shell Centre for Mathematical Education, University of Nottingham, United Kingdom.

Brown, M. 1981, 'Number operations', in *Children's Understanding of Mathematics 11–16*, ed. K. M. Hart, John Murray, London, p. 47.

Cockcroft, W. H. (Chairman) 1982, *Mathematics Counts — Report of the Committee of Inquiry into the Teaching of Mathematics in Schools*, HMSO, London.

DES/WO 1988, *Mathematics for Ages 5 to 16*, National Curriculum Proposals of the Secretary of State for Education and Science and the Secretary of State for Wales, Department of Education and Science and the Welsh Office, UK.

Dickson, L., Brown, M. & Gibson, O. 1984, *Children Learning Mathematics: A Teacher's Guide to Recent Research*, Holt, Rinehart and Winston.

Foxman, D. 1985, 'Missing the point', *Times Educational Supplement*, 19 April, p. 19.

Foxman, D. D., Martini, R. M., Tuson, J. A. & Cresswell, M. J. 1980, *Mathematical Development: Secondary Survey Report No. 1*, HMSO, London.

Girling, M. 1978, 'Towards a definition of basic numeracy', *Mathematics Teaching*, **81**, 13–14.

Hart, K. 1980, *Secondary School Children's Understanding of Mathematics: A report of the mathematics component of the Concepts in Secondary Mathematics and Science (CSMS) programme*, Research monograph, Mathematics Education, Centre for Science Education, Chelsea College, University of London.

Hart, K. (ed.) 1981, *Children's Understanding of Mathematics 11-16*, Murray, London.

Janvier, C. 1987, The interpretation of complex Cartesian graphs: studies and teaching experiments, PhD thesis, Shell Centre for Mathematical Education, University of Nottingham, United Kingdom.

Kerry, T. 1981, 'Talking: The teacher's role', in *Communicating in the Classroom*, ed. C. Sutton, London, Hodder and Stoughton.

Kerslake, D. 1981, 'Graphs', in *Children's Understanding of Mathematics 11-16*, ed. K. M. Hart, Murray, UK.

Onslow, B. 1986, Overcoming conceptual obstacles concerning rates: design and implementation of a diagnostic teaching unit, PhD thesis, Shell Centre for Mathematical Education, University of Nottingham, United Kingdom.

Rees, R. & Barr, G. 1984, *Diagnosis and Prescription — some common maths problems,* Harper and Row, London.

Ruddock, G., Mason, K. & Foxman, D. 1984, 'Concepts and skills: Decimal place value', *Mathematics in Schools,* 3(1), 24–8.

Sewell, B. 1981, *Use of Mathematics by Adults in Daily Life*, Advisory Council for Adult and Continuing Education.

Swan, M. 1978, *Teaching Decimal Place Value: A comparative study of 'conflict' and 'positive only' approaches,* Shell Centre for Mathematical Education, University of Nottingham, United Kingdom.

Swan, M. 1983, *The Meaning and Use of Decimals: Calculator-based diagnostic tests and teaching materials*, Shell Centre for Mathematical Education, University of Nottingham, United Kingdom.

Swan, M. (ed.), 1985, *The Language of Functions and Graphs: An examination module for secondary schools*, Joint Matriculation Board, Shell Centre for Mathematical Education, University of Nottingham, United Kingdom.

Note: The solutions to the Chinese problems in example 3.13 are: 1. Subtraction; 2. Division; 3. Division; 4. Addition; 5. Multiplication.

4 Recontextualizing mathematics: numeracy as problem solving

KAYE STACEY

> Mathematics lessons in secondary schools very often are not about anything.
> (Cockcroft 1982, para. 462)

INTRODUCTION

This chapter considers the relationship between two apparent poles of mathematical understanding: problem solving, often seen to be at the pinnacle of the learning hierarchy; and numeracy, often regarded as the lowest acceptable level of mathematical skill. What have these two to do with each other? It will be shown that mathematical skill developed without regard to problem solving and applications is frequently not useful and hence does not contribute to numeracy. Conversely, taking serious regard of real situations where mathematical ideas arise is important not only to learn how the ideas might be applied, but also for their very acquisition. In the terminology adopted in other chapters, this chapter is principally about the problems of *skill-choosing* and *skill-using*, but it will emerge that these are inseparably linked to *skill-getting*.

The discussion of numeracy in this chapter is principally concerned with what, beyond an understanding of the relevant mathematical ideas, enables people to use their knowledge in realistic everyday situations. However, this focus does not imply that students should first learn the ideas, then add some general problem solving strategies, and finally, if ever, use the ideas and strategies in real situations (although as an interim measure this would be an improvement on much current practice). Applications and problem solving should not be reserved for consideration only after the learning of skills has occurred; they can and should be used as a context in which the learning of mathematical ideas takes place.

It has been common to teach mathematical ideas with little regard to context, trusting that students will later be able to see how to apply the ideas themselves. Both the development of understanding of mathematical ideas and the possibility of using them in real situations are hindered by this decontextualized approach. If the demands of context are re-introduced and treated seriously, both problem solving skills and understanding of mathematical ideas can develop. Hence the title: 'Recontextualizing mathematics'.

The first section explores some of the dimensions of the gap between what students know and what they can use. Numeracy, if conceived of as the accurate performance of algorithms alone, is of little value. The rapid emergence of calculators and computers which can perform routine tasks quickly and reliably is, of course, one reason for this. The reason of concern here, however, is a different one; knowing how to do something is necessary but not sufficient to be able to apply it. Subsequent sections examine some of the skills, strategies and attitudes that students need for closing the gap and how these might be acquired.

The final section returns to school mathematics which is too often overly formal, abstract and decontextualized, and devoid of life. Can we throw away the school maths and survive, perhaps even do better, with a maths sufficient to solve everyday problems as they arise? To answer this, the source of the power of mathematical ideas is examined; it seems that 'everyday' maths alone is not sufficient either. This examination requires a look at the abstract nature of mathematics and the role of the symbol system. The way to harness the power of mathematics is to deal with real examples and real problems, but staying within the environs of 'real maths' is limiting in crucial areas. We cannot throw school maths away either.

THE GAP BETWEEN KNOWING AND USING

It is now well documented that the mathematics that people use in everyday life bears no simple relationship to the mathematics that is taught in school. The following examples illustrate some aspects of this relationship.

Aden: intuitively capable, formally not capable

In the video *Real Maths — School Maths* (Newton 1983) 10-year-old Aden shows that he can work out accurately, quickly and confidently the change when a chocolate bar costing forty-five cents is bought with five dollars. However, Aden is quite unable to obtain a sensible answer to the vertically arranged pencil-and-paper subtraction 500 − 45 which he has supposedly learnt at school. Observations such as this, not just with money, have been documented across the world with children of all ages and with well-educated and poorly educated adults (see, for example, Carraher, Carraher & Schliemann 1987; Hiebert 1989).

The secretary: formally capable, intuitively not capable

Three maths teachers and a young secretary were dispatching orders and completing invoices, which included items like 15 student's booklets at $2.50 each. The secretary used long multiplication, taught at school. The maths teachers worked mentally using a variety of informal methods.

Maxine and Alison: choosing 'primitive' methods

The Medicine question in example 4.1 can most neatly be solved using multiplication and division. However, students tend to choose more primitive methods, based on trial additions. In 371 responses to Medicine, from students in years 5 and 6, answers similar to Maxine's and Alison's were the most common, indicating that most students either did not recognize that the multiplication and division skills they had learned would be appropriate in this situation or did not feel sufficiently confident that they could carry out these operations accurately. In fact, there were remarkably few computational errors evident in these responses — students tend not to select operations which they might not perform accurately (Stacey 1987b).

Example 4.1 Students' responses to the Medicine problem (Stacey & Bourke 1988)

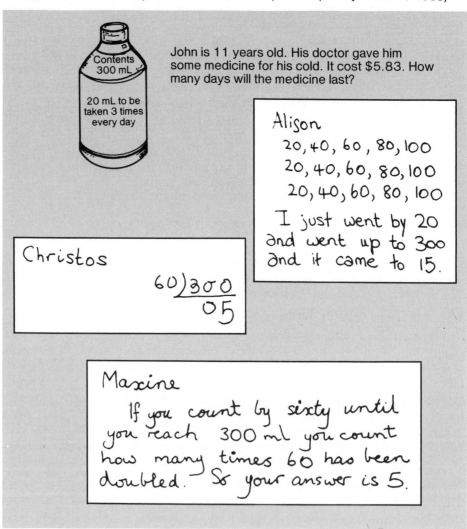

Currency conversion: Inability to choose skills when awkward numbers are involved

The difficulty with recognizing the appropriateness of mathematical skills is not just confined to children and division is a notorious example (see Fielker 1986). In example 4.1, the 'how many' aspect of division is strong and prompts alternative additive responses. When division by a fraction or decimal is involved, however, the user of mathematics who does not recognize that division is appropriate is left without any method of solving a problem. Currency conversion is a typical example. On one occasion, I needed the Australian dollar price for a book priced in US dollars. The senior librarian responsible for ordering and overall budgeting but not for detailed accounts was very familiar with converting Australian dollars to US dollars using multiplication by the appropriate decimal (then 0.72) on a calculator. However, she could only convert US dollars to Australian dollars approximately, by estimation. In fact, she added to the price an amount equal to 0.28 times the price (to compensate for the 'missing' 28 cents per dollar) and knew from experience that her answer would be too small so added a bit. Even though she was adept at both written division and the use of her calculator, she had never realized that dividing by 0.72 on the calculator was the simple answer to her frequent problem.

This incident underlines the importance of both knowledge and strategies. Since it is extremely hard to recognize that division is appropriate in this commonly occurring situation, it is important in schools that students should learn to deal specifically with currency conversions and other commonly occurring situations. Mathematics courses should include all the standard situations occurring in life in the standard problems used to illustrate algorithms and procedures in school. Richard Lesh (1985), after studying the teaching of rational numbers, concluded that there were many commonly occurring situations which were not adequately represented in the standard question types in textbooks. Also, Alan Bell (1984) has pointed out the psychological necessity of treating separately, situations (such as money and temperature) which are the same when fully mathematized (e.g. both use directed number) but which seem different to beginners.

When students are unsure whether division is the right operation or which number to divide into which, one strategy is to replace the awkward numbers by nice round ones and then try to do the problem. This 'trying a simpler problem' is a common strategy used by good problem solvers to supplement knowledge. Since we cannot expect to teach students all the knowledge they will ever need, we also need to build up strategic skills like this.

Advanced students exhibit similar difficulties

Even able students who have apparently demonstrated quite clearly their understanding of mathematical ideas find difficulty in using them. Very often it is because they are unable to mould questions into forms where their mathematical skills can be of use. There are numerous examples of this phenomenon in geometric problems given in the detailed protocols of

Schoenfeld (1985). There are also many examples of students' difficulties in recognizing when techniques of calculus are appropriate. For example, advanced university undergraduates in Poland were asked to develop, from a verbal description, a mathematical model of the process by which the liver converts thyroxine to iodine (Trelinski 1983). This is a continuous process — the liver takes in the thyroxine continuously and processes it. It does *not* take in one batch, process it completely, then begin on the next. The mathematical tools used to describe continuous processes such as this are those of calculus and the students had apparently mastered these. However, most of them only attempted to model the situation as discrete and step-wise. Similar observations have been documented around the world. In Australia, teacher education students studying their third year of calculus, usually do not recognize that the procedures for minimizing functions are applicable to problems about finding a path of shortest length. Yet minimizing a function is one of the main applications of the calculus they have studied. The students adopt a purely experimental approach, drawing paths and measuring their lengths. Their procedural knowledge of how to do calculus seems so tightly bound to specific triggering stimuli that it is not available out of that context.

The situations above illustrate some aspects of the complex relationship between formal knowledge of mathematical procedures and its use in the real world. Whereas mathematical learning should contribute to all aspects of numeracy, instead, for both elementary and advanced students, for the mathematically able and for those who experience difficulty in learning mathematics, it tends to exist separately and is used only when prompted. Even when people have mastered skills at school they often do not use them in everyday situations because another method is better or because they do not recognize that the skill is appropriate or because they do not feel confident in applying it.

In order for a mathematics curriculum to build real numeracy, it needs to develop:
- the ability to make sensible choices about which method to use;
- the ability to recognize major problem types and how to deal with them efficiently;
- confidence in one's ability to carry out the procedure properly; and
- sufficient general problem solving skills so that students can get the problem into a state where their algorithmic and procedural knowledge is of some use. The following sections investigate how some of these skills may be acquired.

MAKING SENSIBLE CHOICES

School mathematics rarely requires students to make any real choice about which skills and ideas should be applied, so they get very little practice at choosing skills. A question which can be done by using calculus to minimize a function is in the calculus chapter and probably even in the maximizing and minimizing section. Even in a climate where problem solving and modelling are now regarded as principal components of mathematics learning, problems are not often given to students without strong clues as to which technique they should use. One teacher recently reacted to my suggestion that he do this thus:

> This question is not in context. You don't just walk into a Year 11 class and put a question like this on them, especially in a formal, traditional school like this. I'd only give this after a relevant chapter. The expectations of the students have to be taken into account. They expect to be given the goods in a particular way and to do something like this would be like dropping a bombshell.

Traditionally, the need to address the application of mathematical knowledge has been met by the inclusion of word problems in the relevant chapter. The word problem provides an easy bridge between calculation and application, in a convenient written form which requires no change in teaching style. But, although they contribute to students' recognizing situations, such as currency conversions, where their mathematics can be applied, they often become 'non-sense' questions which generate non-sense responses. They therefore seem to contribute very little to helping students make *sensible* choices. A much lamented example comes from the 1982 National Assessment of Educational Progress (NAEP; Carpenter *et al.* 1980) testing for 13-year-old students across the USA:

> An army bus holds 36 soldiers. If 1128 soldiers are being bused to a training site, how many buses are needed?

Only 19% correctly rounded the quotient to the next number, whereas 39% either gave the exact quotient or ignored the remainder.

Why does such a large percentage of students give an apparently nonsensical answer? Was it that they simply forgot to round up or that they really thought you can hire a fraction of a bus? Many students did not know how to interpret the quotient and remainder (Silver 1986) and so played safe by giving both, but some are also probably trapped in the peculiar mixture of the real and the artificial that characterizes school learning. They assumed that the examiner did not really want to order buses to transport soldiers but wanted to see if they could use division. Even if the examiner really did want to order the buses, the knowledge that not all of the last bus would be required may be of use: perhaps a smaller and cheaper bus might be available.

Usually, the questions themselves are not nonsense and quite likely may have arisen in real life, but the way they are presented — outlined in just a few words and expecting a single answer response — makes them seem divorced from the real world, stupid and artificial. Conditions of testing and learning, by signalling (clearly or unclearly) the micro-world in which the student is to operate, make an important difference to the answers students give. Unthinking use of algorithmic procedures seems to be produced by the short-answer/short-time testing such as that favoured by the NAEP. For example, Carpenter *et al.* (1980, p. 428) reported that 39% of 13-year-olds in NAEP testing incorporated extraneous information into their answers. In contrast, the testing reported by Stacey & Bourke (1988), where students worked on questions for a longer time and were asked to explain their answers and reasoning, shows quite a different picture. Students like Maxine and Alison were seen as sensible users of arithmetic, who tended to build up answers piece by piece using well-internalized procedures in which they had confidence. Very few of the children's responses showed meaningless manipulation of numbers. For example, the extraneous information of $5.83 and 11 years in example 4.1 was used by only one of the 50 children who were interviewed on this task and in a similarly small percentage of the written responses.

The sociology of the classroom further compounds the difficulties of capturing real-life applications, storing them and then releasing them in good health in class. As one teacher wrote:

> Today I had to teach (in fact, reteach) Year 9 square root and square. They might wonder (if they wonder at all about mathematical matters) when or why anybody would need to find the square root of a number. Shouldn't we begin with the problem or question which contains or suggests the necessity of finding a square root? No; because it's Tuesday, because it is 10.10 a.m. and because you are in Year 9, you will all do square roots NOW. If I get a lesson going about why or when square roots are used, we'll never get through the set exercises. It's crazy!

How then can problems that are easy to use in the classroom be made to seem more real and encourage students to use their mathematics sensibly? Why indeed does the bus question seem simultaneously dull, commonplace and yet unrealistic? What if some soldiers were sick or you could get a smaller bus to take the soldiers left over? Almost all word problems can be criticized in this way for making too many assumptions, but herein lies the key. Making assumptions of this nature is one of the first steps in using mathematics in the real world — an essential feature of mathematical modelling. The difference is not that the assumptions are made, but that, in word problems, they are *pre-made*, without acknowledgement. For the user of mathematics in the real world, making reasonable assumptions is an essential part of solving a problem. Regular class discussion of what assumptions have been made could go some way to making short problems contribute more effectively to developing sensible use of mathematics. Students need to experience, as a matter of course, all phases of using mathematics to solve a problem, and an essential preliminary step is to make assumptions so that the problem is tractable.

One further feature of the teaching environment inhibits the sensible use of mathematics. Earlier, we saw how Maxine and Alison tackled the Medicine problem in example 4.1 using additive methods rather than a more efficient division-based method. In fact, all real instances of whole number division can be tackled by addition. This situation is very common — in the early stages, many new mathematical techniques that students learn do not actually enable them to solve more problems. Equation solving and matrices are other examples. Students can solve the first algebraic equations they are given (like $x + 6 = 7$ and even $2x + 5 = 11$) by inspection, without any need for the standard procedure their teacher is teaching them, and every application of matrices in secondary school can be done without using a matrix. Of course, in each case, teachers are teaching methods that will finally result in students being able to tackle more complicated situations because:

- they are more general (e.g. long multiplication applies with only minor alterations whether the numbers are integers or decimals);
- they can be used routinely when the numbers are awkward and intuition fails (e.g. the formal methods of dealing with ratio problems);
- they lead to new important methods (such as the key idea of 'undoing' an algebraic expression using inverse operations); and
- they are more efficient (e.g. matrix notation is universally used to deal with the enormous sets of equations arising in economic and industrial modelling).

However, the lack of immediate usefulness of new knowledge needs to be recognized by both teachers and students. Teachers often say that students *have* to work out a transformation using matrices (when a diagram will quickly give the answer geometrically) or *have* to solve the equation $2x + 5 = 11$ using inverse operations (when everyone can see that the answer is $x = 3$), or *have* to use division in example 4.1 (when it is easier to use repeated addition). Instead there needs to be a recognition that there are other valid, if more elementary, methods of solving these problems and teachers need to offer some convincing display that the new methods are in fact worth learning. If students believe that new methods just make it harder to do questions they can already do, then the battle for sensible use of mathematics is being lost.

KNOWLEDGE OR STRATEGIES?

This section looks at the question of what it is, beyond a knowledge of mathematical ideas and skills, that enables people to use their mathematics in real situations. Already several examples have arisen of the need for an interplay between content knowledge and strategic skills to use mathematics effectively. Firstly, the usefulness of a 'try a simpler problem' strategy for checking on the appropriateness of dividing one number by another was mentioned. Then, student difficulties in applying calculus were seen to arise not in poor execution of procedures but in an inability to set up the problem so that procedures could be employed. In the calculus problems, an essential first step is to introduce variables — to select central quantities, allocate them algebraic symbols and then use them to express relationships. Until the problem is formulated in a mathematical way, there is no opportunity to implement standard known procedures, for example for minimizing functions. Choosing variables and naming them is an example of an important phenomenon in mathematical problem solving which Davis (1987) has named 'taking charge'. He describes it as, 'the behaviour, frequently displayed by good problem solvers, of feeling free to restructure, revise, or redefine the problem you are working on' (Davis 1987). Perhaps because

mathematics is generally taught using only problems which have been previously 'mathematized', few students exhibit the 'taking charge' behaviour
that characterizes successful problem solvers. Here then we have one
example of an important class of strategic or heuristic skills that are essential
for applying known mathematical techniques.

One of the basic questions underlying problem solving research has been
to assess the relative contributions of the two categories — knowledge and
strategies — to problem solving success. This is an important question
because decisions about the appropriate balance between content and process in a mathematics curriculum relate closely to it. In an attempt to study
problem solving in a 'pure' form, early work tended to use problems which
by their very nature did not depend on extensive background knowledge;
not surprisingly general strategies were found to be effective. But mathematics is different; in the jargon of cognitive science, it is a 'semantically
rich' domain, there is a lot to know and knowing it makes you a much better
problem solver. Later work therefore observed problem solving in
semantically rich domains, where there is potentially a great deal of knowledge that the solver can use. In problem solving situations of this type,
unsuccessful problem solvers tend to rely on weak general strategies whilst
successful problem solvers tend to use powerful strategies specifically related
to the problem (Larkin *et al*. 1980). Classic work comparing chess experts
and novices, for example, which is reviewed by Schoenfeld (1985), showed
that expert chess players derive their superiority not from general factors
such as spatial ability or organization of memory, but from possession of an
extensive vocabulary of perhaps 50 000 configurations of chess pieces stored
in memory. The experts, recognizing a configuration in play, have an automatic response to it, similarly stored in memory.

In mathematics, much of the superiority of 'experts' can likewise be attri-
buted to stored knowledge which gives them the ability to recognize problems quickly and respond automatically with specifically tailored strategies.
Faced with almost all textbook problems, teachers — the expert players in
this game — almost driving on automatic pilot, know 'this is Pythagoras'
or 'this is division'. Routine, unthinking, expert behaviour. Within the
chess-like, artificial world of the textbook exercise, recognition of problem
type is the quick, efficient key to success. Similarly, Lesh (1985, p. 77),
writing about primary students' responses to fraction questions presented in
abstract, structured and real situations, notes that:
- students who understand relevant ideas use them together with powerful
  content-related processes; and
- students who do not have relevant ideas are poor problem solvers, even if
  they are able to use some heuristic strategies.

But what are the implications of this research for developing numeracy?
Does it, in fact, support a curriculum where recognition of standard technique and automated responses are the most important goal? Certainly it
serves as an important reminder in a time when general problem solving
processes are in vogue. Children need maximum opportunities to learn
mathematical ideas thoroughly; knowing more does make better problem
solvers and learning about strategies or process aspects of mathematics *per*

se cannot take the place of that knowledge. However, there is much more to applying mathematics in the real world than there is to playing chess, which operates in one prescribed system. Applications begin and end outside mathematics. Ian Lowe, a Victorian teacher and author, pictures the situation of starting to solve a real problem as standing on the edge of a swimming pool. Before taking a dive into the mathematical world, there is important preparation to be done formulating the problem into a mathematically tractable form, and you must be able to swim. Climbing out on the other side involves interpretation and checking. The problem solving demands for using mathematics are broad and textbook learning is preparation for only one phase of the process.

REAL PROBLEM SOLVING IN THE CLASSROOM: THE WIDER ASPECTS OF NUMERACY

The discussion above has focused on the importance of the different types of skills that are involved in using mathematics in the real world. This section will describe the Numeracy through Problem Solving project set up in England by the Joint Matriculation Board (JMB) and the Shell Centre for Mathematical Education (SCME). This project takes seriously a very broad set of skills required for achieving numeracy with low achievers. It has been selected as a case study because it adopts a logical but extreme approach which raises several important issues. Five modules, occupying between nine and fifteen hours of class time, are available and two are briefly illustrated in examples 4.2 and 4.3. The project targets low ability students aged 14–16 years, it uses real problems in average classrooms and aims for an atmosphere where sensible answers are obtained to sensible questions. In fact, in choosing realistic everyday problems, the project team has accepted that social skills and skills of communication will be of most importance, whilst simple numerical skills are called on only as required.

The project categorizes the skills that are involved in using mathematics on three levels of increasing breadth of application. They are:
1. *technical skills* including algorithms (such as that for finding an average) and routine procedures (such as finding frequencies from a set of data and displaying them on a histogram);
2. *tactical skills* occupying a middle level of applicability, such as selecting the most appropriate method of recording information and presenting it visually; and
3. *strategic skills* which relate to general features of the way in which the problem is approached and the major decisions which have to be taken. They include distinguishing between essential constraints and desirable features, planning and testing, and generating and listing possibilities. (JMB & SCME 1987, pp. 6–7)

The core of the classroom activities consists of situations as close as possible to everyday situations within the constraints imposed by classroom life (timetable, space, numbers involved, etc.). The trialling in about 50 classrooms has explored how tight these constraints are in practice. The problems on which students work are exemplars of wide classes of problems which are important in everyday life. Thus, 'Design a Board game', whilst not an urgent everyday problem in itself, is a feasible classroom illustration of the wide class of design problems (design a kitchen, a garden, a fund-raising competition) that might be encountered in everyday life. The other modules illustrate the 'high-level' application areas of planning and running events, choosing and buying, and giving and following instructions.

The possibility of using activities such as these to develop numeracy raises both exciting possibilities and difficult questions for a mathematics teacher: 'Is this mathematics?' and 'Is this worth the time?' are two fundamental questions. There is, of course, no one answer to the question of time; as previously indicated, the project has been directed at low achievers, whose urgent need to acquire numeracy skills before leaving school is widely recognized and where the futility of teaching more mathematics for its own sake is often painfully obvious to all involved.

The former question, 'Is this mathematics?', is also rather difficult to answer. Whilst a little experimenting with the more difficult situations that can arise in the construction of the paper podium may soon convince a sceptic that there is potentially plenty of mathematics in 'Be a paper engineer' (example 4.2), the mathematical demands of 'Plan a trip' (example 4.3) are basic (e.g. reading timetables, calculating with time and money, finding distances or routes from maps). In fact, the project team do not claim that the demands of problems such as 'Plan a trip' are principally

Example 4.2 Be a paper engineer (SCME & JMB 1988a)

In this stage of the module, students explore the techniques of making gift boxes and pop-up cards. This example shows a challenge based on a card with parallel cuts and folds.

Investigations
Try these . . .

Make up your own examples as well

In this stage you will work mostly on your own using some of the Exploring techniques sheets.

You will try some

■ **investigations**, which ask you to explore what happens when you fold, cut or stick things in different ways,

■ **challenges**, which show you pictures of finished articles that you can try to make.

Challenges
Try to make this winners' podium

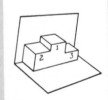

Example 4.3 Plan a trip (SCME & JMB 1988b)

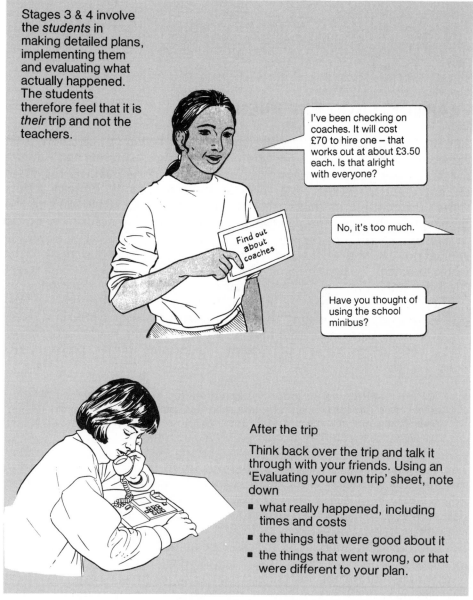

mathematical but they do claim that it is the mathematics teacher who should accept responsibility for developing the broader, not strictly mathematical, skills that are essential for handling real problems (including organizational skills, communication skills and decision-making based on quantitative thinking). In primary schools where there is a general component to the curriculum, it may be possible to argue that the proper place for developing the skills of everyday problem solving is integrated across the curriculum. The Unified Sciences and Mathematics For Elementary Schools project (USMES 1976), for example, saw the right place for real problem solving as being in an integrated study of mathematics, science and social science. The project provided an extensive selection of excellent teachers' guides for undertaking long-term 'challenges' in real problem solving with their classes. But, for most secondary schools, the choice is either to develop the skill of using mathematical ideas within mathematics lessons or to ignore them altogether.

LEARNING FROM EXPERIENCE

The modules of the Numeracy through Problem Solving project have been chosen to exemplify wide classes of problems (design, planning and running events, choosing and buying, and giving and following instructions) which are important in everyday life. Because the intention of 'Produce a quiz show', for example, is that it should illustrate how to tackle some of the problems involved in running events, students' attention needs to be drawn beyond the specifics to the generality of the process. In order to make the general process more obvious to students, a distinct structure is given to the whole problem by presenting the project in four clearly identified stages (JMB & SCME 1987, p. 15) which can be followed in any situation.

The project is therefore an attempt to improve students' skills in real problem solving by providing them with almost real experience in a structured setting. Experience of problem solving, real or mathematical, has always been recognized as a prerequisite for learning to solve problems. As Polya put it:

> Solving problems is a practical art, like swimming, or skiing, or playing the piano: you can learn it only by imitation and practice. . . if you wish to learn swimming you have to go in the water and if you wish to become a problem solver you have to solve problems. (Polya 1962, p. v)

The question of under what conditions one learns from experience has been insufficiently addressed in the mathematics education literature. One exception is *Thinking Mathematically* (Mason, Burton & Stacey 1982) which proposes a theory of 'emotional snapshots' as a way that an individual thinker can capture critical experiences and file them, ready to access in the future. But how can an ordinary pupil in school be helped to learn from experience in the classroom? This emerged as a central question during the extensive observations of teaching that supported the development of *Strategies For Problem Solving* (Stacey & Groves 1985), a set of lesson plans for years 7 and 8. Three essential ingredients for teaching problem solving characterized the program:
- experience in attempting non-routine problems;
- the opportunity to reflect upon these experiences; and
- exposure to some simple problem solving skills and strategies.

During the observations, helping students learn from experience emerged as the major feature of the teacher's role in teaching problem solving. In work of this nature, in order to give students experience, it is essential that the teacher hands over to the pupils the responsibility for decisions, the organization and the path to the solution. However, the teacher cannot adopt a passive role, even as simply a provider of stimulus questions, no matter how intriguing they are nor how beautifully they are packaged. Instead the teacher's activity needs to be deflected from showing and telling towards encouraging reflection. In other words, the teacher's principal role is to provide a context where active looking back can take place. Active reflectors follow ideas through, they think, they discuss and they write (Stacey & Groves 1986). Key activities for a teacher that will encourage this are:

- class discussion of tactical, strategic and emotional aspects of problem solving;
- reporting (oral and written) paths and solutions;
- investigating 'What if . . .' questions that extend the original;
- thinking of independent means of checking the solutions, and
- use of small-group techniques, such as the 'Wimbey pair' technique, so that students have the opportunity to observe their peers solving problems (Woods 1985).

Looked at in a broader perspective, helping children learn how to use mathematics from experience can be seen as one example of a multi-faceted concern to help children really learn from the things that they do in school, principally through the development of certain metacognitive behaviours. In the PEEL project at Laverton High School in Victoria, teachers of six different subjects adopted a variety of tactics in order to attack problems of poor student learning by improving the metacognitive behaviour of the students. Methods included encouraging diary writing for monitoring personal level of understanding, asking 'higher-order' questions of both students and teachers, and a negotiated curriculum. A full account of the first year of operation of the project is given by Baird & Mitchell (1986). In this way, improving numeracy is linked to improving learning as a whole.

HARNESSING REAL POWER FROM AN ABSTRACT SYSTEM

The quotation which began this chapter — 'Mathematics lessons in secondary schools very often are not about anything' — was written after over 300 hours of observation of mathematics classrooms. The irony is that because it is about almost everything, mathematics can appear to be about nothing. The very abstractness that gives it wide applicability to real situations causes enormous difficulties for teaching and, in particular, for teaching which empowers students to use their knowledge in situations outside school. Transmitting a formal, codified system fails to produce sufficient useable knowledge. The Numeracy through Problem Solving project and the USMES project are examples of projects which seek to supplement and partially replace learning the codified system by dealing with mathematical problems as they arise naturally in the context of other things. This final section explores the notion that perhaps the formal and codified system should not be taught at all, and mathematical experiences in schools should be restricted to those that arise naturally. To jump ahead, the conclusion is that whilst intuitive understanding and informal methods are important and should certainly be encouraged, a curriculum which was directed only towards solving immediate problems in the simplest way possible would also not serve numeracy well. To understand why requires a more detailed look at the nature of informal use of mathematics.

The mathematics of primitive cultures, which is seen by d'Ambrosio almost as a variant of common language, is not an abstract system. It differs from one cultural group to another, codifying their popular practices and daily needs and providing the capability of qualifying and quantifying and some patterns of inference. d'Ambrosio observes that while illiteracy is prevalent in the undeveloped world, 'unmatheracy' (innumeracy) is very rare, almost as rare as incapacity for language communication. At school, when children meet the formal symbolic system, the tendency is to lose the capabilities of the 'common language' mathematics, and not be able to replace them by the 'learned' ones. Instead of the two modes of thought supporting one another, d'Ambrosio makes the damning claim that the learned matheracy actually eliminates the so-called 'spontaneous' matheracy, leaving the Third World students more innumerate than they would have otherwise been (d'Ambrosio 1985, pp. 472, 473).

As several of the examples above have illustrated, in our culture too, there is a conflict between the mathematics learnt at school and the mathematics spontaneously used in the outside world. The two ways of thinking are often not well integrated so that school learning has an insufficient intuitive basis and the powerful methods taught at school are not used for practical benefit. Some of the key differences between formal and informal methods are outlined below.

'Manipulation of symbols' or 'manipulation of quantities'

Several authors have characterized differences between formal and informal methods of calculation as a difference between 'manipulation of symbols' and 'manipulation of quantities' (Reed & Lave 1981; Carraher, Carraher & Schliemann, 1987). Hassler Whitney, for example, criticized the view espoused by the 'new maths' movement that mathematics is about number, not quantity (Whitney 1973, p. 290). He stated that, in mathematics education, materials are used in order to develop concepts about pure numbers, but in application numbers are used to find out about quantities. Whitney (1973, p. 293) advocated that children be taught mathematics with real quantities rather than with numbers alone or with concrete materials such as Multibase Arithmetic Blocks which are designed to model the abstract number only.

A precise tool of communication or a personal shorthand

Informal methods of calculation are usually done mentally or as jottings on the 'back of an envelope'. In such cases, mathematical symbolism is not used as a precise tool of communication, but as a personal shorthand, to extend working memory rather than to communicate. Thus children will calculate $5 \times (3 + 7 \times 4)$ by writing mathematical nonsense such as:

$$7 \times 4 = 28 + 3 = 31 \times 5 = 155$$

Or they will write a pseudo-algebraic answer such as '6c + 7d' (meaning 'there are six cats and seven dogs') to a question which asks them to find c, the number of cats and d, the number of dogs from certain information (Stacey 1987a).

The difficulty with writing the symbol system precisely is of much less immediate practical consequence than difficulty with reading it precisely. For example, testing at one Melbourne secondary school revealed that two-thirds of year 8 students did not distinguish the order in division, so that they gave 6 as the answer to $2 \div 12$. This simple difficulty with using notation cuts these students off from effective use of a calculator when following written instructions involving division.

Cockcroft, the Chairman of the Committee of Inquiry into the Teaching of Mathematics in Schools (England and Wales), saw communication as central to the importance of mathematics in the educational system:

> Many would of course immediately reply that [mathematics is important in school because it] is 'useful', but in doing so usually imply that the way in which it is useful is somehow different from the usefulness of some other school subjects. Pressed further, I believe that those who react in this way would argue that it is useful because it provides a unique and particularly effective means of communication. (Cockcroft 1986, p. 328)

Intentions signalled by context or symbols

The strength of informal mathematics is shown when abstract questions are not involved and intentions or instructions are signalled by the context, rather than by written symbols. Even though no complicated calculations are required, an abstract question such as 'What is the value of y if $9 - 6 = y - 9$?' is surprisingly difficult. MacGregor (1989), for example, found that only 37% of year 9 students answered it correctly. Like the division difficulties referred to above, student difficulties with this question seem to arise in large part because there is no clue from the context as to what should be done. Common misconceptions operate unhindered, so that pupils produce answers such as:

- $y = 6$ (by a process of matching terms on left and right sides of the equation),
- $y = 3$ (because $9 - 6$ gives 3 and equals is interpreted as 'gives'), or
- $y = -6$ (because $9 - 6$ gives 3 and then you have to take away the 9).

If a mathematically equivalent question arose in a context understood by the pupil, finding the answer would be very easy. If, for instance, a friend bought an article for $6 and sold it to me for $9, and then I wanted to sell it and make the same amount of profit as she did, it would be easy to find the answer: first she made $3 profit, now I need to make $3 profit so I will have to sell it for $12. In the terms used by Margaret Donaldson (1978), we tend to exhibit a capacity to interpret, understand and calculate at the level of 'human sense'.

There are two further points to note here. Firstly, although it is known in an operative sense, in the real context people would not make explicit the fundamental relationship which is expressed so concisely by the algebra:

$$\text{her profit} = \text{my profit}$$
$$9 - 6 = \text{my selling price} - 9$$

Locating such underlying relationships and expressing them explicitly is fundamental to the use of algebra and this in turn allows one to use the power that manipulation of symbols provides.

Secondly, the informal procedure is perceived step-wise, rather than as the whole that the equation presents. At each step, the elements involved are 'closed', the difference between selling price and cost price, for example, being perceived not as a relationship ($9 − $6) but as one definite thing ($3).

Compare the length of the verbal description of the profit problem with the conciseness and manipulability of the equation. Formal mathematics deals well with combining operations ($10 \times 2 + 3$, $\cos 2x + \sin x$, etc.), and is able to work simultaneously with the whole relationship or set of relationships as one object of study. Applications of mathematics to technical areas require this, whether it is to compare the growths of different populations over time, to understand the flow of electricity through a complicated circuit, or to estimate the value of an investment taking into account interest rates, inflation and taxation. An important limitation of informal mathematics is that it works best operating one primitive step at a time, getting one answer at each stage to carry on to the next step.

These are three of the key differences between formal and informal mathematics. If numeracy is to be interpreted as a capacity to deal well with simple numerical tasks that arise in everyday practical contexts, such as shopping, paying bills and measuring, then an informal mathematics without a well-developed symbol system can serve people well. If, however, we adopt the broader definition of numeracy that has been advocated in other chapters then the strategy of teaching 'real' mathematics only as it arises in response to everyday demands will not be sufficient. Being able to read and write the symbol system precisely, and to handle relationships simultaneously and as entities, are then crucial skills. Whereas students' experiences of learning mathematics should arise from the real world and build upon common sense, teaching mathematics must also go beyond this.

CONCLUSION

This chapter has been concerned with skill-choosing and skill-using and their relationship to skill-getting. The relationship between knowing and being able to use skills and between operating formally and informally was shown to be a complex one, for adults and children of all abilities. Offering genuine practice at skill-choosing and creating a classroom environment which values sensible answers to sensible questions are first steps towards making school knowledge more useful in the real world. The relationship between knowledge and strategies is crucial to an analysis of students' abilities to solve problems. Clearly, there is a dynamic interaction between the content of mathematical ideas and the processes used to solve problems based on those ideas. Sound knowledge of powerful mathematical ideas is essential, but so too are a range of strategies for formulating problems into mathematical terms and for checking and interpreting answers. These strategies are best developed in conjunction with experience of all stages of problem solving. In order to learn from these experiences, the teacher needs to guide students towards active reflection on the processes involved. The ideal situation for developing skills for solving real-world problems seems to be by re-creating real-world problems in the classroom. There are substantial difficulties in doing this but the teaching materials provided by the Numeracy through Problem Solving project and the much earlier USMES project show how it might be done in fairly typical classrooms. Finally, there was a recognition that if students are to reap the benefits of the particular power of mathematics, it is not sufficient to find intuitive methods for solving individual real-world problems. Formal skills need to be developed alongside informal skills, but both can be done better if the contexts within mathematics are given a fuller consideration in the curriculum.

REFERENCES

Baird, J. R. & Mitchell, I. (eds) 1986, *Improving the Quality of Teaching and Learning: An Australian Case Study — The PEEL Project*, PEEL Group, Melbourne, Victoria.

Bell, A. 1984, 'Short and long term learning — experiments in diagnostic teaching design', in *Proceedings of the Eighth International Conference for the Psychology of Mathematics Education*, eds B. Southwell, R. Eyland, M. Cooper, J. Conroy & K. Collis, IGPME, Sydney.

d'Ambrosio, U. 1985, 'Mathematic education in a cultural setting', *International Journal of Mathematical Education in Science and Technology*, **16** (4), 469–77.

Carpenter, T. P., Corbitt, M. K., Kepner, H. S., Lindquist, M. M. & Reys R. E., 1980, 'NAEP Note: Problem Solving', *Mathematics Teacher*, **74**, 427–32.

Carraher, T. N., Carraher, D. W. & Schliemann, A. D. 1987, 'Written and oral mathematics', *Journal for Research in Mathematics Education*, **18** (2), 83–97.

Cockcroft, W. (Chairman) 1982, *Mathematics Counts: Report of the Committee of Inquiry into the Teaching of Mathematics in Schools*, HMSO, London.

Cockcroft, W. 1986, 'Inquiry into school teaching of mathematics in England and Wales', in *Proceedings of the Fifth International Congress on Mathematical Education*, ed. M. Carss, Birkhauser, Boston, 328–9.

Davis, R. B. 1987, '"Taking charge" as an ingredient in effective problem solving in mathematics', *Journal of Mathematical Behavior*, **6** (3), 341–51.

Donaldson, M. 1978, *Children's Minds*, Fontana, Glasgow.

Fielker, D. 1986, 'Which operation?' Certainly not division!, *For The Learning of Mathematics*, **6** (3), 34–8.

Hiebert, J. 1989, 'The struggle to link written symbols with understandings: an update', *Arithmetic Teacher*, **36** (7), 38–44.

Larkin, J. H., McDermott, J., Simon, D. P. & Simon, H. A. 1980, 'Expert and novice performance in solving physics problems', *Science*, **208**, 1335–42.

Lesh, R. 1985, 'Conceptual analysis of mathematical ideas and problem solving processes', in *Proceedings of the Ninth International Conference For the Psychology of Mathematics Education*, ed. L. Streefland, State University of Utrecht, Netherlands.

Joint Matriculation Board & the Shell Centre for Mathematical Education 1987, *Assessment of Numeracy Through Problem Solving*, Joint Matriculation Board, England.

MacGregor, M. 1989, *Students' Errors in Constructing and Interpreting Algebraic Equations*, PhD thesis, University of Melbourne.

Mason, J., Burton, L. & Stacey, K. 1982, *Thinking Mathematically*, Addison Wesley, London.

Newton, W. 1983, *Real Maths — School Maths* (video), Victorian Ministry of Education, Melbourne.

Polya, G. 1962, *Mathematical Discovery, Vol 1*, John Wiley, USA.

Reed, H. J. & Lave, J. 1981, 'Arithmetic as a tool for investigating relations between culture and cognition'. in *Language, Culture and Cognition: Anthropological perspectives*, ed. R. W. Casson, Macmillan, New York.

Schoenfeld, A. H. 1985, *Mathematical Problem Solving*, Academic Press, Orlando.

Shell Centre for Mathematical Education & Joint Matriculation Board 1988a, *Be a Paper Engineer* (student's booklet), Longman Group UK Limited.

Shell Centre for Mathematical Education & Joint Matriculation Board 1988b, *Plan a Trip* (student's booklet), Longman Group UK Limited.

Silver, E. A. 1986, 'Using conceptual and procedural knowledge: A focus on relationships', in *Conceptual and Procedural Knowledge: The Case of Mathematics*, ed. J. Hiebert, Lawrence Erlbaum, Hillsdale, New Jersey.

Stacey, K. 1987a, 'Children's informal mathematics: Building on strengths and identifying weaknesses', in *From Now To The Future*, ed. W. Caughey, Mathematical Association of Victoria, Melbourne.

Stacey, K. 1987b, 'What to assess when assessing problem solving', *Australian Mathematics Teacher*, **43** (3), 21–4.

Stacey, K. & Bourke, S. 1988, 'Testing mathematical problem solving', *Research in Mathematics Education in Australia*, December, 12–29.

Stacey, K. & Groves, S. 1985, *Strategies For Problem Solving*, Victoria College Press, Melbourne.

Stacey, K. & Groves, S. 1986, 'Getting the most out of problem solving', in *Mathematics Teaching: Challenges For Change, Australian Association of Mathematics Teachers Eleventh Biennial Conference*, eds BCAE Mathematics and Computing Department.

Trelinski, G. 1983, 'Spontaneous mathematization of situations outside mathematics', *Educational Studies in Mathematics*, **14** (3), 275–84.

Unified Sciences and Mathematics For Elementary Schools 1976, *The USMES Guide*, Education Development Center, Newton Massachusetts. (Available as an ERIC document.)

Whitney, H. 1973, 'Are we off the track in teaching mathematical concepts?', in *Developments in Mathematical Education*, ed. A. G. Howson, Cambridge University Press, London.

Woods D. (ed.) 1985, *Problem Solving News Vol 36* (Jan), McMaster University, Ontario.

5 Beyond the mathematics classroom: numeracy for learning

ANNE CHAPMAN, MARIAN KEMP AND
BARRY KISSANE

INTRODUCTION

The Cockcroft Report (1982) refers to numeracy as the ability to cope confidently with the mathematical demands of everyday life. For students, 'everyday life' includes study-related activities; indeed, it is characteristic of our educational processes that most students of mathematics are simultaneously students of other subjects and disciplines. As John Ling has suggested:

> For teachers of all subjects, the most important link between subjects is the fact that it is the same pupils who are trying to learn all of them. (Ling 1977, p. 3)

Common to all of the learning activities in which students engage is a need for literacy. A similar case might be made, perhaps with a little less force, for a corresponding need for numeracy.

Especially during the 1970s, the importance of language across the curriculum was recognized and many teachers were persuaded that 'Every teacher is a teacher of literacy'. There are two complementary aspects of literacy embodied in this slogan. On the one hand, literacy is seen as an important constellation of skills and abilities necessary for effective citizenship, both in and out of the workforce, and one goal of schooling is to help students develop such functional literacy. On the other hand, literacy can be regarded as a tool for learning — a tool that is necessary for students to efficiently cope with the demands of schooling itself. This chapter argues a parallel case for numeracy. In particular, we suggest that it is now time to consider the complex (and often unrecognized) mathematical demands of learning various subject areas and to ask whether a comparable case for numeracy across the curriculum should be made, and an equivalent catchcry, 'Every teacher is a teacher of numeracy' at least contemplated.

Analogous to literacy, there are common mathematical features of instructional media across the range of school subjects. Also in common with literacy, many numeracy skills may best be developed in the contexts in which they are needed. Unfortunately, the level of public awareness of numeracy has not obviously risen beyond numeration, and the extent to which mathematical concepts and skills are embedded in curriculum activities other than mathematics and physical science has not been well understood. The intention of the present chapter is to highlight some subject-specific demands upon numeracy and to suggest some ways of accommodating them.

The chapter consists of four broad sections. In the first, we look at the range of types of meanings present in written and oral communications, and explore the numeracy requirements for students to come to grips with these. We conceive these requirements in terms of students making transformations from one form into another. In the second section, we detail the kinds of activities demanded of students in social studies — an area of the curriculum not generally regarded as quantitative in character — and make some remarks based on observations of student and teacher handling of these requirements. The third section examines the numeracy requirements of the study of some interdisciplinary tertiary courses, again not regarded as particularly quantitative. We present several case studies of student attempts to deal with course requirements as these pertain to numeracy. The fourth and final section of the chapter explores some of the implications of our conception of numeracy for the school curriculum.

SOME TRANSFORMATIONS

We believe numeracy is, in part, concerned with understanding messages. It is useful to think of the process of constructing meanings as one of making *transformations* of messages from one kind of representation into another. The first act necessary to extract meaning from unfamiliar material involves a decision to transform the material in some way. Everyday conversation, spoken in a familiar tongue, can usually be understood easily and quickly, requiring little transformation. Also, much of the ordinary text one reads in daily life can be understood with little conscious effort and fairly rapidly. To the extent, however, that full understanding of text requires transformations of the text amongst representations, this takes time and often conscious effort. Rather than expend such time and effort, many people (including students) gloss over essential meanings, assuming they are unimportant or simply beyond their comprehension. Indeed, and worse, there is frequently insufficient time for dealing with spoken material, where it is not possible to backtrack and actively engage with the material; to do so may jeopardize an understanding of the rest of the material. It seems likely that students will need help in learning when and how to make such transformations.

Students are expected to deal with messages represented in one of four forms: verbal (both written and oral), symbolic, graphical and tabular. In order to better 'understand' the message, transformations may be needed between different linguistic forms (for example, from the language meanings and usage of a particular discipline into those of another discipline or into the more colloquial language of daily life — we need to 'say it in our own words') or between verbal and non-verbal forms. We will focus here on those transformations which demand mathematical understanding of some kind. For instance, the use of a sketch graph, the careful reading of a table of information, or the re-reading of a passage with careful attention to the precise meaning of essentially mathematical terms, all take a good deal more time and effort than students or their teachers may expect to need when reading.

It is frequently not clear to students that transformations, in general, are needed to understand new material. That these transformations sometimes have a mathematical flavour is often even less clear to them. Few students realize that, even in subjects not obviously mathematical, they will need to deploy mathematical understanding to make sense of subject specific matters. Even for a numerate person, this is not always a conscious process.

Two different contexts make numeracy demands: a curriculum may include activities that require, and are known to require, numeracy for successful completion. Examples include questions that ask students to interpret a table or a graph or even passages of text where numerals and mathematical symbols act as flags, indicating that mathematics may be needed. It is likely that teachers will see that they have a role to play in helping students with such tasks. In some cases, however, teachers may be unsure of their own or of their students' abilities to deal with overtly mathematical material, and may simply skip such aspects of the curriculum.

The second context is more subtle, and occurs when mathematical ideas are embedded in messages, and are not highlighted as mathematical. Students are not directly instructed to deal with these mathematical ideas explicitly. Rather, they may encounter them while attempting to read passages in texts. They may not even recognize that numeracy skills are required to deal with the message. An example is a passage of text describing an essentially mathematical relationship, but which does not include any numbers or symbols. Some words and phrases that are often used with mathematical intonations are: increasingly, recently, rising/falling, more/less/faster/slower, after tax, together, altogether, except for, included/excluded, and in addition. General mathematical concepts like these and other more specialist terms such as inflation, mortality/fertility, enlargement/dilation and speed/velocity/acceleration are frequently found in text, and not obviously flagged to readers as having precise mathematical meanings. Terms such as inflation, enlargement and acceleration, for example, connote the idea of 'getting bigger' but the terms are used technically to denote change of size, whether 'getting bigger' or 'getting smaller'. Similarly, fertility and mortality can refer to the state of an individual, but often refer to birth and death rates for populations.

Often statements that appear not to make sense are a result of a reader or listener thinking of a word in its colloquial sense while the writer or speaker used it in its technical sense. The reader or listener, to make sense of the statement, needs to ask questions: Will it help if I sort out the differences between positive inflation, negative inflation, increasing inflation and decreasing inflation?; 'When they say "fertility increased" do they mean that the women and men were more able to have children or do they mean that the rate of births increased? And how are these related in this case?' Often students do not recognize that they need actively to decide how to deal with such complexities and, in any case, find it hard to do so, frequently giving up the struggle in favour of accepting someone else's meaning or no meaning at all.

In what follows we describe briefly some of the possible transformations a numerate person might make in order to make sense of unfamiliar material outside the domain of mathematics but which includes mathematical ideas. These examples illustrate the kinds of tasks comprising the repertoire of a numerate person, and suggest an agenda for teachers wanting to assist their students.

Transformations into and out of verbal form are especially important, since many messages are presented in this way. In the school context, obvious examples include giving an oral report to others, responding to teacher questions and producing a written summary. As noted above, mathematical concepts are frequently embedded in a passage of text, so that it is not clear that numeracy skills are needed in order to understand or make sense of it. Example 5.1 is taken from a history text intended for senior high school students:

Example 5.1 An extract from a history textbook (Barcan *et al.* 1982, p. 242)

> In the 1960's, enrolments in tertiary education had grown. But after 1975, the tide started to turn. Since 1971, the birth rate had fallen, and gradually enrolments in the primary schools started to fall. After the recession of 1974, fewer teachers resigned, for fewer alternative jobs were available. The fall in the resignation rate, together with the reduced number of pupils, meant a reduced demand for teachers. Enrolments in teacher-training courses in colleges of advanced education and, to some degree, in universities, fell.

The extract, clearly, is of considerable linguistic complexity but it also requires students to deal with some difficult mathematical ideas concerned with rates of change and their consequences, and there are no clear flags to the reader to indicate that this is so. For some students, a *verbal → graphical* transformation may help to make sense of the first two sentences. A rough sketch such as that shown in figure 5.1 may be sufficient. (In practice, of course, such a sketch would be hand-drawn, with little regard for accurate scales and titles.) For other students, a similar sketch may be constructed in the mind rather than on paper.

Likewise, understanding 'The fall in the resignation rate, together with the reduced number of pupils, meant a reduced demand for teachers' may require that a student make a diagrammatic representation of the relationships involved, such as figure 5.2.

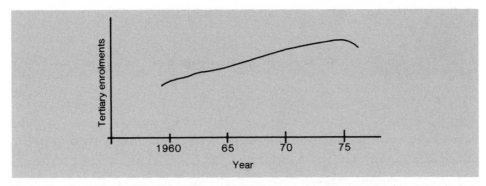

Figure 5.1 A rough sketch of the changes in tertiary enrolments described in example 5.1

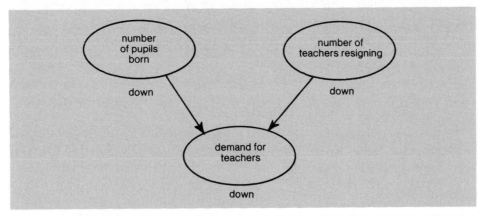

Figure 5.2 A diagrammatic representation of the relationships involved in the demand for teachers (example 5.1)

These representations may help readers to paraphrase the passage, or, as we have said, to express the ideas 'in their own words'.

It is not difficult to imagine a conversation in a television current affairs programme or even a lecture that contains material of this kind. In such cases, people often must transform the message from the oral verbal form to their own representation of the meaning. Given the complexity of the message, which is partly a function of the mathematical concepts, many people are likely to have trouble making such transformations, especially if there is limited time to do so.

Few mathematics curricula deal explicitly with the process of reading tables and yet quantitative information is often presented in the form of tables for efficiency. Whether child or adult, those seeking information in a library may find themselves trying to interpret tabular information.

Consider example 5.2 which is taken from *Yearbook Australia 1988*. To interpret this table, it is first necessary to understand the structure provided by the headings. In common with many such tables, the headings are nested under each other. Numeracy skills are needed both to see what is being 'totalled' to get the two 'total' figures and also to accept that the process of rounding the numbers to the nearest thousand leads to apparent inaccuracies, rather than real errors (for example, the total production of

Example 5.2 Production and export of dried vine fruit for 1988 (*Yearbook Australia* 1988, p. 521)

	Production				Exports			
							Total	
Year	Raisins	Sultanas	Currants	Total	Raisins/ Sultanas	Currants	Quantity	Value f.o.b.
	'000 tonnes	'000 tonnes	'000 tonnes	'000 tonnes	'000 tonnes	'000 tonnes	'000 tonnes	$m
1980–81	5.7	50.7	4.8	61.1	50.1	1.9	52.0	75.5
1981–82	5.8	78.5	5.9	90.2	38.5	0.8	39.4	49.5
1982–83	3.9	64.9	4.7	73.4	57.1	2.4	59.5	59.7
1983–84	1.4	69.0	4.6	75.0	51.6	0.9	52.5	54.1
1984–85	2.1	60.1	5.7	67.8	61.5	1.0	62.4	58.0
1985–86	5.2	72.9	6.3	84.4	48.4	2.9	51.3	71.3

DRIED VINE FRUIT: PRODUCTION AND EXPORTS (dried weight)

dried vine fruits in 1980–81 is given as 61.1 in the first line of the table, although 5.7 + 50.7 + 4.8 = 61.2).

To further interpret the table, it is necessary to look carefully at relationships amongst the elements of the table. This is not an easy task, and will take some time. For example, the relationship between production and exports needs to be determined. In general, exports are likely to be less than production, assuming that long-term storage is not undertaken, but this is not obvious without some thought. Interpretations of these kinds can be thought of as *tabular → verbal*. In fact, the table consists of at least three tables, because of the nested headings. There is a table each of Production, Exports and Value f.o.b. (freight on board). Recognizing this requires students to make a transformation of the *tabular → tabular* kind.

For each of these tables, there is a discernible trend over the years shown. Indeed, this is the reason for presenting a table of information, rather than merely the figures for a single year. To understand the table fully students must deal with these trends. To do so probably requires a sketch of some kind (perhaps a sketch in the mind, rather than on paper?). Recognizing that this is an appropriate way of dealing with the information, and having the necessary skills to draw a sketch quickly (rather than draw a graph painstakingly by plotting each data point carefully) are essential aspects of numeracy. Examples of suitable sketches are shown in figure 5.3. (As with the earlier graph, these are drawn more neatly here than would likely be necessary.) These are examples of *tabular → graphical* transformations.

Students are taught how to draw graphs generally, but frequently are not taught how to do it *roughly* (i.e. back of envelope sketch); nor are they taught *when* to do it. Typically, in the mathematics classroom, they are told explicitly by teacher or textbook to draw a curve or a graph, rather than taught how to decide which situations will be helped by doing this and what to do once they have drawn one. Hence, most of the graphs students are taught to draw are not drawn for their own purposes — rather they are

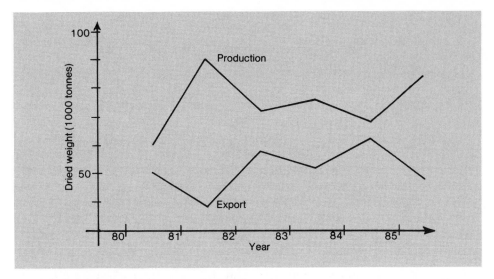

Figure 5.3 Graphs of data given in example 5.2

drawn for a distant audience, and so details of presentation loom large. A graph drawn to help oneself understand some information is a more private affair and more fleeting in character.

In example 5.2 some of the trends indicate that there are sizable fluctuations in this industry, perhaps due to seasonal factors. Examples are the marked increase in total production in 1981–82, and the relatively small proportion of sultanas exported at the same time. These relationships are subtle, however, and only appear after some efforts are made to interpret the raw data. Deciding to make such an effort is a crucial first step, and one that students will undertake only if they have the confidence and the numeracy skills to do so. This is an essential difference between tasks which explicitly make numeracy demands and tasks in which the numeracy demands are more implicit; in the latter case, students themselves must decide what to do, rather than merely follow instructions or answer questions posed by someone else.

Interpreting tables makes fresh demands on the ways students use their mathematics — fresh numeracy demands. For example, it is often necessary to read up as well as down and from right to left as well as the usual left to right. Attention is needed to read headings and footnotes to check definitions of terms and restrictions on the data presented. Also, it is usually necessary to look for structural relationships between columns and rows (e.g. identify the base for percentages, or the way in which numbers have been added to give totals).

A common need is for skills concerned with *graphical → verbal* transformations. A focus in mathematics curricula has been on the construction and interpretation of correct graphical representations of statistical information (for example, note the concern for 'lying' with statistics!). But this is not much help to students who have to interpret improper diagrams in textbooks or newspapers. Even if not 'correct', they need to be interpreted. The graph in example 5.3 appeared in a daily newspaper.

Example 5.3 A graph taken from the *Weekend Australian* (Cribb 1988)

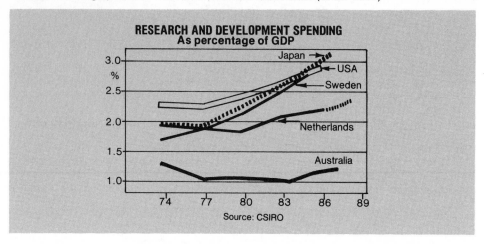

RESEARCH AND DEVELOPMENT SPENDING
As percentage of GDP

Source: CSIRO

Graphical purists might complain (rightly) that the vertical scale is misleading because it has no zero point, that the years for which the data are plotted are not clear and that it is not even clear which parts of the graphs pertain to the Netherlands and which to Sweden. But, despite these flaws, the graph still has a message, and is informative. In general terms, readers should conclude that: research and development (R&D) spending in Australia is rather stable, unlike that in some other countries where it is increasing; relatively little of Australian gross domestic product (GDP) is allocated to R&D, in contrast with other countries; it is not possible to compare R&D spending directly in various countries without knowing their GDPs; and, despite visual appearance to the contrary, Japan, USA and Sweden spend a little more than twice the percentage of GDP on R&D that Australia does. Interpreting the graph requires a recognition of the meanings of the terms (notably GDP) and the significance of the subheading and the horizontal scale, which indicates that the major message of the graph is likely to be the ways in which the values concerned are changing over time.

Conciseness is not always a virtue, and one of the problems of mathematics texts is that a lot of information is conveyed succinctly using (algebraic) symbols. This can be frightening to a novice, and even to experienced people. This possibly accounts for the relative scarcity of demands that students interpret symbolic material outside mathematical contexts (and why it is rare for symbols to appear in newspapers or magazines). School curricula tend to avoid symbols with the notable exceptions of physics and chemistry, where their use is generally in tightly controlled circumstances (e.g. F always refers to force and Na always refers to sodium). Thus, transformations to and from symbolic messages to other kinds of messages are less common than other kinds of transformations. Perhaps they are so obviously mathematical in character that there is a clear set of rules for dealing with symbolic messages (including, of course, avoiding them altogether).

SOCIAL STUDIES IN SECONDARY SCHOOL

This section includes some examples from materials provided for social studies students in their final year of compulsory schooling. We will show at least some of the mathematical aspects of these activities. Social studies was chosen because, although it is not generally considered to be particularly mathematical by either students or teachers, it makes a variety of numeracy demands upon students. Since social studies is a core part of the school curriculum for almost all students for the ten years of compulsory schooling, these demands are made of practically all students.

Even a superficial examination of social studies curricula will reveal the extent and sophistication of some of the mathematical/numeracy skills that students need if they are to achieve the curriculum objectives. Two major areas are, firstly, map work incorporating similarity, scales and bearings, and secondly, the interpretation and construction of statistical and other graphs, tables and diagrams. The latter require not only an understanding of how to transform information but also how to compute percentages, rates and angles. By year 10, students are expected to understand Gross National Product, the Consumer Price Index, inflation, birth and mortality rates. A knowledge of probability and sampling techniques is essential for dealing with topics of weather prediction, market research and opinion polls, and to interpret data concerning issues such as drug trials, vaccines, fluoride treatment, smoking and alcohol use. Finally, to achieve some of the purposes of social studies curricula students need to know how to use formulae (such as the kind used in determining repayments on a loan), and how to estimate and check the validity of their computations.

In the space available it is not possible to give examples from all the aspects listed above, however we will illustrate some of the range of numeracy skills needed. The first major area mentioned above is that of map work. In this component of the social studies course students acquire 'mapping skills' which are generally viewed by the students as something belonging to social studies and perhaps being useful for an orienteering course. In fact a large proportion of these mapping skills rely heavily on mathematical skills such as measuring (both lengths and angles), calculating bearings, using scales, calculating or estimating gradients, understanding latitude and longitude, appreciating the different kinds of projections of the world's surface area onto two-dimensional maps, drawing sketch maps to illustrate different relative sizes of populations or crops from tabular information and so on. The fact that these are called mapping skills in one context and mathematical skills in another may help to obscure the connections.

The first example (example 5.4) includes questions related to maps of Tasmania and South Australia. Even this short set of questions involves scale conversion, angles, and area and an understanding of the mathematics involved. Certainly year 10 students have already been introduced to these numeracy concepts at a less sophisticated level earlier in their school life.

Example 5.4 Questions relating to maps of Tasmania and South Australia (Armstrong 1981, p. 25)

1. What is there at the following map references: 913335, 905245?
2. Find on the map and give the six figure map references for: Jervois Oval, a windpump, Tailem Bend.
3. What is the bearing of the summit of Denison Hill from Bee Tree Hill, relative to the grid north?
4. What is the area of irrigated land on the map?
5. How far is it, to the nearest kilometre, from the ferry at Tailem Bend, to that near East Wellington (i) as the crow flies (ii) by river?

Example 5.5 Questions relating to reference and location skills and scale conversion tasks (Scott 1982, p. 58)

1. If you were to walk from Mackey Lookout to Bent Lookout, what would happen to the height of the land and the steepness of the land?
2. What landforms would you observe from Bent Lookout?
3. The photograph [provided for the students] was taken somewhere in the area above 1500 metres. Give the grid references for three places where the photo may have been taken.

Example 5.6 Questions involving interpretation of a table (Bennetts *et al.* 1988, p. 158)

Europe, average % growth in GDP 1960–1970 and 1970–1980		
Country	1960–1970	1970–1980
Austria	4.7	3.9
Denmark	4.6	2.9
Finland	—	2.9
France	5.6	3.9
Greece	7.6	5.1
Eire	4.3	3.9
Italy	5.6	3.0
Netherlands	6.0	3.1
Norway	6.6	4.4
Portugal	6.3	4.7
Spain	7.5	4.1
Sweden	4.6	1.5
Switzerland	4.7	0.8
United Kingdom	2.8	2.3
West Germany	4.7	2.9

Source: *Geo-search* 1983

(a) What does the table indicate about current and future economic growth?
(b) What is the relationship between economic growth, the supply of national resources and technology?
(c) What does this information suggest about future living standards in Europe?
(d) What steps can be taken to ensure the maintenance of standards of living and quality of life in Europe?

The extract in example 5.5 is from the year 8 social studies curriculum and involves reference and location skills and scale conversion tasks. Such activities include transformations from the graphical representation to other forms including verbal and symbolic.

Students are frequently asked to read and interpret data that are presented in tabular form. Example 5.6 is a table, together with a list of questions prepared for students in year 10.

Students need to look at two columns of figures and decide what these tell them about current and future economic growth. As with reading any table, the first step is to decide what information is accurately presented. In this case, students need to interpret the phrase 'average % growth in GDP' in the heading. In addition, they need to see that each line of the table presents data for a different country in two separate decades. It is easy to become bogged down with the details of such a table, and miss the 'big' picture — in this case, that economic growth was generally a good deal lower in the seventies than in the sixties. A graphical representation of the data might be helpful in this regard. This would involve a *tabular → graphical* transformation in order to see the trend more clearly. A possible graph is shown in figure 5.4.

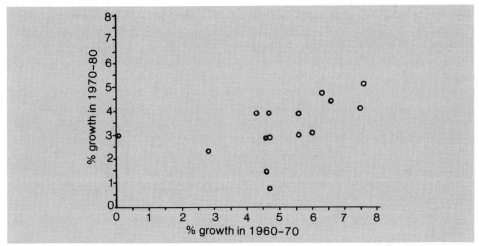

Figure 5.4 A plot of the data in the table in example 5.6

We observed students as they worked on this task. They could see quite clearly that the figures were smaller in the second column for most cases and all students interpreted this as a fall in the standard of living.

Parts (b), (c), and (d) required students to make predictions about the future, based partly on the information in the table but also requiring additional information. It was suggested to students that they draw sketch graphs to illustrate their answer to part (b) but most found it difficult to do so. Whether this was due to a lack of understanding of the meanings underlying the terms or to inexperience with drawing sketch graphs is unclear. The most obvious errors were related to students' apparent belief that the scales could decrease away from the origin. Furthermore, the students all read 'national resources' as 'natural resources'!

In example 5.7 students are explicitly required to construct appropriate graphs to illustrate information taken from a local government report requiring another *tabular* → *graphical* transformation.

Example 5.7 Interpreting percentages (Bennetts *et al.* 1988, p. 114)

Do we use prison as a punishment in Western Australia more than do other states?

In the table below are statistics on the percentage of superior-court convictions leading to sentences of imprisonment.

Percentages of convictions leading to imprisonment sentences, superior courts:

| | Most serious offence by state | | | | |
| | NSW | VIC | QLD | SA | WA |
			Percentage		
Offences against the person	57	52	46	43	75
Offences against property	52	52	44	38	66
Drug offences	74	82	82	18	74
Total, all offences	56	52	46	38	70

Draw a pie or bar graph showing the contrast between states, in the percentage of convictions in superior courts leading to imprisonment.

The table includes information concerning percentages of convictions leading to imprisonment, the meaning of which is by no means obvious at first glance. Neither is the meaning of 'most serious offence by state' clear. Once they have made sense of this terminology, or even if they haven't, decisions have to be made about whether a pie or bar graph is more appropriate. Neither the columns nor the rows add up to 100 per cent and the students interviewed were confused about how to draw a pie graph. Should you just add up the numbers and divide by 360? That the numbers do not 'add up' may imply that some of the categories overlap but this is not self-evident.

Of the students asked to complete this task, those who constructed a pie graph found it difficult to decide exactly how to begin and 'unusual' totalling and dividing took place. Bar graphs were drawn using the 'total' figures in the bottom row. None of the students we interviewed queried why the data indicate that the imprisonment rate for drug offences in South Australia is much smaller than for other states. Is it typographical error, or are the data collected differently in South Australia, or is the law different in South Australia, or are there simply fewer drug-related crimes in South Australia? Part of the skills of reading a table include the ability to assess what seems to be reasonable and what stands out as being an extreme value and may need to be checked.

For this task, the students are asked to construct a graph but it is not clear what the purpose of that graph would be since the question of whether we use imprisonment as a punishment in Western Australia, put above the table, could probably be answered equally well by an examination of the table itself. It is not always true that *any* picture is easier to understand than a table and in this case the construction of pie or bar graphs may be inappropriate — a line graph may have been more effective.

In example 5.8 students are again required to make sense of some data presented in a tabular form and to present their conclusions in graphical and verbal forms.

Example 5.8 Percentage of work-force in levels in industry (Curriculum Branch 1984a)

Percentage of work-force in levels in industry					
Country	% primary	% secondary	Country	% primary	% secondary
W. Germany	8.2	38.9	Sweden	7.7	28.6
UK	2.7	36.0	Austria	16.4	29.8
Italy	17.5	31.1	Switzerland	7.6	48.4
France	12.3	26.3	Denmark	9.7	27.0
Spain	24.9	24.1	Finland	20.6	25.8
Netherlands	6.9	26.0	Norway	11.9	24.9
Belgium	4.0	31.7	Ireland	26.5	20.9
Greece	40.4	16.4	Luxembourg	10.2	47.4
Portugal	31.1	26.8	Iceland	14.8	20.1

(a) Construct pie diagrams indicating distributions of the work-force in a selection of countries in Western Europe.

(b) Write comments on possible reasons for these distributions and describe how the distribution of the work could affect population distribution for the country as a whole.

In this case, students are required to make decisions about the way the data should be organized into pie graphs. The students interviewed were concerned by the fact that none of the columns or rows add up to 100% and that the decision to select the countries is up to them. There are no values for the tertiary sector of the work-force which, therefore, need to be calculated on the assumption that the percentages will add to 100%. Few secondary students have been encouraged, in mathematics classes, or, it seems, in social studies classes, to perform such tasks unless explicitly told to do so.

Perhaps, more significantly, the students are told to construct pie graphs and the implication seems to be that this will help them to see differences in distribution more clearly. That a student may find another representation easier to use or, indeed, find the table itself adequate appears irrelevant. It is important that students are given sufficient opportunity to construct graphs from data, but they also need to see some purpose in producing representations of information. It is difficult to escape the notion that in social studies classrooms, as in mathematics classrooms, the construction of graphs is seen as an end in itself and students are asked to do so in situations where very little advantage can be gained. Earlier, we remarked that students rarely draw informal sketch graphs, perhaps because they do not recognize their usefulness. It may be that the students have not learned to regard graphs as serving the purpose of illumination because they are expected to produce graphs at the discretion of the teacher or textbook, and because they are expected to produce neat, accurate, detailed and correct graphs rather than those of the 'back of the envelope' kind.

As well as making sense of data collected and already in tabular or graphical form, students need to be aware of how such information might be gathered and the implications of the means of data collection. This knowledge is particularly relevant to their understanding of surveys and Gallup polls to ascertain people's opinions of or actions involved in topics of national or local interest. The sampling techniques employed by those conducting surveys are based on mathematical concepts in the areas of statistics and probability. Some of the activities included in the year 10 curriculum require students not only to interpret polls but also to undertake surveys of their own. Example 5.9 assumes numeracy skills related to an understanding of statistics.

Example 5.9 An excerpt from a Social Studies Teachers' Guide (Curriculum Branch 1984b)

> Students could plan and conduct a survey on Australian overseas tourism, to find out, for example,
> • The age groups that most frequently travel overseas.
> • The percentage of people who have travelled overseas.
> • The most frequently visited region or nation.
> • The impact of the visit on the tourist.
> • How the visit has influenced the person's lifestyle.
> • The nation or region people would most like to visit in the future.
> Students should interpret their findings and summarize them on a large chart.

This and other examples require students to be able not only to design and implement questionnaires using appropriate sampling techniques, but also to analyse them. This involves *verbal* → *symbolic* transformations. In addition, they need to decide on appropriate methods of dealing with averages and to transform the verbal data into graphical form.

Example 5.10 consists of a short but mathematical piece of prose from which students are expected to perform mathematical calculations in order to draw meaningful conclusions.

Example 5.10 An example of mathematical prose (Bennetts *et al.* 1988, p. 142)

> Only 7 percent of Denmark's population is employed in agriculture, yet enough food is produced to allow 70 per cent to be exported. One Danish farmer can produce enough food fo feed 115 people.
>
> Write a paragraph on the significance of these statements to both European and world food production.

This provides an interesting example of *verbal* → *verbal* transformations. It would be very easy to overlook the full implications of this statement. The students concluded that Denmark was producing plenty of food, and therefore the country was able to export freely to Europe and to parts of the rest of the world. Included in the prose are two bases for percentage. One of them refers to a percentage of the population and the other to a percentage of the amount of food produced by that proportion of the population. Students were not aware of the possibility of setting up proportional models and did not pursue the calculations necessary to get a clear mental picture of the extent of food production.

All of the examples included here indicate a need for numeracy skills. The examples are by no means unusual in this respect; they are just a small sample from many, some more and some less overtly mathematical. All students follow a course which includes questions such as those above. All students need to have acquired the relevant mathematical skills, to know when to apply them, and to know how to interpret the results that they obtain.

NUMERACY AT THE TERTIARY LEVEL

We have seen something of the range and types of numeracy demands expected of students at the lower secondary level. In this section, we look closely at some examples of the kinds of numeracy demands placed on tertiary students by non-mathematical courses and, more specifically, how students deal with those demands.

Every first-year student entering Murdoch University, Western Australia, is required to take one of three interdisciplinary foundations courses in their first semester. The six students in the following examples were all enrolled in one or other of these courses, none of which are regarded by students or staff as making heavy mathematical demands upon students. Students were interviewed individually and asked to discuss excerpts from a selection of 'typical' readings for their course. By examining some responses we hope to at least provide an insight into some of the numeracy issues and problems facing students.

Transformations of the *verbal* → *verbal* kind are particularly important for listening to lectures and associated activities, such as note-taking and making sense of those notes. Oral messages are presented quickly and often students can do little more than jot down key words for interpretation later. If mathematical ideas are deeply embedded in an apparently non-mathematical statement, they may go unnoticed by the listener or become lost in the broader context of the topic. Lecture note-taking itself fosters particular transformations as students develop idiosyncratic methods of recording significant information. For example, they may write full sentences or use abbreviations, sketch graphs, construct tables, draw diagrams or use combinations of these.

Tertiary students are generally expected to do considerable background reading for their courses. Mathematical ideas represented verbally in written texts present particular problems and students vary in the ways they relate a mathematical term or concept to an apparently non-mathematical text. Those with a strong mathematical background or who feel confident in their mathematical ability may successfully integrate what they know with the current situation. Those who feel less competent, however, may not be able to balance a mathematical concept with a non-mathematical context. As a result, they disregard the mathematics they know in favour of what they regard as a more appropriate meaning.

The process of constructing meanings from *verbal → verbal* transformations is exemplified in example 5.11 taken from a paper which 'addresses issues of development in resource regions of northern Australia and presents recent research results concerning miner's attitudes towards commuting'.

Example 5.11 Interpreting mathematical prose (Newton & Brealey 1979)

> The radius that could be projected would obviously depend on the mode of transport chosen for the journey to work.

Two students, Sean and Alan, were asked to read a portion of the article which included this statement and then interviewed. Each assigned non-mathematical meanings to the word 'radius' (the meaning of which is taught early in secondary school mathematics) in an attempt to make it fit the context of the text. Asked to define *projected radius*, as used here, Alan's immediate response was to replace the term with another which fits the sentence, but may alter its meaning; 'the length of the journey'. Brief reflection, however, caused him to ponder the particular associations of the word radius. Thus, he attempted to understand the author's *intended* meaning ('Well, I suppose they're picturing a circle. Like, with the work places around the town.'), imagining a graphical representation of the textual message.

Sean, on the other hand, did not identify the word radius, in this context, with a circle. All other references in the text to the journey to work contain words such as distance or length and this may have underpinned Sean's understanding of the radius as 'how far it's going to be from the town to the work, depending on what sort of transport they'll be using. . .' He stated that the word 'radius' could easily be replaced by 'distance'.

Another example of *verbal → verbal* transformation is provided by the same students' responses to an article entitled *The Education of Australian Elites* (Higley *et al.* 1977), which discusses the results of research on the educational backgrounds of Australian elites. The text is dense in information, containing statistical data both in verbal and tabular forms and requiring, at the very least, interpretations of the *verbal → verbal* and *tabular → verbal* kinds. The article provides many examples of mathematical ideas in written text.

Example 5.12 (Higley *et al.* 1977)

> . . . the final sample of 370 persons included at leas` three quarters of the population that we think most observers would agree constitute the top position holders in the sectors studied.

Here, the wording of the definition of the final sample is confusing and, again, Alan and Sean provided contrasting strategies of dealing with the mathematics they encountered. Here is Alan's interpretation:

> What he's saying is that they had to get a certain amount, a sample together and what they did was they got all the people who they thought might be . . . or who they thought most people would say were included in the elite and they were top position holders. They put them all together and they drew out 370. As it turned out, 370 was three quarters of what the entire population would have thought (you know, that most people who looked at it would have thought) were top position holders and they just drew it out of a whole sample they put together. And so they're saying there that the majority of them are probably Australian elites.

His assertion that the authors gathered up all those that most people would include in the group of elites and then drew out 370 is unreasonable and unlikely, yet he saw no problem with this. Similarly, he had not considered how many people the entire population considered to be top position holders. An algebraic investigation (e.g. $370 = \frac{3}{4}n; n = 493$), a transformation from *verbal* → *symbolic* in this case, would have shown that that number was very small and unlikely, possibly resulting in a rethinking of the meaning of the statement.

Sean's understanding of the composition of the final sample was similar to Alan's:

> It's a bit confusing. Umm . . . three-quarters of the population . . . It's messy . . . you couldn't say it was three-quarters of the population which *occupied* top positions, so it couldn't be that. But it could be three-quarters of the actual people who occupied top positions. So, you've got a whole range of people . . . a whole lot of people who occupy the top positions and they've, umm . . . included three-quarters of the whole number. And three-quarters of that number is equal to the 370, yeah, it could be.

However, Sean tried to interpret the authors' description in several ways to see which made the best sense. He formulated a mathematical equation (three-quarters of that number is equal to the 370), but did not attempt to solve it in order to find out what that number was.

As in the secondary school, many texts, particularly in the social sciences, contain graphs and tables in an essentially verbal context. Unlike secondary school texts, however, tertiary subject texts do not tend to provide activities or even instructions dealing with when and how to make transformations between representations. Often, the lack of signals results in the non-verbal parts of texts being regarded as unimportant to the text's overall meaning. Consider, for example, how Sean and Alan dealt with the table in example 5.13, also from the article, *The Educations of Australian Elites*.

Alan read the text at a consistently rapid rate, ignoring the table altogether. When asked about the meaning and purpose of the table, he replied:

> Well, it's showing you . . . well, look! You've got the results in their words, because they always talk about it in words, don't they? The table shows where that comes from. Well, when the sample was taken, which was around 1975 I think, it's showing you how many elites have got all these different classifications like basic schooling and post-grad degrees. It's comparing that to people who are in other kinds of . . . um . . . occupations, and to other elites who are in things like unions.

Example 5.13 Table showing the highest education level attained by Australian elites (Higley *et al.* 1977, p. 52)

HIGHEST EDUCATION LEVEL ATTAINED BY AUSTRALIAN ELITES												
Education Level	all elites in 1975	Males aged 45 or more in 1973	Individual Elites									
			Busi-ness	Trade Unions	ALP	L. NCP	CPS	Media	Vol. Assns	Aca-demics	N
Basic schooling	15	60	6	67	24	12	4	11	2	0	55
Apprenticeship	2	17	0	9	7	0	0	0	0	0	6
Senior secondary	17	7	21	9	24	27	6	34	5	0	61
Non-degree tertiary	11	13	21	2	7	6	2	26	10	0	39
University degree	30	3	39	4	24	38	49	16	38	5	108
Post-graduate degree	25	0.2	13	9	14	17	39	13	45	95	89
Totals	100	100.2	100	100	100	100	100	100	100	100	
N =	358	1362	89	45	29	48	49	38	40	20	358

Alan considered the table to be a support or reference for the authors' results, but less relevant for the reader than the verbal report. He had faith in the authors' interpretation of the data and saw no need to verify this by drawing his own conclusions. His view of what the table was about was from a structural rather than a statistical perspective. He focused on the variables and their relationships rather than the numerical data. A sketch graph might have helped this student clarify and interpret from these relation-ships; that is, a *tabular → graphical* transformation.

In contrast, Sean, the other student, read the article slowly and carefully, often interrupting his reading of the verbal text to look at the table. He saw no discrepancy in the level of difficulty in reading the words and the table, stating that he preferred to see the data to which the authors referred, using it to make sense of the text. The table complemented the rest of the article, making it an important aspect of the whole rather than an added extra:

> When they make a statement like, 'Australian elites do not deviate from this pattern', you have to go back and check it. If it's something stated, I'd always look for something to back it up. As I said, the table really complements the rest of it. Actually, I prefer to see something like that, with the data. It makes more sense than if they just explain it themselves. You know, you can compare one thing with the other.

He considered that the authors are making assumptions about the education of Australian elites based on the data contained in the table. His own role as reader was to evaluate the authors' conclusions in light of his own interpretation of the data. Unlike Alan, Sean did not accept without ques-tion the authors' assertions and conclusions.

The same information can be represented in different ways; verbally, graphically, symbolically and pictorially, but students may make different meanings from different forms. The emphasis in tertiary study on extensive reading means that students need to read quickly. Inevitably, those who read fast or skim-read tend to focus on verbal representations. Diagrams are seen as extra, often unnecessary, illustrations of points already stated in words. Symbols, too, may be disregarded when one skim-reads. It seems reasonable to suggest that students who do read each representation for meaning gain a better understanding of the text as a whole by integrating different perspectives. For a particular student, one form may present a clearer picture of a concept than another, although different forms may emphasize different aspects of one idea. The following example shows how one student considered that alternative representations of an idea can be useful in providing a comprehensive description or understanding of a principle or idea, while another saw diagrams and symbols only as illustrations or examples and therefore not really essential to understanding.

The two students, Carol and Chris, were given the extract shown in example 5.14, which contains three representations of Kepler's laws. Carol read through the whole excerpt carefully, then re-read the equations and diagrams more slowly. This shows an awareness that the different types of text require different rates and styles of reading. She stated that this text would be more difficult to read for someone without a strong background in mathematics or science. In this process, she became aware of an error in the diagram. The verbal form of the second law states that the line joining a planet 'to the sun' sweeps out equal areas in equal time intervals but the diagram shows the areas swept out by the line joining the planet to the *centre* of the ellipse and not the focus which, according to the first law, is where the sun is. Carol knew that Kepler's laws have the same meaning whether expressed verbally, pictorially or symbolically and could use this to compare representations. She said that the diagram did not help her understand the laws, but that the equations were necessary. She readily made transformations amongst representations, translating words into symbols and vice versa and felt that the different forms of presentation were interrelated and together provided a comprehensive description of Kepler's laws. The third law, for example, she thought was meaningless without a graphic representation.

Example 5.14 Kepler's laws expressed verbally, symbolically and graphically (Theimer 1973, pp. 20–1)

Verbal
(1) The planets travel in elliptical orbits about the sun, and the sun is at one focus of the ellipse.
(2) The line joining a planet to the sun sweeps out equal areas in equal time intervals.
(3) The ratio of the squares of the revolution periods of two planets is equal to the ratio of the cubes of their mean distances from the sun. Figure 2.8 explains these laws.

Symbolic
. . . the equations representing Kepler's third law:

$$\frac{\tau_1^2}{\tau_2^2} = \frac{\alpha_1^3}{\alpha_2^3} \quad [2.2]$$

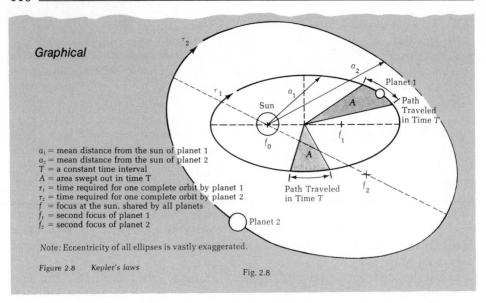

Graphical

a_1 = mean distance from the sun of planet 1
a_2 = mean distance from the sun of planet 2
T = a constant time interval
A = area swept out in time T
τ_1 = time required for one complete orbit by planet 1
τ_2 = time required for one complete orbit by planet 2
f = focus at the sun, shared by all planets
f_1 = second focus of planet 1
f_2 = second focus of planet 2

Note: Eccentricity of all ellipses is vastly exaggerated.

Figure 2.8   Kepler's laws

Fig. 2.8

In contrast to Carol, Chris focused his reading largely on the words. He saw the equations as examples or illustrations of the laws, rather than as alternative representations. Their application was evident in equation 2.2 and its subsequent worked example. School mathematics often involves the use of 'worked' followed by 'practice' examples and Chris' association with the symbols in this case may stem from such experience:

> Yeah, well, it [the diagram] is attempting to illustrate what he's sort of saying and like in the second law, for instance, 'The line joining a planet to the sun sweeps out equal areas in equal time intervals'. He's trying to sort of demonstrate what he means by area. Essentially, as far as that goes, the first law just says that, 'the planets travel in elliptical orbits,' so it shows the elliptical orbits and how the sun sort of focuses, so it's showing one and two, but as far as three is concerned, it doesn't really show much of anything, which is probably why they show it in these symbols [equation 2.2].

Chris saw no discrepancy between the verbal description of the planets' orbits and the pictorial representation. The diagram, like the equations, was seen as an example. For Chris, the different representations were considered to be distinct parts of the text, while Carol saw an interplay between them. Chris' preference for the symbolic form was evident. He saw a purpose in the equations. They could be used to solve problems, whereas the diagram was less useful. He remarked, 'Well, if I hadn't read the laws, I wouldn't be able to get much information from the diagram about them'.

Chris tended to read the names of the symbols, rather than reading them for meaning. For example, when asked to read equation 2.2 aloud, he replied, 'T one squared . . . well, tau one squared over tau two squared equals alpha one cubed over alpha two cubed'. Carol, on the other hand, referred to the ratio of squares of the revolution periods when reading the same equation aloud, using a *symbolic → verbal* transformation to make meaning.

A final example shows two very different approaches to reading an apparently non-mathematical text which requires mathematical thinking. The reading is an extract from *Being Mentally Ill* which discusses a recent study of the role of the mass media in sterotyping mental illness. This reading is mostly verbal, with the graph and table in example 5.15 included in the text.

Example 5.15 Graph and table included in the text of *Being Mentally Ill* (Scheff 1960, pp. 69, 70)

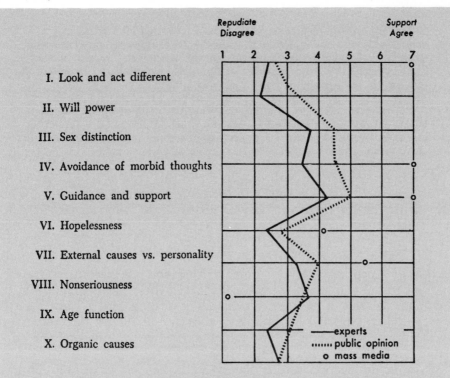

FIGURE 1[15]

COMPARISONS OF EXPERTS, THE PUBLIC, AND THE MASS MEDIA
ON THE 10 INFORMATION FACTORS

NUMBER OF TELEVISION PROGRAMS DEALING WITH
MENTAL ILLNESS, 1951–8

	1951–3	1954	1955
Documentary programs	2	2	2
Other (features and films)	1	12	37

	1956	1957	1958
Documentary programs	2	1	1
Other (features and films)	122	169	72

Two more students, Maryanne and Patrick, were asked to read and comment on this extract. Maryanne read the excerpt quite slowly, re-reading several parts. She paid a lot of attention to the table, but only briefly scanned the graph. In giving a summary of the text, she did refer to some information she gained from the graph, but quickly dismissed it as unimportant. Her ability to understand the graph left her no option but to accept the author's interpretations and conclusions without question. This was not necessarily typical of Maryanne, however, as her involvement in reading the table shows:

> It gave me this quite precise, vivid factual information. I could look at it very quickly and sort out that in '56 only .2 documentary programs were made. I'm familiar with numbers, but the chart was . . . sort of alien. That's why I spent time figuring out the table. I could make sense out of it. Like, those little circles under mass media didn't have any meaning for me. But 'documentary programs,' that has got a meaning for me. So has 'other features and films,' I knew what they were talking about. I suppose you could say I didn't have to think too much. I mean, I got something out of it, because I *could*. I suppose that if I could have known what the chart meant, then I would have paid more attention to it.

Maryanne's confidence with numbers and this type of table allowed her to become more actively involved in the process of making meaning. While recognizing the importance of having access to the information contained in the table, she seemed to be unaware of the extent of her own role. 'Sorting out', 'figuring out' and 'making sense' will almost certainly result in the reader having a better understanding of the text, than would uncritically accepting a writer's point of view and conclusions. Maryanne's reactions to the graph and the table illustrated these two extremes. On the one hand, her lack of experience and skill in dealing with a particular type of presentation rendered her unable to address it at all. On the other hand, her familiarity with numbers and tables allowed her to interpret the information and thus *own* her interpretation.

Maryanne understood, and explained well, the concept of ratio. She was asked to explain the sentences (in example 5.16) which followed the table.

Example 5.16 Interpreting proportions (Scheff 1960, p. 57)

> Once again we see . . . that the other features outnumber the serious programs with a ratio of the order of 100 to 1. Apparently, moreover, this disproportion was not decreasing.

She did not use mathematical language, but nevertheless made a successful *verbal* → *verbal* transformation, explaining clearly her understanding of a ratio as a comparison between quantities and also that this relation is determined by the number of times one number contains the other.

> It means that for every 100 feature programs you've only got the 1 program that had any real information. Well, the 100 beside the 1, they're not compatible. You've got a huge gap there and nothing is happening to put it in proportion . . . To make that gap smaller. It's getting bigger — the gap. That's bad, because you're giving a heck of a lot of inaccurate information to the public, practically nothing correct.

Her understanding of the disproportionate relation between the number of feature films and the number of serious programs appears to be based on intuition. She did not regard the terms discussed as abstract or mathematical, but directly related to the present context. Her interpretation was thus relative to the context and informal. She did not take time to reason things through, but voiced her immediate insights.

Another student, Patrick, also had trouble making sense of the graph in example 5.15. His problems, however, were with the irregularity of the diagram rather than his own knowledge and skills. This problem is real, as the ten factors should, but do not, correspond to the ten lines on which the level of agreement is represented. Patrick questioned both his own perceptions and the presentation of the data. He felt that the onus was on him, as reader, to figure out a way to interpret the graph.

Patrick explained that a ratio of the order of 100 to 1 means 'there's a hundred times more of the one thing happening than the other'. He then applied this meaning to the text, stating that it did not seem true that the other features outnumbered the serious programs with that ratio. He assumed that the author was approximating:

> Yeah, approximating. He's probably a sociologist. It would be interesting to find out what happened in the next few years. Like, there's some suggestion of vast growth here [1956, 57] with a fall off here [1958] and if it was continued, does this mean a kind of . . .? [points upwards] It might be interesting to find out.

Patrick agreed that he was visualizing a graph here, because it might be clearer and make more sense. It might assist him to draw a graph of a type with which he is familiar to illustrate the data contained in the table. Nevertheless, Patrick stated that he preferred to read verbal text. He had the following to say about tables and graphs:

> Harder to read. My alertness sort of changes. I can read words without too much of a problem. I can get ideas and sort of be actively working on it like I've made these little circles and marks and things as I was going through the text. I did see significant things. I'd get more kind of attentive and slightly more . . . I suppose far away was a feeling of dread somewhere there when I saw the tables. But you know, you have to pay more attention to get any sense out of it.

Patrick and Maryanne have illustrated how attitudes towards mathematics can affect how students deal with the numeracy demands they encounter. Maryanne's attitude seems to be tied to her background of little formal mathematics. She perceived her problems to stem from lack of mathematics content. However, once Maryanne found that she could deal with some of the mathematics in the text, she went on enthusiastically and successfully to address other, similar, material. Without learning any more content she was actually able to make better use of the mathematics she already knew and thus to enhance her understanding of the whole text. Patrick, on the other hand, preferred to read quickly and thus tended to skip the mathematical material where possible, addressing it only in response to specific questions. The inevitable result for students like Patrick is that whole parts of a text may be missed altogether, thus limiting learning.

IMPLICATIONS

By necessity we have provided only a few examples of the mathematical demands of study in a small range of subject areas, mainly in the social sciences, but they serve to illustrate our contention that the numerate person needs far more than computation skills alone and that there are important numeracy skills involved in making sense of information across a range of apparently non-mathematical fields.

In order to be able to effectively call upon mathematical skills to assist in the understanding of new material one needs to recognize when mathematics will help, have the needed mathematical skills and have confidence both in one's judgement and in the use of the mathematics. Very often students need to learn more mathematical content in order to reach a 'reasonable' level of numeracy for their home, work or study circumstances, but it is our contention that they more often need to learn to make better use of the mathematical skills they already have. Sometimes this is as simple as starting to notice when mathematics is needed or might help! Indeed, one of the most important things that students can gain from school mathematics is the attitude that mathematics really *can* help.

Of course, we already teach students the mathematical *content* demanded by the tasks presented in this paper. Nonetheless, a great deal of anecdotal evidence and our preliminary research indicates that students cannot cope with many of the numeracy demands of other subjects. One teacher, who taught both mathematics and social studies to the same students, remarked that the transfer of skills from mathematics to social studies was inadequate. He commented that students were often reluctant to apply the same level of mathematical expertise to a problem in social studies as they would to a problem in mathematics. Often we are exasperated at what we regard as inadequacies in students that lead them not to 'apply' their mathematics in new contexts. Reassuringly, whole research areas have developed around the question of 'transfer of training', effectively letting us off the hook about what it is we actually teach in mathematics.

We suggest, however, that for many students this is an almost inevitable consequence of the way we conceive of and teach mathematics, both within mathematics classrooms and 'across the curriculum'. Many of the strategies we adopt for teaching mathematical skills (whether in mathematics classrooms or in other subjects such as social studies and science) do not encourage the kind of executive skills needed for the independent use of mathematics, and may actually inhibit them.

Consider tables and graphs for example. It is vitally important that students learn how to interpret tables and graphs, even those which are difficult to fathom or downright misleading. It is equally important, however, that they come to see graphs and tables as purposeful and personally useful. While we continue to ask students to produce tables or graphs for no other reason than because we asked them to, and require that they draw graphs in order to make interpretations that are as easily made without the graphs, and keep imposing on them our view of the most appropriate way of making sense of data, it is unlikely that students will come to see graphs as a powerful, personal and purposeful tool for their own understanding. It is further unlikely that they will use them unless they are told explicitly to do so. If they are not encouraged to make executive decisions about their own learning and are even discouraged from doing so, then they are unlikely to make executive decisions elsewhere, particularly in situations that seem school-like.

Even when asking students to interpret graphs in mathematics, we often use 'cleaned up', 'unmessy' figures which have little to do with the real uses of tables and graphs. Our intentions are good — we do not want to confuse students by introducing too much complexity — but real uses of mathematics are complex and real users of mathematics often do not care for the subtleties of presentation and style that teachers of mathematics like to see. We do not remove the complexity by failing to deal with it in mathematics classrooms; we simply ensure that the mathematics we teach is rarely used for the purposes we intend.

As we have also suggested earlier, in our commitment to teaching students to recognize misleading graphs we have often disregarded both the evocative nature of many imperfect graphs and the fact that many such graphs do a perfectly reasonable job and are not necessarily misleading. Futhermore, we have what could almost be considered a fetish with the various parts of a graph — the title, the scale, the labels — and neatness and accuracy. Teaching about graphs often is seen as teaching about how to put these parts together accurately and neatly, and their assessment a matter of counting the number of these parts that are correctly and neatly placed. Students are taught to despise products which do not have all the appropriate parts, they are disciplined by negative comments or low marks if their graphs are untidy and show evidence of a rushed job. That the essential purpose of most graphs is to be informative often is overlooked; certainly few of the students who have worked with the various examples presented earlier in the paper have had this sense of graphs.

While learning to produce correct and visually appealing representations of data may be a commendable objective, it should not be at the expense of learning to make decisions about when a graph might help and the useful skill of producing quick illustrative sketch graphs. The practices described in the previous paragraph, whether they occur in mathematics or other subjects, are likely to inhibit the development of these latter skills.

Increasingly, however, the importance and necessity of developing the understanding and skills needed to produce such sketch graphs is understood, and is now included explicitly in Australian mathematics curricula. In chapter 3, Malcolm Swan points to some of the kinds of experiences that are likely to be productive in this regard.

Map work provides another example of how the development of numeracy skills 'across the curriculum' is often inhibited. Several skills related to and, often, essential to mapping are taught in the mathematics classroom. 'Similarity', 'scale drawing', and 'coordinate geometry', for example, are all clearly things students learn in mathematics. And they are generally taught as distinct and even unrelated topics. In social studies, on the other hand, students learn mapping skills. It is probably regarded as a broader, less mathematical topic than those just mentioned. And it is useful, too, even outside the classroom. But as we have shown in earlier examples, mapping activities in the social studies classroom typically involve transformations such as graphical to verbal, or graphical to symbolic representations. They require specifically mathematical skills, but, again, this must be made explicit. Students may well have the necessary skills, but fail to recognize their relevance in the current context.

Teachers of mathematics must provide students with activities designed to show the purpose of a particular skill. The sense of purpose must extend beyond the classroom. This means that actual tasks from across the curriculum should be used. The applications of a mathematical concept in particular situations and contexts can be used to enrich and extend understanding of that concept. Children will learn to develop their mathematical capabilities in a range of situations if they experience an appropriate balance and interplay between skill-getting and skill-using (Open University 1980). Recognizing and taking up opportunities to use mathematical skills can motivate or require students to refine those skills, or to learn more or different skills. Skill-getting in the mathematics classroom might deliberately involve ideal, neat, and cleaned-up examples and problems, but, as we have shown in this paper, the mathematical tasks confronting even lower secondary students outside the mathematics classroom are of considerable complexity and noise.

We propose a critical stance towards numeracy, one which focuses on mathematics in *use* and in *context*. This involves seeing numeracy (and, perhaps, mathematics) as serving the purpose of other fields and subjects. We need to help students at all levels recognize the potential in mathematics for learning and problem solving in all situations. We need to help them ask, 'will mathematics help here?', even though the answer might be 'no'. There are a number of ways we can do this, for example,

- teaching students to 'unpack' mathematical words embedded in text;
- teaching students to read symbols as meanings, rather than names or labels;
- emphasizing the interpretive aspects of problem solving; and
- explicitly asking for several ways of doing and understanding mathematics.

As students progress from secondary to tertiary level study, it is expected that they have already acquired a variety of skills. They are generally assumed to be both literate and numerate, although criticisms of the levels of 'standards' in these areas have become commonplace. As with secondary school, dealing with text involving mathematics is a major part of tertiary study, and numeracy skills are thus important for *all* university students.

The traditional approach to numeracy in most universities is the provision of bridging and remedial classes in mathematics. The aim of such 'catch-up' courses is to prepare students for university courses which demand a particular level of mathematical content. Even for those universities that embed such things within a 'Learning skills' or 'Study skills' framework, the approach to numeracy often tends to be the provision of lessons that focus on such things as fractions and basic algebra and possibly the construction of decontextualized graphs. An implication of the examples presented here is that not knowing enough mathematics is not always the real problem for students. Therefore, while more mathematics would be valuable for many students, it is neither necessary nor sufficient in order for them to be able to make better use of the mathematics they already have.

We have seen that, in some cases at least, students do not have the necessary skills to use the mathematics they 'know', even when they have supposedly learned 'enough'. Furthermore, it seems that some students who are quite confident that they know a lot of mathematics do not use it at all and that others who do not have very much mathematics can still make sense of mathematical material in context if they are able to access and make use of what they do know.

CONCLUSION

In this chapter, we have considered some of the numeracy demands made on secondary and post-secondary students in situations and subjects which they may not consider to be particularly mathematical, and suggested that the mathematical demands may indeed be considerable and complex. These issues are, however, of relevance beyond the learning of formal subject specific material. If students have not learned how to use mathematics across the curriculum unless explicitly asked to do so, it is unlikely that they will use mathematics beyond the mathematics classroom.

Whether at home, work or study many people are required, to a greater or lesser extent, to access material which involves mathematics in some way or another. Indeed, adequate reading of daily newspapers increasingly demands many of the skills we have highlighted in this paper. Reading successfully, whether reading newspapers, magazines, reference books, reports, or academic articles, is likely to demand some mathematics. So too is listening to a daily news broadcast, a documentary, a lecture or the evidence presented in a trial. In school, activities are provided which direct and structure students' actions and help to prompt ways of understanding oral or written material. Such help is not usually available, however, outside the school setting where people are likely to be responsible for their own understanding and their own learning strategies. To meet this responsibility, people need numeracy skills which they are entitled to expect as an outcome of a mathematics education, and which should be explicitly taught to them in schools.

REFERENCES

Armstrong, P. 1981, *Reading and Interpretation of Australian and New Zealand Maps*, Longman Cheshire, Melbourne.

Barcan, A., Blunden, T., Dwight, A. & Shortus, S. 1982, *Modern Australia: The World and Australia in the Twentieth Century*, Macmillan, Melbourne.

Bennetts, R., Forrestal, P., Tutt, K., Harrison, J., Gardiner, D., Armstrong, R. & Atkinson. A. 1988, *Looking at Society: Trends and Turning Points*, Longman Cheshire, Melbourne.

Cockcroft, W. M. (Chairman) 1982, *Mathematics Counts: Report of the Committee of Inquiry into the Teaching of Mathematics in Schools*, HMSO, London.

Cribb, J. 1988, 'A dark age dawns in Australia', *Weekend Australian* 1–2 October, p. 25.

Curriculum Branch 1984a, *Social Studies K–10 Syllabus Materials, European Studies, Resource Sheet 12*, Education Department of Western Australia, Perth.

Curriculum Branch 1984b, *Social Studies K–10 Teachers Guide*, Education Department of Western Australia, Perth.

Higley, J., Smart, D. & Pakulski, J., with Deacon, D. 1977, 'The educations of Australian elites', *Education Research and Perspectives*, 4 (2), 52–62.

Ling, J. 1977, *The Mathematics Curriculum: Mathematics across the Curriculum*, Schools Council Publications, Blackie, London.

Newton, P. W. & Brealey, T. B. 1979, 'Computing mining: Toward the rational development of resources regions in tropical Australia', *Mining Review*, April, pp. 6–11.

Open University 1980, *PME Mathematics Across the Curriculum*, The Open University Press, Milton Keynes, UK.

Scott, L. 1982, *Our World in Change 1: People and Places*, Jacaranda Press, Brisbane.

Scheff, J. 1966, 'The social institution of insanity', in *Being Mentally Ill*, ed. J. Scheff, Aldine, Chicago.

Theimer, O. H. 1973, *A Gentleman's Guide to Modern Physics*, Wadsworth, California.

Yearbook Australia 1988 No. 71, Australian Bureau of Statistics, Canberra.

Beyond the mathematics classroom: numeracy on the job

JOHN FOYSTER

WHAT MATHEMATICS DID YOU USE TODAY?

We can argue about definitions later but, as you read the next few para-graphs, please develop a case study about yourself, just as I am about to do. I will set down here a list of the mathematical tasks I performed today. I'll also list some common mathematical tasks I didn't carry out; let me start with some of those.

First, I did not use, at all, subtraction or multiplication or division. No, not once. When I buy things in a shop I trust people, and neither tot up the prices of individual items nor check my change. When I started writing this paragraph I thought that I hadn't had to add things either but, now that I think about it again, I realize that this afternoon I was writing a system of classification on a whiteboard and at one stage I counted how many categories there were in the classification, and as a check counted how many were in each column and then added the totals. But that was it, today, for the four basic functions.

Today, as it happens, wasn't one of those days when I used any higher mathematics as part of my job. If I drove a car, then I would certainly have used mathematical skills from time to time, mainly geometrical skills which mightn't be recognized as such. But I don't and so I didn't.

I did a bit of estimation, as we all do, both of distance and of time. I didn't estimate magnitudes of numbers, or of numbers of things, though.

Apart from this self-confessed mathematization of the world, I did no mathematics today.

But while I'm confessing, and to allow you a little more time to reflect on the mathematics you did today, let me admit that, although I didn't deliberately set out to avoid mathematical activities today, I think that today was a below-average day for mathematics on the job for me.

For instance, yesterday I did some stuff which is undeniably mathematics

— quite specifically some statistics, mainly using Fisher's exact probability test (something I found out about in a book, not in a class). At the same time I gave some attention to Yule's Q and Pearson's Chi Square and the phi coefficient and a few other useful numbers which are relatively specialized; no one ever 'taught' me about them either. I hasten to assure you I didn't calculate any of these coefficients — I let the computer do that.

And I also let the computer draw some graphs. But not many.

At work I don't use my specialized training in mathematics (which happens to be an out of the way area of Applied Mathematics). I do use specialized mathematics, as I've indicated, but specialized in a quite different area. I don't just use the kind of statistics I've mentioned above, however. Various kinds of algebra do enter into my job from time to time.

Now, where do you stand? What mathematics did you actually use today? Let me place just one restriction on your answer; don't include any teaching of mathematics to others. That's a rather specialized field; I add the restriction because such a distinction is important, otherwise we would be led to believe that Latin, for example, is more significant in the twentieth century than it actually is.

Well, do you actually use a lot of mathematics? Was what you did more or less than you first thought? And I wonder whether you and I would agree on what was mathematics, especially if we generalized the argument to include activities that we observed others to be involved in. Were we to debate about levels of numeracy, it is quite possible we couldn't agree about what numeracy and numbers are.

After all, to take an extreme case, 'numbers' is a word which has culture-specific meaning. To be a numbers man in New York in the days before state lotteries became vastly popular meant one thing. To be a numbers man in Canberra, Australia, means quite another (or not, depending upon your political attitudes). The skills required of 'the numbers man' depend on where he lives.

The meaning of 'numeracy' also depends on where we come from. From a pedagogical viewpoint we may hold to one definition or another of numeracy, but in the world outside school and its pedagogues the real meaning of numeracy depends on the users, each of whom believes a personal understanding to be a universal one: everyone knows what you mean by numeracy — until you start to consider specific activities. To understand what actually happens we need to take the discussion further than this.

This chapter is based in part upon a study I conducted in 1986, which was funded by the Curriculum Development Centre (CDC), and in part upon the report of that study, *Mathematics Beyond the Classroom* (Foyster 1988). The study was intended to find an answer (or answers) to the question 'What mathematics do young workers actually use?'.

THE MATHEMATICS OF YOUNG WORKERS

By 1985, a substantial amount had already been established about the answers to the question 'What mathematics do young workers actually use?'. For over sixty years researchers in Australia and elsewhere have been trying to describe exactly what mathematics is needed using quite straight-forward methods. For example, as long ago as 1960, that remarkable and progressive educator Henry Schoenheimer, who might not readily spring to mind as a researcher in this area, had completed a masters' thesis titled 'What arithmetical calculations do people perform? A review of current practice in the Ivanhoe electorate of Melbourne, Victoria'. More recently, significant studies in the United Kingdom, New Zealand, and Australia have illustrated just how complex the matter was. The results of these studies, taken together, ought to discourage simplistic assumptions about the level of mathematical competence of young Australians.

Graham Hunt's study (1979) of the mathematics involved in carpentry illustrates just how complex an apparently simple area may be. Hunt identified almost 200 mathematical and carpentry skills, and obtained information about those skills from almost 500 young carpenters. The findings were complex, but the following bring some of the issues to the fore:
• the number of different skills was large but the number used in any one job was relatively small;
• less than half of the existing content of maths training, up to the Advanced Trade Certificate level, is used at the workface; and
• those in the industry most easily identify as mathematical the four functions, but they less readily see as mathematical other important (and certainly mathematical in a technical sense) tasks, such as those involving geometry, for instance.

In other words, a person working in a particular job in the carpentry trade:
• is likely to use only a few mathematical skills out of a much larger range of skills used in the trade as a whole;
• will have been taught a large amount of trade-specific mathematics which is not actually used; and
• will probably identify as 'mathematical' largely those skills involving the four arithmetic functions.

Such evidence as there is tends to confirm this pattern in other vocational areas; a given worker will, at a particular stage in his or her working life, use skills which might be easy to define, but they will be different from skills used at other stages of the same worker's career, and may differ depending on just which area of the given trade the worker is operating in.

In a later publication, Hunt (1980) reported the outcome of his study of the interaction between instruction and performance: over the three years of their training, he indicated, apprentices did not significantly improve their capacity to perform mathematically in paper-and-pencil tests but, Hunt believed, their capacity to perform practical tasks in which mathematics is hidden or embedded may have increased. Perhaps, in other words, we find mathematics easier if it is not identified as mathematics.

Other studies in the late 1970s and early 1980s, in particular those produced by Cockcroft (1982) and Fitzgerald (1986), reported findings across broad areas of employment. The preparation of students to use mathematics in their working lives is dealt with extensively in these reports; amongst common elements one often finds the circumstances described at length by Fitzgerald:

> The first point to draw attention to is that although in any one occupation various employees' achievements in mathematics at school were usually spread over a wide range, such mathematical elements as existed in the work rarely seemed to be the source of much difficulty and were generally dealt with both competently and confidently. Yet, in spite of this, an impression which came through very strongly, sometimes when discussing the work, sometimes through the more personal discussion, was of a widespread lack of confidence among employees concerning their ability in mathematics. (Fitzgerald 1986, p. 32)

This lack of confidence amongst the competent, which Hunt also remarks upon, is disturbing both in itself — for those of us who love mathematics — and in terms of what it means about the teaching of mathematics. If young people are competent at the mathematics they require, why do they lack confidence about mathematics, especially when it is presented in the school (paper-and-pencil) context?

Part of the explanation for this lies in the nature of the experience of mathematics which young people have at school; this is a matter to which I shall return in the latter part of this chapter. Some description of the sources of misunderstanding about numeracy and mathematics on the job should precede that.

SIX ISSUES ON THE JOB

To illustrate some of the problems I will describe a sample of six situations in which differences of opinion about the levels of mathematical ability of young workers might arise. It should be emphasized that this is only a sample. Once the general nature of the difficulties has been appreciated, it will be possible, firstly, to look at what schools do, and secondly, at what they might do.

Manipulation of symbols

It is sometimes said that young workers cannot manage simple algebra; a first response has to be a question about the source of irritation. Sometimes it isn't so much algebra as an interesting example of a change in fashion with respect to a particular problem-type leading to misunderstanding. The fact that there are several ways of solving algebraic/arithmetic problems which involve symbol manipulation leads to different understandings about what mathematical skills are possessed by young school-leavers.

The way in which substitution into formulas is commonly handled has changed in recent decades. In the more distant past the emphasis was on manipulation of the formula to produce an algebraic expression with the unknown variable on the left of the equals sign, followed by substitution into this expression. Nowadays it is increasingly common for students to substitute numerical values into the original expression, and then manipulate the numerical expression to determine the unknown variable. Thus, if we are given $d = vt$ and are required to find the value of t given values of d and v (say $d = 12$ and $v = 2$), then in the old style we would first obtain

$t = d/v$ and then substitute to obtain $t = 12/2 = 6$. Nowadays many students would solve this problem by writing $12 = 2t$ and then $t = 12/2 = 6$.

Students using the latter method would have less practice at algebraic symbol manipulation and if tested on their capacity to solve applications by setting up a symbol manipulation exercise will seem to have less skill, whereas if asked to solve the whole problem they would perform as well or better than students using the old approach. It does not matter here whether the reader thinks one method or the other is superior; what matters is that we recognize that what appears to be a decline in skill may in fact be substantially a change in fashion. We do not, after all, these days expect year 12 students to be proficient with a slide rule.

Natural versus mathematico-symbolic language

A significant problem which arises in a discussion of numeracy or mathematics is simply that speakers fail to distinguish between different manifestations of mathematics. Bailey (1981) found it fruitful to distinguish between 'Specific tasks incorporating mathematics' or STIMs (that is to say, tasks which a mathematician might analyse to discover some mathematical content), and 'Mathematics incorporated in specific tasks' or MISTs (that is, the mathematics which the mathematician would extract from or identify in the STIM). I believe that any analysis of numeracy/mathematics in the workplace must make this distinction; and we need to be wary of seeking out mathematics in every nook and cranny, of 'mathematicizing the world picture'. I shall give an example which will serve a dual purpose: to show how closely mathematics can be tied to students' interests, and to suggest that such efforts may easily be counter-productive. In his *The Real World and Mathematics* Hugh Burkhardt cites, as a relevant illustration of some mathematics, the following:

> An attacking player on the left touch-line starts to run at 8 m/s and at 45 degrees to the touch-line towards the goal; at the same moment the mid-field player, 32 metres away at right angles to his run, passes the ball so that it just reaches the running attacker 3 seconds later. At what angle should the mid-field player aim the pass and at what horizontal speed? (Burkhardt 1981, pp. 6–7)

This may be an interesting description of a real-world situation, but it is also the production of a seemingly rabid mathematizer. You and I know that the mathematics is embedded in that situation, but one of us at least doubts that the player who mathematizes will be a better player and we probably agree that in this situation we are looking for good football players rather than good mathematicians.

Although we are not likely to encounter so extreme an example in any examination of the workplace, neither can we afford to ignore the risks associated with identifying particular tasks as mathematical. I have already quoted from Alan Fitzgerald's work about the lack of confidence young people (and older people?) have when told to manage a mathematical task.

It is not just knowing that one is doing mathematics which can be disadvantageous. Because of this lack of confidence, and perhaps because of negative feelings about mathematics, it is often found to be the case that mathematics is done in the workplace in ways quite different from those expected in school, and one common difference is the avoidance of algebraic symbols, perhaps associated with the lack of confidence described above.

One reason for workers avoiding algebra is that they work with a concrete and not an abstract world. An Australian study (Thiering, McLeod & Hatherly 1987) cites a plain language case from the area of building:

$$(\text{common rafter})^2 = \frac{1}{2}\,\text{span}^2 + \text{rise}^2.$$

This will have more meaning for almost every reader of these words than:

$$h^2 = a^2 + o^2$$

which is what is taught in schools; the first form, which we recognize and understand, is not, of course, generally taught in schools. School mathematics favours abstraction and generalization, as opposed to the concrete representation which, as we have just seen, is so clear to the common reader.

This establishes one clear difference between school and work. There are, of course, several more.

Which skills are identified as being 'necessary'?

Late in 1988, I was part of a group evaluating a year 12 Accounting course in South Australia. The subject is attracting students and growing quickly, and those involved in the redevelopment of the course wanted to be sure that they were serving the needs of employers, as the number of students taking the course would probably double over the next five years, and most of those taking it will move directly into the work-force.

Members of the evaluation team (which included a couple of practising accountants, I should add) carried out, as one part of the evaluation study, a small telephone survey of employers. Useful as the survey proved to be, the members of the team were especially disappointed by one thing; when they asked employers what outcomes they would like students to have from the course, what the employers had in common was a wish that students have developed 'figure skills'. To the accountants conducting the survey this was a let-down, just as it was to the teachers involved in the survey, for the ability to add correctly long strings of numbers by hand did not play a large part in the year 12 Accounting course; indeed, the ability to add long strings of numbers correctly by hand does not play a significant part in any year 12 courses in South Australia. Those developing the year 12 Accounting had expected that more sophisticated demands would be made of their students, and had designed the course accordingly.

Such disparities of perception are common, not rare. Do young employees anywhere in Australia now devote a significant part of their working lives adding long strings of figures without the benefit of the help of a machine? It scarcely matters. What seems clear is that for many (if not all) occupations the views that are commonly held about the mathematical/numerical content of the occupation are much simpler than the reality; people need to use a much greater range of mathematical skills than we originally conceive.

The instance cited earlier concerning carpentry is, if not wholly typical, at least indicative of the range of skills required in some jobs. In my report for the CDC, I indicated one reason why it might seem that basic arithmetic skills appear so important: 'the skills required [in most jobs] are so diverse that only the basic ones are held in common and thus, by default, become descriptors of what is expected' (Foyster 1988, p. 31).

A more sophisticated view recognizes that the ability to add long strings of numbers is not vocationally relevant, but identifies that ability as a surrogate for more meaningful abilities; we shall return to this point later.

Whatever the skills required, what boosts them?

Different groups have different views not only about what specific mathematical skills are needed, but also about what general approaches might best prepare young people for work. An interesting but unpublished study by Ken Clements & John Scarlett (1977) reveals some surprises in this area.

The study compared the attitudes of various groups (notably employers and teachers) towards some of the matters under consideration. One of the suggestions canvassed in the study was that apprentices should be given a rigid 'trade-only' mathematics course rather than a general mathematics course. The group most strongly opposed to this suggestion was the employers. There can be very many reasons for opposing such an approach, but this strong expression of opinion must be borne in mind when considering the question of preparation. The attitude of employers is easy to understand, given what we have seen above about spurious specificity in courses which are established in the belief that a small group of skills will suffice for most jobs.

The same study reported some opinions of these same groups about the importance of various possible emphases in mathematics teaching in schools. There were strong agreements but also some small but notable differences between employees and teachers: in Victoria *employers* gave higher rankings than high school teachers to 'training students to think logically' and 'enabling all children to see how mathematics is used in everyday life', while the *teachers* gave a higher ranking than employers to 'making sure that all students have the mathematics necessary for their expected occupations'. Both groups, however, gave a low ranking to 'making sure that all students have a foundation for further advanced mathematical study'; the irony of this will be discussed below.

Mathematics in use and mathematics at school

There appears to be at least one genuine difference between what happens in school and what is expected on the job which will give rise to disagreement between employers and teachers. The situation is well summarized by Bailey:

> A consideration with most employers is speed and ease of working. They want employees to be near as possible 100% accurate with all the work they

do and they want it done quickly. It will not pay them to work their employees at the upper limit of their mathematical ability, because errors will occur and work will slow down. The call for higher qualifications than are necessary seems to rest partly on the assumption that succeeding at a higher level of Mathematics makes the lower levels easier to cope with. (Bailey 1981, p. 214)

Teachers, and educators generally, see these matters differently; these differences extend to all of education, not just mathematics education. Firstly, they do not place the same emphasis on speed. Secondly, they do not, despite an increasing familiarity with, and rhetoric inspired by, mastery learning, place the same emphasis on getting things right. One of the reasons teachers don't place so much emphasis on getting things right is that they recognize that students, when learning, need encouragement. Another reason is that public examinations do nothing to encourage the notion of mastery.

Throughout a student's secondary mathematics schooling, the prevailing pedagogical view is that each step towards mastery should be rewarded. There is nothing strongly objectionable about this. The difficulty with the approach arises when the student masters nothing, lurching from one partial understanding to another, the teacher seeking desperately for signs that something — anything — has been understood and, finding some such evidence, rewarding it with 'marks for method'. As a result a student who at year 11 level still cannot reliably factorize an algebraic quadratic will be getting some marks for method in an exercise whose satisfactory completion relies crucially upon such a factorization because the student can ape the teacher's chalkings at a board (but not get a right answer).

Students need such encouragement; but they also need to learn about what mastery means by actually mastering mathematical techniques. It is here that the external examinations set in mathematics do some of the greatest damage, for they are pitched at such a standard that very few students can show mastery of the whole range of expected skills, while a majority of students are confused about the whole examination. As recently as the late 1970s it was common in most of Australia for students to be able to perform satisfactorily in these year 12 public examinations — to 'pass' — while getting around 30% of the marks available. Although there has been some movement, it is still the case for most secondary students that at the highest level at which they will be expected to perform they can 'get through' with not much mastery. (A strong contrast here would be with music performance examinations where a much higher standard, in terms of the examples dealt with, is expected.)

Associated with this practice of ignoring strict requirements of mastery is a disinterest in pressing students on the matter of speed. While the prevailing practice in mathematics education is to have students muddle along with ideas they barely understand, one can scarcely demand accuracy and speed. Indeed, the structure of much mathematics 'learning' in textbooks — long lists of 'examples' to be solved — encourages neither of these traits. There is comparatively little reward for being right if all that follows is more, much more, of the same. Such texts encourage the belief that being wrong is natural and that only mindless repetition can lead to success. And then, since we want students to have the maximum opportunity to show that they can be successful, we cannot demand speed; every opportunity to work and rework must be extended to the student.

Much of this is pedagogically sound but ignores the reality of the world of work, where speed and accuracy matter. Making the transition between the two realities is a task which appears to be left up to young people, and this may demand too much.

Skills tested in selection

The interface between school and work is an extended one; one section which has proved particularly troubling has been the matter of selection tests used by employers. From the employers' viewpoint these could be used to show how ill-prepared students are for work; from the schools' viewpoint these could show how out of touch employers are with the realities of school.

It is easy to appreciate the foundations of both views. In defence of the employers' views, one has only to note that the discussion of mathematical needs on the job has indicated that the diversity of mathematical skills actually needed is so great that looking for common elements reduces one to considering very basic mathematics. Furthermore, we could argue that ability to perform very basic tasks might be a reasonable predictor of more sophisticated mathematical tasks. Indeed, when interviewing employers in preparing my own report I heard exactly this view presented several times. And the view can go further; some employers indicate that they would like to use selection tests which do test mathematical tasks that are more sophisticated but cite two objections — cost and availability, both of which make sense.

In examining the employers' needs we must also, however, consider that the selection test is but part of the selection process; interviews and school records also play a part. The reality is that the selection test is more often than not just a simple filtering device, necessary from an economic viewpoint because, nowadays, the number of applicants usually outstrips the number of positions by so large a ratio. (One unintended consequence of this ratio is that the selection test in practice does not have to be highly accurate, since there will be many more suitable applicants than there are positions available. The selection test must eliminate the majority of the unsuitable candidates; it will not make much difference to employers if at the same time it removes some of the suitable candidates, of whom there are far too many.)

The viewpoint of the schools is also easy to understand. If, for example, an employer's test relies on arithmetic tests but bans the use of a calculator when everyone, at school or on the job, uses a calculator, one can understand the annoyance teachers might feel. This picture changes somewhat, however, when we remember that the employer is not using the selection test to find out whether the student can carry out the basic arithmetic tasks, but as a surrogate for testing more sophisticated mathematical skills.

Another reason why the employer does not use more sophisticated testing is that the employer wants to test potential employees on common mathematics experiences. Some employers will argue that the range of offerings at schools now makes it necessary to retreat to basic arithmetic to find this common ground.

This may nevertheless not be the best and most useful common ground. There are cases in which the employers' zeal for fairness is implemented in impractical ways, as in those cases when, seeking an appropriate and impartial test of arithmetic skills, the employer reaches back into the past and produces a venerable test which includes items about rods, poles, and perches, something which still happens twenty and more years after the introduction of the metric system to Australia.

These six examples (and more which could have been cited) show that misunderstandings, between schools and others, about numeracy (broadly construed) can easily arise. In some cases it is possible to take steps to ameliorate the situation, but others may prove more intractable. Where do schools stand as they prepare to confront these problems?

WHAT MATHEMATICS STUDY IS AVAILABLE TO STUDENTS?

What capacity have schools to respond to the challenge of providing mathematics courses that enhance numeracy on the job? Such a question entails some consideration of what schools offer and how students perceive what is offered.

Courses in mathematics play a central role in the secondary school curriculum; mathematics is almost invariably, though not always, regarded as a compulsory subject (along with English). Mathematics is usually described as being sequential in nature and this, together with its perceived importance in the curriculum, leads to its frequent use as a sorting mechanism, at several levels, to identify elite students. In much of Australia, as students at successive years in the middle secondary school fail to 'keep up' they are relegated to a sort of educational second (third, fourth) division; mathematics performance is a major source of information when streaming students.

Because the model for mathematics learning in so much of the Australian secondary school is a deficit one — students relegate themselves to lower levels by failing to perform within a course designed to prepare Australian teenagers for higher and higher levels of mathematics study — the context for study of mathematics by those not making the grade is not a course designed for practical use of mathematics in a working environment, but rather a course for those who 'haven't made it'.

Students and their parents know this well, and this leads to students struggling to remain with the elite mathematics classes for as long as possible; and when the student drops out of the race it is reluctantly, with a feeling of failure, and a belief that mathematics is unpleasant or difficult (a view which the majority of textbook writers labour at mightily to encourage). The next section considers some objective evidence about the study of mathematics in secondary schools.

Why students study mathematics

Whatever we argue about the necessity for numeracy may have little or no effect on what students choose to do. Most students, of course, continue to study mathematics of some kind until late in their secondary education. Our concern here is primarily with what kind of mathematics students should learn. But students themselves may choose to study (or not study) mathematics for reasons which we cannot afford to ignore. The next paragraphs deal with the 'select' group of students and the mathematics they choose.

Part of my present work involves the coordination of the evaluation of year 12 subjects in South Australia. In 1987 the organization in which I work, the Senior Secondary Assessment Board of South Australia (SSABSA), surveyed an anonymous sample of the 1986 students who had taken the publicly examined mathematics subjects (either Mathematics 1 and Mathematics 2, for those taking double mathematics, or Mathematics 1S, for those taking a single mathematics). In each case 500 students were approached for their opinions and the response rate in each case was just under 60%. The four-page survey covered a range of issues, only three of which will be mentioned here.

First, we asked the students to indicate the relative importance for them of several possible reasons for studying mathematics at year 12. The students responded on a five-point scale (from 'very important' to 'very unimportant'). Tables 6.1 and 6.2 show the percentage choices for four of the possible reasons.

Table 6.1 Students taking double mathematics

Reason	Opinion rating (%)				
	Very important				Very unimportant
I like the subject	27	34	24	10	6
I chose the subject for vocational reasons	24	16	29	12	19
I chose the subject in preference to [school-assessed subjects] because I needed a university entrance score	44	17	10	4	25
I took the subject to get a higher tertiary entrance score	32	25	24	12	8

Not only do the two groups of students agree about the relative importance of these possible reasons, but there is considerable agreement in absolute terms between the two groups. (At this point readers may wish to assess their knowledge of useful mathematics: how would you decide whether there is a statistically significant difference between the answers given by the single and double mathematics students? If you do not know the specific

Table 6.2 Students taking single mathematics

Reason	Opinion rating (%)				
	Very important				Very unimportant
I like the subject	24	28	28	9	12
I chose the subject for vocational reasons	19	17	21	13	29
I chose the subject in preference to [school-assessed subjects] because I needed a university entrance score	42	17	8	7	26
I took the subject to get a higher tertiary entrance score	25	26	21	14	14

statistical test then you should assume that your mathematical preparation has been inadequate for reading this chapter, and presumably this book.) It is clear from the tables that reasons associated with further study are regarded as more important than liking mathematics or needing mathematics for work.

Although gender differences are not discussed elsewhere in this chapter, it may be useful to report without comment that in 1986 females in South Australia were more likely than males to rate highly the response concerned with liking mathematics, and less likely to rate highly the strictly utilitarian responses.

The second issue I want to take up here is what students did after they left school. Because we asked the questions in the year after the students had completed their year 12 studies, we were able also to find out what they found themselves doing after completing year 12.

Table 6.3 shows the percentages of students reporting themselves being in various categories, for both the single and double mathematics students.

Clearly, although these students had seen tertiary study as an important factor in their decision to study year 12 mathematics, relatively few of them continued their studies of mathematics at tertiary level. Perhaps the most significant figure to reflect on is that only 36% of those who studied double mathematics at year 12 (that is, devoted 40% of their year 12 studies to mathematics) went on in the following year to study any tertiary mathematics at all.

It should be noted that in states in which tertiary prerequisites are described, mathematics is one of the most commonly-listed subjects, if not the most-often cited. Such a situation shapes year 12 choices for both students and schools.

The third and final issue to be reported briefly from the 1987 study concerned what students had liked and found useful in 1987 from their year 12 studies. Whether students had taken single or double mathematics had little effect on their answer to these questions. Both groups of students reported Matrices and Calculus as the topics they had liked most at year 12. And their responses to the question 'Which topic have you found most useful in 1987? echoed that opinion, for Calculus came in second for both groups of students — some distance behind 'None'.

Table 6.3   1987 Destinations of 1986 year 12 mathematics students

Post year 12 activity	Year 12 subject (%)	
	Double mathematics	Single mathematics
Not studying or using mathematics	13	20
Doing any tertiary study	63	52
Doing university studies	38	17
At a tertiary institution, studying some mathematics	36	20
At university, studying some mathematics	24	6
At secondary school, studying some mathematics	13	17

For South Australian students who have studied these publicly examined subjects and — given the similarities between the states — probably for many students in the other states in Australia, questions about what kind of mathematics should be studied make little sense. Many of these students, who must be considered a sort of mathematical elite, have uses for mathematics that have little relation to the kinds of argument being advanced for numeracy in this volume. Firstly, these students collectively identify as the most important reason for studying mathematics their own aspiration to university study, although only about 30% of them will go straight to university from year 12. Secondly, these students (most particularly those taking double mathematics) cite as an important reason their wish to obtain a higher tertiary entrance score. These two major reasons which year 12 students give for studying mathematics have little to do with using mathematics in the sense we have been thinking of, but much to do with making use of the non-mathematical advantages conferred on those who can prove their membership of an elite. It is appropriate to consider them here because of the influences they have on the structure of mathematics teaching in secondary school, but the wider political and social implications of this are beyond the scope of this chapter.

Using mathematics — and being used by mathematics

The use of mathematics as a major selection device during secondary schooling in Australia will not be discussed further here; it will be assumed. The argument will, firstly, consider the uses made of mathematics by those who have already been selected into year 12 mathematics and then the uses made of mathematics by those who do not study year 12 mathematics.

Students of year 12 mathematics may be categorized in four groups.
1. Those students who go on to study at a tertiary institution and make direct use of the mathematics they studied at year 12 as they study mathematics at the tertiary level.
2. Other students who go on to study at a tertiary institution and make indirect or direct use of the mathematics they studied at year 12 as they study non-mathematics subjects at the tertiary level.

3. Other students who go on to study at a tertiary institution and make no use of the mathematics they studied at year 12 as they study non-mathematics subjects at the tertiary level.
4. Finally, those students who do not go on to study at a tertiary institution and who may or may not make use of the mathematics they studied at year 12.

Each of these groups — all of them elite, in the mathematical sense espoused in most of Australian secondary schooling — makes use of mathematics 'on the job'. What does using mathematics mean to them?

Group 1

The majority of those in the first group will study mathematics to support their main field of study. Others will pursue a purely mathematical line of study. But all of them will have studied courses at year 12 which are intended to prepare them for this further year of mathematical study; the courses offered at year 12 follow traditional contents established by (if not still wholly determined by) university staff members.

In some cases, however, tertiary staff taking mathematics and mathematics-related courses are not satisfied that the traditional year 12 courses are suitable preparation for their tertiary courses. In South Australia, for example, staff at the South Australian College of Advanced Education have indicated that they would prefer their students to have taken one of the school-assessed mathematics courses. An area in which discontent is particularly likely to arise is statistics, which does not fit comfortably within some traditional elite mathematics courses, having become more important in the decades since the old courses were designed.

Group 2

These students are in much the same situation as the students in the first group; many of them will have been comfortably prepared for the mathematics they will use in their studies, while some will not.

Group 3

Many of these students make use of mathematics in quite different ways from those in the first two groups. Some may have once intended to study mathematical subjects further but abandoned the idea. But because the elite mathematics subjects lend themselves to other uses they are popular, not just for their mathematical content. One way or another, the elite subjects become the key to tertiary study. Two of these ways are described below.

Firstly, students who take double mathematics gain a bonus in the race for a tertiary place because of the high correlations which exist between the two mathematics subjects. The bonus (or bonuses) arises because the similarities between the subjects often allow students to benefit twice from learning one piece of content; trigonometry learned in one of the subjects does not have to be relearned for the second, and so on. This makes gaining marks easier for all students. But because of the high correlations anyone who does well in one subject does well in the other, boosting the aggregate.

In South Australia — the only state for which I have contemporary figures — the correlations between the two double mathematics subjects are as high as it is technically feasible for them to be.

Secondly, and here I refer particularly to those students who saw getting a higher tertiary entrance score as important, most states use a selection device which relies upon an aggregate of scores in year 12 subjects. These states also have some kind of inter-subject scaling process which helps boost the aggregate of those studying highly-correlated subjects *and* is reputed to boost the aggregates particularly for those students who take mathematics/science subjects. It is for this second reason that many students choose mathematics even if they have no intention of further study.

It is true that the inter-subject scaling processes appear to favour the mathematics/science subjects. This is, however, a reflection of the fact (assumed in the second reason) that mathematics in particular is used as a selection device in secondary schooling; schools stream students into mathematics and then, some years later, wonder why it is that mathematics students receive higher tertiary aggregates.

Such circumstances ensure that many students have not had appropriate mathematical experiences at school, in terms of the interests they are likely to follow later in life. This theme will be returned to at the conclusion of this section.

Group 4

These students, who do not go on to tertiary study, are least likely to have their mathematical needs satisfied by the present mathematics courses. They may have chosen to study mathematics, either single or double, for one of the reasons already given above, but their studies have been within a curriculum designed for others.

It is with this fourth group that the notion of 'mathematical needs' has been introduced formally, although this has been implied in the reference earlier to some disillusion with 'traditional' year 12 courses.

Once one moves to consider the situation of those not in the four elite groups such a notion becomes more important for, in addition to these four groups of students who collectively take the elite mathematics subjects at year 12, there are three further groups: those who take alternative (usually school-assessed or school-designed) year 12 mathematics courses, those who take no mathematics in their year 12 studies, and those who do not reach year 12. Their positions and learnings *vis-à-vis* mathematical preparation for working lives, though varied, are driven by the same factors — mathematics courses designed almost exclusively as a preparation for the study of mathematics at a tertiary institution.

Before directing our attention towards these three latter groups, we ought to establish the relative sizes of the groups. In other words, what proportions of a typical student cohort fall into the different categories? We can make reasonable estimates for South Australia in 1987, based on the data from the SSABSA survey. In table 6.4 we assume, as a round figure, a generous 70% retention rate to year 12 (actual figure is in the mid-60s) for 1987.

Table 6.4 The relative sizes of the seven categories of secondary students

Category	Number	Percentage of year 12	Percentage of cohort
Group 1			
Students of tertiary mathematics	1628	10.1%	7.1%
Groups 2 and 3			
Tertiary students using secondary mathematics	1622	10.1%	7.1%
Group 4			
Non-tertiary	2892	18.0%	12.6%
Group 5			
Year 12 alternative mathematics	2714	16.9%	11.8%
Group 6			
Taking no year 12 mathematics	7233	45.0%	31.5%
Group 7			
Those not reaching year 12	6895		30.0%

If we interpret this table pessimistically and accept the notion that the traditional year 12 mathematics programmes (which are designed for students in the first group) determine the nature of secondary school mathematics, then it follows that the secondary mathematics curriculum is driven by the mathematical needs of 7% of the students. Another 7% mainly use the selection power of the mathematics subjects, as opposed to their mathematical content, to reach tertiary education. Of the remaining young people those in the fifth group, just under 12%, benefit mathematically by taking courses other than the traditional academic mathematics course; the majority will, however, have taken all, or almost all, of their mathematics studies in an environment antithetical to their mathematical needs.

Is this not unreasonable criticism of existing traditional mathematics courses, driven by the needs of the 7%? Do not others benefit from exposure to this kind of learning? Some may, but there is altogether too much evidence that many other students experience the wrong kind of mathematics during their secondary schooling. In *Mathematics Beyond the Classroom* (Foyster 1988) I cite many examples of this evidence. Such an indication of curriculum exclusivity may seem extreme. It is, however, quite consistent with Fensham's remarks regarding science education (cited in Westbury 1988); in his view existing courses serve about 20% of the population at the expense of the other 80%. The figures suggested in this chapter are rather harsher but I believe, with respect to mathematics at least, more accurate.

What are the consequences for the 'others'? What are their mathematical needs?

I have thus far said little about the details of the study menitoned at the beginning of the chapter; most of the time went into contacting young workers in a range of occupations and discussing with them the mathematics they used. At least partly because of the way they were identified they were almost all enthusiastic about mathematics (enthusiastic enough to talk to me about it, mostly in their own time). There were two other factors which brought them together. Firstly, they were almost all unsuccessful at mathematics in secondary school. Those who were unsuccessful generally reported being unhappy with the way they were taught, and often identified someone who, later in their lives, had let them see that mathematical ideas could be mastered and used. They reported, some of them, being shunned in secondary school because they were dumb at mathematics, but they now earn their livings using mathematics directly or indirectly: they all know a lot more mathematics now than when they left school. Secondly, they now enjoy mathematics; they can see its power in their lives — to make their lives more productive. Mathematics is no longer a bogey.

A different approach in the construction of school mathematics courses might lead to a better outcome for those thousands of students, who like the young people I refer to above, found little benefit from their school mathematics but, *unlike* these young people, were not lucky enough to get a job in which they could discover the joy of mathematics. In *Mathematics Beyond the Classroom* (Foyster 1988, p. 3) I suggest two possible improvements:

• improving school mathematics so that there is less subsequent avoidance of things mathematical, probably by involving those outside the immediate education community more fully and directly; and

• making sure that students take the right mathematics courses.

I shall return shortly to consider possible improvements in school mathematics for those who, unlike you and me, have not been successful in studying mathematics courses in Australian schools in the 1980s.

However, there is one way in which the young workers discussed differ from you and me. They do more mathematics, more often, than we do. At least it is true for me and, if you have done the task set out at the beginning of this chapter and have discovered that you devote less than, say, one-third of your working time to mathematics that counts in your job, then it is true for you also.

Is it true, is it possibly true, that we live in a society which allots the tasks that depend upon the use of real mathematics to those with least training, to those who have 'dropped out' of mathematics? I hope that the answer is 'no', but the evidence I have seen is discouraging.

CAN ANYTHING BE DONE?

Present practices in the teaching of mathematics are well entrenched. We cannot assume that a few changes can reform the learning of mathematics. But we can certainly avoid changes that will produce learning programmes which are even worse than the present ones. For example, it is clear that taking a narrowly vocational view of mathematics learning and focusing upon 'trade maths' would be a backward step. The notion of a core curriculum in mathematics would be easier to accept if one could feel happy about the likely core. Unfortunately, the likely core would be disastrous for mathematics learning — an emphasis on 'basic skills' devoid of a context for that learning.

If we are able to avoid taking a vast step backwards, we may be able to make some progress forward. We might imagine a classroom in which learners choose to use mathematical skills to solve problems because such techniques are appealing; we might imagine textbooks without answers at the back; we might imagine learners inventing mathematics rather than itemizing it. Progressive steps have been outlined in many publications and even demonstrated in some classrooms, but there has been little widespread impact because of community attitudes which include, in a large measure, teacher attitudes. If there is one step forward which is essential it is a recasting of the notion of what mathematics teachers do and how they teach, because the greatest single barrier to improved mathematics learning for the children of Australia remains the present teaching of mathematics, at all levels.

CONCLUSION

In my discussion of the Clements & Scarlett report on the attitudes of various groups, I omitted one small point: participants in the survey were asked to rate emphases in mathematics, as we have seen. One of these emphases was 'To see mathematics as an enjoyable and satisfactory activity'. One group of teachers in Britain ranked it in first place, employers ranked it in fourth place, and Victorian teachers ranked it fifth (out of six).

As it happens, I enjoy mathematics, and so do those I was lucky enough to interview in 1986, even though our mathematical backgrounds are so different. When, in our concern for societal functioning, we focus our attention upon numeracy and its attainment we run the risk of perceiving mathematics as having only utility and ignoring the capacity of mathematics to add pleasure to our lives. Mathematics is, I think, quark-like for most people — difficult to grasp and certainly strange. But we are unlikely to understand how to make it useful until we acknowledge and use its truth, its beauty, and its charm.

REFERENCES

Bailey, D. 1981, *Mathematics in Employment (16–18)*, University of Bath, Bath.

Burkhardt, H. 1981, *The Real World and Mathematics*, Blackie, Glasgow.

Clements, K. & Scarlett, J. 1977, *The Mathematical Needs of Beginning Apprentices in Victoria*, Monash University, Melbourne.

Cockcroft, W. (Chairman) 1982, *Mathematics Counts: Report of the Committee of Inquiry into the Teaching of Mathematics in Schools*, HMSO, London.

Fitzgerald, A. 1986, *New Technology and Mathematics in Employment*, University of Birmingham, Birmingham.

Foyster, J, 1988, *Mathematics Beyond the Classroom*, Curriculum Development Centre, Canberra.

Hunt, G. 1979, *The Identification of Mathematical Co-requisites in Carpentry*, Massey University, Palmerston North.

Hunt, G. 1980, *The Analysis of Learner Competencies in Carpentry Training*, Massey University, Palmerston North.

Thiering, J., McLeod, J. & Hatherly, S. 1987, *Trade Mathematics Handbook*, TAFE National Centre for Research and Development, Adelaide.

Westbury, I. 1988, 'Who can be taught what? General education in the secondary school', in *Cultural Literacy and the Idea of General Education*, eds I. Westbury & A. Purves, NSSE, Chicago.

7 Evaluating assessment: examining alternatives

LYNN S. JOFFE

INTRODUCTION

Assessment is an integral part of the educational process, and is strongly bound up with the curriculum. It should not be treated as an appendage to be tacked on. Since assessment should reflect the curriculum, taking a fresh look at numeracy necessitates a review of how it is assessed and for what purposes.

As has been discussed in other chapters, our understanding of what it means to be numerate is changing, resulting in related curricular developments. Generally though, assessment is not keeping pace with these changes. This is creating difficulties for teachers. Many are loath to replace old content with new or to alter their working practices, until they are sure how to assess and evaluate the efficacy of such reforms; yet they are being pressed to do just that. Employers too are finding that existing assessment procedures are no longer providing adequate information about prospective trainees and employees. The need for change in assessment is not change for change's sake; it is necessary in order to establish whether students are being educated appropriately for the changing needs of society and the workplace.

The current emphasis appears to be on encouraging flexibility and adaptability in thinking. Consequently, we need to concentrate on how students plan, make decisions and solve problems, rather than whether they can regurgitate chunks of content that have been fed to them in a stylized form. This requires that teachers evaluate students' thought processes as well as their knowledge of facts. As anyone who has attempted it will know, the former is a far trickier process.

So, how do we assess students' problem solving skills and their application of knowledge to real-life situations? What of their estimation skills and do they have 'a feeling for measurement' (Cockcroft 1982, p. 24)? Do we abandon all previous tests in favour of new assessment procedures or can we adapt existing tests to serve current needs more effectively?

There is much debate as to the most appropriate and effective methods to harness such information. This paper offers brief reflections on past practices, with suggestions for necessary amendments. Discussion then moves on to address issues related to the assessment of numeracy in the 1990s and perhaps beyond.

WHAT IS WRONG WITH PRESENT PRACTICE?

The main criticism of the present system of assessment in most States and Territories in Australia is that it is limited, both in what is assessed and the means of assessment. Traditional assessments often do not tell us what we want to know about our students. Standardized written tests assess a limited range of skills, the results of which are often interpreted as a measure of 'intelligence'; and finally, such assessments may have a deleterious effect on the curriculum. Let me elaborate.

The shortcomings of current assessment

In schools, many of the new K—12 syllabuses [e.g. Mathematics Framework P—10 in Victoria (Cribb *et al.* 1988); Years 1 to 10 Mathematics Sourcebooks in Queensland (Department of Education 1987)] emphasize the need to encourage students to be active participants in the learning process, rather than passive receptacles of facts and figures. More time is to be devoted to practical work, problem solving and group discussion. In tertiary training and the workplace, rapid, on-going changes are creating a demand for flexible trainees and workers, who are able to adapt their knowledge as technology advances. However, by and large, means of assessing these now much-valued skills are not widely available.

Not only that, there is a general feeling of uncertainty about whether they can be assessed. Until more detailed directives are given, refuge is being taken in traditional batteries of tests and assessments, despite the fact that, in many cases, they are patently inappropriate for the task. So, on the one hand, classwork is being extended to include options for developing and demonstrating knowledge, while on the other, there is still a prevalence of assessments that separate skills from meaning:

> . . . student work is evaluated via pencil-and-paper tests; students' thought processes on reasoning skills are not considered. This fragmentation, the emphasis on pencil-and-paper procedural skills, and a simplistic form of evaluation have effectively separated students from mathematical reality, enquiry, and intellectual growth. (National Council of Teachers of Mathematics 1987, p. 2)

In Brazil, Carraher (1988) found that many students who failed to carry out computations and calculations in the school situation were able to do similar tasks competently in out-of-school contexts that were central to their lives, like working in the market. Are we making fair assessments if we count those children as innumerate on the basis of their school performance? The issues of need and relevance appear to be central to this debate.

There is evidence that mismatches between school mathematics and out-of-school mathematics exist for many children from all sub-cultural groups in Australia (e.g. see chapters 2 and 4). These mismatches are likely to be a particular problem for children whose home culture is most different from the mainstream culture of the school. Amongst Aboriginal students, those who lead more traditional lifestyles provide an obvious and somewhat extreme example of the potential disjunction between school and community mathematics (Graham 1984).

Many children do not achieve well in our school system, but cope in the everyday world. These discrepancies appear to highlight difficulties in how we measure and ascribe proficiency and success, with important consequences for the opportunities open to such individuals.

The National Council of Teachers of Mathematics (NCTM) argue that:

> Students should learn that mathematics is more than a collection of concepts and skills to be mastered [and] . . . demonstration of good reasoning should be rewarded even more than students' ability to find correct answers. (NCTM 1989, p. 3)

Similar assertions are contained in all the new Australian State and Territory curricula in mathematics; yet, because the predominant (often sole) means of assessment is still through written tests, only those parts of students' knowledge that are thought to be accessible through the written mode are assessed. With the ever-increasing changes in work practices to accommodate new technology, employers and selectors for further training are finding that there is a need for more broadly based evaluation procedures, that provide information beyond a written test score.

At a recent seminar held jointly by the Mathematics Education Department at Deakin University and the Mathematical Association of Victoria, employers and spokespersons from the Commission for the Future claimed that existing selection techniques for apprentices were too limited and were not related to the type of skills that industry required; current tests were seen as too narrow. The tests in question are the basic proficiency tests which are widely used to select potential employees. By and large, they serve to identify specific, usually decontextualized skills, like arithmetic computation. Scores are used to make judgements about potential suitability for a post, even though the tasks comprising the test protocol may bear little relationship to what is actually required on the job.

Selection on this basis may mean that some suitable potential employees are eliminated prematurely. Findings from large-scale studies have indicated that many students, who were apparently unable to perform required computations in isolation, were able to do so within a context in which such information was needed. For example, in the Assessment of Performance Unit (APU) studies (Foxman *et al.* 1985), some students who were seen as 'not good at sums' performed adequately when asked to plan, shop and organize a party for six people, so that each guest got the same amount.

In this case, numerous multiplications and divisions of six were involved, but were not seen as problematic by the same students who could not 'do' the decontextualized versions, apparently because they did not perceive the calculations in the two situations as similar tasks. In other cases, students labelled as 'low attainers' were able to cope competently with complex problems, like organizing a class trip (see later in chapter), when the situation was presented in a practical way. Their teachers expressed surprise at their achievements. Findings like these cast considerable doubt as to whether we give students full credit for their knowledge and understanding, when we assess in a limited way.

Limitations of written tests

By their very nature (that is, they are written) standardized tasks comprise a circumscribed range of skills. This does not mean that they are of no value, rather that the limitations of information that can be gleaned from them should be recognized and not used beyond its intended purpose. The major weaknesses of many standardized written tests relate to the actual content of the majority of tests, to confusion about what is being assessed, and to the assumption which often underpins their construction, namely that numeracy is a unitary trait.

Firstly, many written tests which claim to test numeracy do not directly address skills that are useful in real life, but rather try to infer something about the ability to apply mathematics in context from the ability to remember decontextualized facts or standard written procedures. The items selected for inclusion often tell us little except that students have good skills for manipulating numbers. For instance, what is a reasonable answer to the question in example 7.1?

Example 7.1 An item from Test Booklet 2A of the Progressive Achievement Tests in Mathematics (Ward & Farish 1984, p. 6)

Which of these sentences is true?

A $\quad \dfrac{3}{7} \times \dfrac{7}{9} = \dfrac{63}{21} = 3$

B $\quad \dfrac{3}{7} \times \dfrac{7}{9} = \dfrac{21}{16} = 1\dfrac{5}{16}$

C $\quad \dfrac{3}{7} \times \dfrac{7}{9} = \dfrac{10}{16} = \dfrac{5}{8}$

D $\quad \dfrac{3}{7} \times \dfrac{7}{9} = \dfrac{21}{63} = \dfrac{1}{3}$

E $\quad \dfrac{3}{7} \times \dfrac{7}{9} = \dfrac{27}{49}$

'Who cares?' might be the most polite answer one could expect. What is this telling us about a student's mathematical competence and, more importantly, what is the relevance of an item of this sort in a test published in the mid-1980s? The problem is that as long as items like this appear in tests, similar material will remain part of the curriculum. Teachers, whatever they might think about the educational value of such examples, will not eliminate them from their classwork if doing so is going to disadvantage their students when they are taking tests.

Another criticism of many written tests is that items do not reliably assess what they appear on the surface to be trying to assess. For example, in an assessment of students' understanding of money, what is it that we are trying to find out in a question like: 'What fraction of $10.00 is 1 cent?' Is this a question about money or about fractions? If one wants to know whether a student knows how many cents are equivalent to $10.00, as appears to be the case here, would it not be more appropriate to ask: 'How many cents make up $10.00?' or 'How many cents would you get for a $10.00 note?' or 'You have been saving cents in your money-box, you take them to the bank to swap them and they give you a $10.00 note. How many cents did you give them?'

The particular wording and presentation used in written questions can also markedly affect the responses given. For an APU item on symmetry, the success rates for written items fell by as much as 20 per cent when the term 'line of symmetry' was used, compared with similar items when more familiar words such as 'reflection' were used (Foxman 1987). How should such results be interpreted? Does this imply that these students did not understand the concept of symmetry or was the associated language the confounding factor?

The required mode of response can affect outcome. Many students, who apparently cannot answer written questions on some topics, can often demonstrate their knowledge if they are allowed practical apparatus or if oral answers are permitted. For example, Joffe (1981) found that children who gave written answers such as $\lvert p d \rangle \frac{2}{1}$ in response to a question about money, were able to provide the correct answer orally: 'one pound, six and a half pence'. There are many instances like this in other areas of mathematics as well.

If students' proficiency is determined on the basis of their written performance alone, we have to question what it is we are assessing — mathematical concepts or ability in written representation. Whilst the latter may be an important skill, it certainly should not be regarded as the equivalent of the former.

Written tests do not allow students with difficulties in this mode to reveal their true levels of competence. Sue Willis provides another example:

> Ransley (1980) describes a group of children who failed an ASSP item which required them to read the time on a picture of a clock face and who were later interviewed. Almost all of these children could tell the time on a real clock, state the time represented on a picture of a clock face and indicate that they understood the period of the day represented. What they could not do was express the time in written form — possibly an important skill but certainly not the same skill — and yet failure on the item would generally be interpreted as an inability to read the time. (Willis, S. 1987, pers. comm.)

As Willis suggests:

> Such examples are legion as are the converse examples of children who produce, on cue, rote standardised procedures and responses but are unable to use this knowledge in different contexts. (Willis, S. 1987, pers. comm.)

There are drawbacks to many of the written tests on the market; however, multiple-choice tests are possibly the most limited assessment alternative. The forced-choice answer format tells you little about what a student understands by the questions and gives no information about the thinking underlying their choice of response. Arguably more information could be gained by asking similar questions but allowing students to supply their own answers and, where possible, their working out. Of course the reason for the popularity of multiple-choice tests is that they are relatively quick and easy to administer and mark.

If multiple-choice tests are the only option, then the type included in the *ACER Mathematics Tests Series ALM1–6* (ACER 1971–79) seems a reasonable choice. Here, each test is devoted to one aspect of the curriculum, rather than a hotch-potch, and it is possible to build up some picture of pupils' performance in each area.

Another criticism of many standardized tests is that the underlying assumption appears to be that performance in mathematics is a single measurable trait that can be summarized in a single score. This assertion is considered untenable by most respected mathematics educators (e.g. Krutetskii 1976).

Of particular concern are written tests such as the *Progressive Achievement Tests in Mathematics* (Ward & Farish 1984). This is a type of test that has been widely favoured in the recent past, though its value must be questioned in the light of research findings and pedagogic considerations. Taking Test 2A in this series as an example; the test consists of fifty-seven multiple-choice questions, covering a range of mathematical topics, to be completed in forty-five minutes. Although there are some interesting and creative questions in this protocol, the major concern is that it is a hotch-potch of items — some relating to fractions, some to shape, some to codes and others to length.

The usefulness of a score derived in this way needs to be considered since it is not clear what a composite score based on these items would indicate. Such a score is potentially misleading. What if two students both get scores of 10, one by getting some questions correct and the other by getting a different set of questions correct? They both get the same score, does this mean they both have the same level of proficiency?

Over-interpretation of test results

A general problem with assessment is that test results are often used to imply more than is valid. One may calculate a score and rank students but what can this tell us about what they can and cannot do? Very little! The assumption that because a student can answer one or two questions about a topic she or he is proficient in that area is questionable. As suggested in the previous section, it is equally questionable to infer something about 'mathematics performance' from a smorgasbord of items. Ability is often inferred from achievement on a written test and standardized tests are used to stream students with little acknowledgement of the limitations of such tests. Programmes like those conducted by the APU Mathematics Team at the National Foundation for Educational Research (NFER) in the UK, report consistently that there are many students who are able to achieve at a far greater level than their written test results have suggested. Conversely, teachers have often been surprised that some seemingly high achievers have had difficulty demonstrating and applying their knowledge in practical situations. This serves to emphasize that achievement in one situation and general ability should not be confused.

We can say little about ability *per se*. The wide-ranging differences in achievement that can be seen, depending on what questions are asked, who is asking, what mode is considered acceptable for response, and so on, make it difficult to say with any degree of conviction whether achievement in a test reflects some underlying ability. This needs to be borne in mind when scores are extrapolated to support predictions beyond the limits of the test design.

The assessment-led curriculum

There is no doubt that the formal written methods used to assess the rank students have had an enormous influence on classroom practice. Most teachers have firm pedagogic beliefs about what constitutes good teaching; often, however, these are in conflict with the pressure to 'get students through' tests and examinations. This leads to 'teaching to test', where emphasis is placed on what might appear on a test paper rather than on exploring relationships within mathematics that might enhance understanding.

The present reality is that many teachers feel pressured to get through the syllabus, often in a rush and sometimes despite students rather than with them. Getting through the syllabus is equated with the teacher having presented it in class (having 'taught it') rather than with students having learned it. Unfortunately, most syllabuses are unrealistically large, thus not allowing the majority of students to develop their understanding in all areas. The choice appears to be twofold: one can give everyone a small taste of all topics and not spend too much time on any, but, in so doing, possibly disadvantage students by not giving them time to develop skills that they may need in life generally. Alternatively, one can spend more time on fewer topics and perhaps disadvantage students at test time.

As discussed earlier in relation to example 7.1, inclusion of inappropriate and outmoded material in published tests can perpetuate its inclusion in classroom work. Test constructors have a responsibility to consider this when devising and updating instruments. Teachers and other test-users also have a responsibility to be vocal in opposing the use of protocols that perpetuate bad practice. The move in numeracy is towards learning for meaning, use and application and a similar move must be reflected in assessment techniques.

Usually, higher achieving students and their teachers successfully play the system, particularly in upper high school. Here the aim is to prepare for the exams, often by adopting the correct format and style with less concern for understanding and application. Lower achieving students are often seen as inappropriate for that level of work — students are moulded by the system, the system is not moulded to suit the students. Sometimes alternative 'maths-for-everyday-life' classes are offered and despite the often excellent and relevant content, neither students nor teachers view them as more than a sop to the 'real' system. Such exercises are denigrated by the term 'vegie maths'. Ironically, it is proficiency in this vegie maths and the way it is taught (often in practical situations) that employers are seeking. It is often not assessed formally either.

The Australian Association of Mathematics Teachers (AAMT) discussion document on assessment asserts firmly that 'assessment should follow the curriculum and not lead it' (AAMT 1988). Whilst this should be our goal, in some circumstances, assessment may lead the curriculum in positive ways. For example, in the next section the results of APU assessments of decimal concepts will be reported. Such assessments have helped to heighten teachers' awareness of problems associated with certain traditional teaching practices. This has led to creative new approaches such as those described by Malcolm Swan (chapter 3).

Also, there are instances where an honest acknowledgement of the power of assessment over teaching practice has led to this power being used to change teaching practice in what are considered to be productive ways. For example, in Britain, many teachers who were loath to introduce practical and group work to students, especially in high schools, have had to do so, because assessment exercises, like those conducted nationally by the APU provided such encouraging results. These were supported by the Cockcroft Committee's findings (Cockcroft 1982) and are likely to form part of the forthcoming national standard assessment task programme in the UK.

Of course, in neither of these cases could it be said that assessment led the curriculum in the sense that it determined goals, but certainly it led the real curriculum as it happens in classrooms.

What is assessed is valued

It is not only in preparation for employment that we need to consider assessment issues. From the first assessments in school, value is placed on the tasks that are included in test protocols. If students, their parents and teachers are to appreciate that a wide range of aspects of performance can be assessed, we need to ensure that diversity of content and response modes are a feature of evaluation from year 1 on to year 12.

Generally, however, practical work and discussion in mathematics and its assessment, if practised at all, are seen in the early primary years. They then tend to be phased out. This situation needs to be reconsidered. It is disappointing, for example, that, in an otherwise useful bank of tests developed by the Education Department of Western Australia (1986), practical testing, which is the core of their assessments for years 1–4, is phased out after year 5.

Similar criticisms of their assessment systems have been voiced by the

English and American educational communities respectively and have resulted in major revisions. In the UK, a new evaluation at school-leaving age, the General Certificate of Secondary Education, was introduced, comprising large components of open-ended, investigational work and a summative assessment format. In late 1989, a new national mathematics curriculum for students from year 1 onwards is to be introduced. The associated programme of assessments is likely to involve a number of components including oral, practical and written modes (Department of Education and Science and the Welsh Office 1989; Task Group on Assessment and Testing 1987). In the United States, a new document relating to standards in curriculum and evaluation has just been published, with similar aims (NCTM 1989). Their conclusions too have relevance for the Australian situation. The following section will, therefore, draw on work from Australia, the United Kingdom and the United States.

HOW MIGHT ASSESSMENT METHODS BE IMPROVED?

In order for assessment to be a more valuable source of information for students, teachers and selectors alike, we need to broaden the range of what we assess and how we do this and alter the traditional expectations of assessment procedures.

Changing the emphasis

The NCTM committee (1989) summarize neatly some shifts in emphasis that are likely to encourage positive developments in the area of assessment. They suggest that increased attention be paid to some elements with a concomitant decrease in reliance on others.

Increased Attention	*Decreased Attention*
• Assessing what students know and how they think about mathematics	• Assessing what students do not know
• Having assessment be an integral part of teaching	• Having assessment be simply counting correct answers on tests for the sole purpose of assigning grades
• Focusing on a broad range of mathematical tasks and taking a holistic view of mathematics	• Focusing on a large number of specific and isolated skills organized by a content-behavior [sic] matrix
• Developing problem situations that require the application of a number of mathematical ideas	• Using exercises or word problems requiring only one or two skills
• Using multiple assessment techniques, including written, oral, and demonstration formats	• Using only written tests
• Using calculators, computers and manipulatives in assessment	• Excluding calculators, computers and manipulatives from the assessment process

- Evaluating the program by systematically collecting information on outcomes, curriculum, and instruction

- Evaluating the program only on the basis of test scores

- Using standardized achievement tests as only one of many indicators of program outcomes

- Using standardized achievement tests as the only indicator of program outcomes

(NCTM 1989, p. 191)

Getting more from existing written tests

However wide-ranging the changes in assessment under discussion, the intention is not to dismiss the value of some current techniques. Some form of written test is likely to prevail for the foreseeable future. What is needed is more creative exploitation of the potential of such tests. It is possible to extract a great deal of information about students' performance in certain areas, by using a traditional short response pencil-and-paper test. For example, important insights can be gained into students' understanding by asking them to attempt items and then talk about how they worked things out. The following response pattern emerged from a written test that was part of an APU Mathematics Survey of 15-year-old students.

Table 7.1 Questions from an APU Mathematics Survey of 15-year-olds (Foxman *et al.* 1985, p. 34)

Question 1: Which of the following numbers has the largest value?		Question 2: Which of the following numbers has the smallest value?		Question 3: Which of the following numbers has the smallest value?	
A*	0.625	60% dpi	A	0.625	34% ls	A	0.625	4%
B	0.25	0%	B	0.25	3%	B	0.25	2%
C	0.375	0%	C	0.375	2%	C	0.3753	36% ls
D	0.125	0%	D*	0.125	37%	D*	0.125	43%
E	0.5	33% ls	E	0.5	22% dpi	E	0.5	13% dpi
Other		5%	Other		1%	Other		0%
Omit		2%	Omit		1%	Omit		2%

*   represents the correct answer.
dpi   indicates the response obtained by the 'decimal point ignored' error.
ls   indicates the response obtained by the 'largest is smallest' error.

An initial surprise was the difference in the numbers of students selecting the correct responses to questions 1 and 3 respectively; the success rate for seemingly similar items drops from 60 per cent to 43 per cent — why? And why, in questions 2 and 3, are there major shifts in the distribution of answers?

In this case, little working out was shown, so students were interviewed and asked to explain their thinking. What emerged was that students made two predominant errors in relation to ordering decimals, reflecting a deficit in understanding place value. The first finding, which was apparently not too surprising for many teachers, was that a large group of students (sometimes as many as 20 per cent of the sample) treated decimals as if they were whole numbers. When trying to order decimals or identify target numbers, these students ignored the decimal point (dpi) and treated decimals as if they were whole numbers.

This explains the difference in the number of seemingly correct responses to questions 1 and 3. In question 1, many students chose the correct answer using an incorrect strategy. The relatively high success rate reflects this; it includes students who got the right answer based on correct reasoning and students who got the right answer based on erroneous reasoning.

In question 3, the strategy of ignoring the decimal point leads students to select '5' (option E) and obtain an incorrect answer.

However, as can be seen from the other responses, that is not the full story. What of the students (over 30 per cent in the above examples) who select another predominant alternative? Here a more sophisticated belief emerges: it appears that many of these students believe that the longer the digit string the smaller the number, irrespective of the relative size of the digits in each place value holder. For question 3, such students will choose 0.3753 as the smallest number because it has the longest string of digits on the 'getting smaller' side of the decimal point. When, as in question 2, the longest digit strings are of equal length, some students apparently believe that largest is smallest, so that 0.625 is regarded as a smaller number than 0.375 or 0.125.

Numerous other examples of this type of item have been collected and subsequent interviews with students support these explanations. When presenting these findings to groups of teachers their reactions are often ones of disbelief: 'It certainly does not happen in my classes', is a comment often heard. Challenged to put this to the test, and after talking to their students, teachers have had to admit, albeit reluctantly, that many of their students do hold these beliefs.

Many illuminating findings about students' understanding of seemingly straightforward aspects of the mathematics curriculum have been collected in this way by the APU Mathematics Team (Foxman *et al*. 1985; Mason & Ruddock 1986) and the CSMS programme team (Hart 1980). Further examples in relation to interpretation of graphs are given by Malcolm Swan (chapter 3) and Lesley Booth, of the James Cook University, who has studied students' beliefs and difficulties with algebra (see Booth 1984, 1986).

From this type of work has come the recognition that:

- traditional test questions can be used to initiate a valuable diagnostic process, as well as to serve as an end product;
- we need to talk to students about their understanding of aspects of numeracy, to find out what beliefs underlie their responses;
- we must be sensitive to the language in which problems are couched since terminology used can radically influence the outcome; and
- we should ensure that, as far as possible, items in tests cannot be selected as correct, for the wrong reason. This depends, of course, on the test constructor having a thorough understanding of common misconceptions across a wide range of mathematical topics. It is also particularly difficult to control when a multiple-choice format is used.

Teachers may argue that they do not have time to question every student about every response. Of course, that would not be reasonable. What is certainly possible is that teachers (individually or as a school staff) look at response patterns drawn from ongoing tests and, if there is a grouping of responses to particular types of items, ask selected students to describe how they got their answers. This, as can be seen from the examples above, can provide illuminating detail about students' mathematical ideas which can, in turn, lead to the kind of interventions described by Swan (chapter 3).

Very often, when students are asked about their methods of working, their immediate reaction is that their answers must be wrong. Generally it is clear that students are not used to talking about mathematics; they see it as a written subject in which things are right or wrong.

Other forms of assessment

To the extent that we broaden the scope of the curriculum, we have to also broaden the range of contexts in which students can respond and teachers can assess. In effect, this may mean quite significant changes in what we regard as acceptable opportunities for students to show what they can do.

Firstly, teachers use ongoing assessment all the time in their classes to make judgements about how students are coping: whether students understand, whether there is a need to recap, etc. Teachers identify students with difficulties and those of excellence, often without recourse to a test. It is part of a teacher's training and professionalism to use judgement and insight into students' performance. Yet, when it comes to what is seen as 'formal assessment', neither teachers nor other users of test results, see this ongoing assessment as legitimate. Ironically, what is seen as good enough for students most of the time is not seen as an acceptable basis for important judgements, like end-of-year tests and school leaving certification. Teachers' assessment skills need to be valued, recognized and built upon rather than minimized. As part of the APU programme such skills were harnessed to enable the development of interactive assessment techniques.

Secondly, we need to take seriously the possibility of interactive assessment in its many forms. As the term suggests, interactive assessment allows for communication between the teacher and individual students or groups, to allow for oral presentation and reporting back, clarification of tasks and ideas by both parties, and modification of problems by the inclusion of 'what if . . .' questions and other techniques, discussed below.

To structure an interactive situation, and to provide a standard format for the presentation of tasks and the collection and recording of information, a detailed script is often used. This is to ensure that students have the same start and that any modifications that are made follow a set procedure. The extent of teacher intervention during the task is recorded and used in analysing students' responses. On completion of the protocol, there are also opportunities to ask questions which may or may not be included in the more 'structured' part of the assessment. These include non-directed questions like 'Can you tell me more about that?' and 'How did you decide which option you were going to choose?'

Extended tasks have been used interactively to assess a range of skills and processes, including those normally measured through conventional tests. For example, one of the APU tasks required students to plan a class trip (see chapter 4), given a choice of activities, timetables, menus and a budget (Joffe 1985a, 1985b). Similar tasks were completed by individuals in one survey and by groups of three students in another. An adaptation thereof, used in an Australian study (Cooper, Joffe & Smith 1988), is given below.

For both individual and group presentations of this task, teachers use a script that specifies how the problem is to be introduced, what questions may be asked by students and answered by teachers, and in what ways. Teachers are instructed not to deviate from the script, except at specified points. This is necessary to ensure that the presentation of the task is standard, and gives all pupils similar opportunities. (This is the same procedure adopted for administering standardized tests.) Modifications to the task, like the simplification and extension discussed below, are also scripted. Of course, in group tasks, there is also interaction amongst participants and, where relevant, this is assessed.

The assessment task — an example

Example 7.2 'Plan a trip' assessment task (Cooper, Joffe & Smith 1988, p. 6)

> Your school is in Wombat Creek and you are in charge of planning a class trip to Beaut Billabong and Karri Karri Peak. You have to decide what you will do during the day, what meals you will have and what trains you will catch. Everyone will do the same activities and have similar meals.
>   *So, you have to decide:*
> • What activities you will do. You must choose 3 activities and they take one hour each. You cannot do all 3 activities at Beaut Billabong.
> • What meals you will have. Remember meals are only served at certain times. You are not allowed to bring sandwiches or packed lunches.
>   You have $4.50 to spend per person. The school pays for the trains, so you do not have to worry about that.
>   Make an easy to understand plan of your day, for your Headteacher, so she / he can contact you if necessary.

The type of task outlined in example 7.2 (materials illustrated in figures 7.1–7.3) enables us to assess a wide range of skills, both general and specific.

The general skills include:
Students' general approach to the task:
• How do they conceptualize the problem for themselves?
• Where do they start?
• What do they select as salient features of the task?
Students' methods:
• Do they use a systematic and/or trial and error approach at different times? Is such usage appropriate?
• What planning, if any, is demonstrated?
• What working out, if any, is shown?
• What happens when plans do not work? What changes are made?

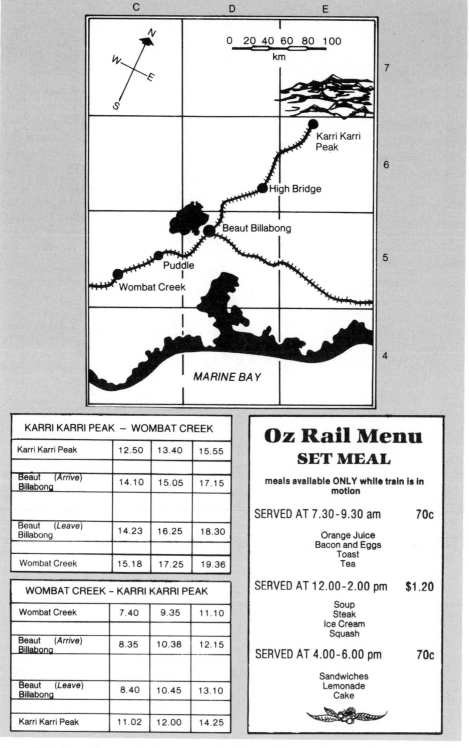

Figure 7.1 Class trip — each item presented on a separate card

Figure 7.2 Beaut Billabong — activities and cafe menu

Completing the task and reporting back:
- Do students resolve the problem to their satisfaction and/or to the teacher's satisfaction?
- Are all the task requirements met?
- Are they able to report back?
- Is their written plan a good reflection of their oral report and of any discussion the teacher overheard?
- Is the need for amendment mentioned?
- Are improvements suggested?

Attitudes throughout the task:
- Are students interested, enthusiastic, withdrawn, nonchalant, etc., to begin with?
- Does their attitude change as they work?
- How does this relate to perseverence on the test? Are signs of frustration apparent? Do students give up easily?
- What are their feelings on completion of the task?

The specific skills would include the following:
Timetables:
- Can students read a timetable properly?
- Can they use this information in their planning? (This distinction is

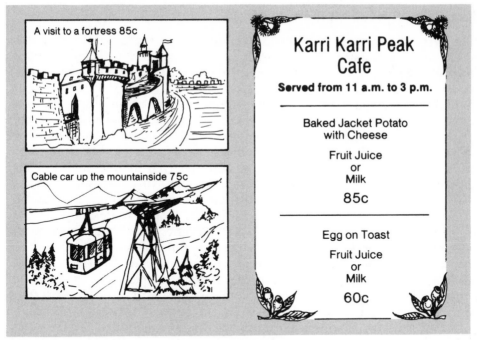

Figure 7.3 Karri Karri Peak — activities and cafe menu

important, many students were apparently able to read timetables, but could not integrate the train times in their planning.)

• Can students use the 24 hour clock? . . . the 12 hour clock?
• Can they convert from 12 to 24 hour times and vice versa?

Money:
• Do students keep within budget?
• Are calculations correct?
• What working out is shown?
• What errors are made?

Maps:
• Can they use coordinates?
• Do they use compass points correctly?

Many of the tasks included in *Mathematics at Work* (Treilibs 1980/1; Lowe 1988) could be similarly adapted to provide useful and engaging assessments, as could the tasks included in modules from the Numeracy through Problem Solving project (Swan, Gillespie & Binns 1988/9).

The general skills can be assessed using a four-point rating scale. For example, the rating for starting on the problem, looked something like this:

    0   no idea
    1   some idea, required help
    2   competent start
    3   ideas developed before start and implemented well

Criteria for the ratings were established by groups of teachers after they had observed numbers of students working. A sheet was then compiled of the criteria for each aspect and used for recording. Specific skills can be evaluated in the manner suggested in the section on practical testing.

Assessing the full attainment range

One of the shortcomings of traditional testing is that students are either able to answer set questions or not. Credit is often not given for what students know if they cannot demonstrate it to test-level. In the interactive mode, students are able to demonstrate their knowledge rather than write about it, and the interview format provides opportunities to question students about their methods and solutions, where appropriate. Problems such as the Class Trip, can be tackled in a variety of ways, at a variety of levels. One way of giving students credit for their achievements is to differentiate by outcome. Here ostensibly the same problem is given to all students. They then tackle it using the range of knowledge and skills available to them.

In example 7.2 the most sophisticated responses from 11-year-old students (and 15-year-old students on a similar, though more complex task) yielded a fully integrated day in which travel times, meals and activities all dovetailed and the budget was not exceeded. Other day-plans satisfied all the criteria but left students waiting for long periods for trains. Some students acknowledged this and made allowances like, 'Oh, we will go shopping for souvenirs in the time before the train leaves', or 'We will play some games to pass the time till the train goes'. Others did not allow sufficient time for all the activities or meals and mentioned this in statements like, 'We will be able to see the fortress from the train' or 'We will have to eat lunch while walking to the station'.

Figure 7.4 Cards which can be used to increase the complexity of tasks

Some students cannot cope with all the complexities of such a task. In cases where it becomes evident that students are unable to use the time-tables, for example, these are removed. This is done in a non-threatening way such as the teacher saying: 'It is your lucky day, the principal has decided that you are going by coach. Plan your day so that you leave school at 9 o'clock and each part of the journey, activities and meals take one hour'. In this way it is still possible to assess whether students can cope with the complex integration task and other aspects of the problem when they are not hampered by their inability to interpret a timetable. Similar adjustments can be made with the monetary aspect of the problem; simpler prices can be given to make the calculations easier.

The beauty of tasks such as the Class Trip is that they can be easily modified to accommodate students whatever their level of achievement. This is a variation on simply differentiating by outcome. For students who are able to meet all the task requirements adequately, it is interesting to increase the complexity of the task. This allows evaluation of the adaptability of their skills and knowledge. Once such students have completed their plans, the teacher selects a change of circumstances that necessitates amendments. These changes are presented to the students on cards, such as those show in figure 7.4.

Using the extensions to make the problem easier or harder allows for the assessment of what students can do to their fullest capabilities, rather than within the narrow range described by many protocols.

Assessment with practical equipment

Skills and knowledge can be tested using practical apparatus. In Western Australia, such assessments are used for students up to year 4. An example from the Ministry of Education's Baseline Tests (1986) is given in example 7.3 (over page).

Other more complex graded examples developed for 11- and 15-year-olds respectively can be seen in work by Joffe (1985a, 1985b).

Lack of time and insufficient apparatus are reasons often given for resisting such assessment. There are ways round this; the circus or work station method, for example. Here, a variety of tasks, involving the use of practical apparatus, are set up round the classroom. Students work at each station successively, recording their findings (see Foxman 1987 for further details). A British standardized version of a practical class test will be available in early 1990 (Foxman, Hagues & Ruddock, in press).

Profiling

Since numeracy is developmental, a promising alternative is the longitudinal approach, in which the focus is on development of understanding and competence over a period of time. Here, a range of techniques can be used to build up a comprehensive picture of performance — a profile of strengths and weaknesses. Students' progress can also be measured against their previous achievements rather than a perceived absolute. Progress records of this type can accompany students throughout their schooling.

Example 7.3 A Ministry of Education Baseline Test (Education Department of Western Australia 1986)

MEASUREMENT TEST : YEAR 4

M1.

Teacher Instruction

Measure the length of this hammer in centimetres.

Equipment

Toy hammer [or any object approximately 15cm or 20cm long], rule.

Marking Scale

3. Able to accurately measure hammer.

2. Able to measure hammer without guidance. Has an error of plus or minus 1cm.

1. Able to measure hammer with clues given. *"Line up the zero mark on the rule with the end of the hammer." "What number is closest to the end of the ruler?"*

0. Unable to measure hammer with clues given in 1.

M2.

Teacher Instruction

Put these containers in order starting with the one that holds the most.

Equipment

3 containers each with a different capacity [vary by approximately 20-30ml]. Beans, rice or water for measuring. Measuring cylinder.

Marking Scale

3. Able to demonstrate full understanding and accurately measure containers.

2. Able to measure containers with guidance but with inaccuracy through spilling, incomplete filling, incorrect reading of measuring cylinder.

1. Able to measure containers with clues and assistance given. Need assistance to use measuring cylinder: *"What will happen if you fill this container with beans and tip them into the measuring cylinder?"*

0. Unable to measure containers after clues given in 1.

ASSESSMENT OF NUMERACY INTO THE 1990s AND BEYOND

There are a range of inhibitors to the kind of change needed in assessment practices. There are problems of inexperience on the part of teachers and fears about lack of comparability with newer assessment strategies. There are also, dare I say it, certain conflicts of interest, and there is habit (often called tradition).

Teachers' inexperience in a range of types of assessment

A large number of teachers who see the value of alternative forms of assessment are reluctant to try them because they do not value or have confidence in their own assessment skills and seek reassurance in externally devised tests.

For some, their concern about using forms of assessment like group work and project work is that they will not be able to keep track of all the activity that is taking place. Many are worried that they may disadvantage students by their judgements, particularly with complex and open-ended tasks. These are realistic concerns; however, with good training and practice it is possible to minimize such risks. In this context, it is worth considering how much information we are losing by the circumscribed way we assess students' performances at present.

If there is a real commitment to change in assessment practices on the part of ministries of education, there is also an obligation to provide sufficient funding to allow extensive in-service and pre-service training. Occasional one-day in-service courses will not be sufficient if the issue is to receive adequate attention. Through education of teachers and the public, fears about personal bias affecting assessment outcomes can be tempered by increased teacher confidence and trust by the community in the professionalism and skill of teachers.

Comparability

One of the reservations about adopting a broader range of assessment techniques has been the issue of comparability. The feeling seems to be that whatever one may or may not have been able to determine from traditional test results, at least they were comparable. However, as can be seen from the APU model in Britain, comparative assessment is possible in other modes, even at a national level, so it should be feasible at a state or territory level. It is conceivable that more progressive, wide-ranging assessments using open-ended responses could be used. Much depends on the provision of adequate training for teachers.

Conflicts of interest

Students' results, especially those at school-leaving age, have become a political issue. The perennial debates about effective schooling, in which political parties engage, sometimes retard development rather than enhance it.

An issue that surfaces at periodic intervals is the back-to-basics one. As recently as 1988, Nick Greiner, now premier of New South Wales, then Leader of the Opposition, suggested the introduction of basic proficiency tests. He is quoted as saying, '. . . the whole idea behind the policy was to find out whether they [students] were learning to add up at an early age' (Morrison 1988). Seemingly equally narrow is the means by which such skills would be assessed. The use of multiple-choice question papers is proposed, with marking and analysis to be carried out by computer.

According to Dr Max Dunston, Head of the Testing Centre at Wollongong University, this exercise would be beneficial for all:
• the Education Department would get accountability data and the knowledge that improvements are being made [how?];
• teachers would get data to guide teaching [how?];
• students would receive data to guide learning [what?];
• parents would receive information on their children's performance [in what?].

In view of the foregoing discussions in this chapter, many of these assertions would be questionable. Most importantly, what kind of teaching would be guided by the results of tests which assess only the things accessible by timed multiple-choice tests. Is 'adding up at an early age' to be amongst the most important achievements we require of our students?

Not according to Dr David Widdup, Executive Director of the Federation of Australian Scientific and Technological Societies (1988), who dismisses the back-to-basics push. He maintains that employers no longer need employees to act as substitute calculators; they need numerate students, who can think mathematically to analyse and solve problems (Dawson 1988).

A major issue in this debate is that policy makers and classroom teachers are too far apart; the needs and concerns of these two groups are often very different and there appear to be few occasions when there is real communication between the two. There is little point in ignoring the reality that educational issues are affected by non-educational factors. Sensible and useful assessments need to address the needs of students, teachers, parents, politicians and employers — it is essential that these groups negotiate an acceptable and practicable compromise if assessment is going to be useful more generally.

Tradition

Assessment has lagged behind curricular development at every stage of innovation. This means that current modes of assessment have been in use, without much modification, for a long time.

In some States and Territories, even in recently updated syllabuses, the rhetoric concerning new initiatives in style and content is not being matched by suitable assessment procedures. Examples of this can be seen in the latest Mathematics Sourcebooks issued by the Department of Education in Queensland (1987). Here, every effort has been made to promote the enhancement of teaching and learning. The aims of the years 1–10 programmes are admirable, as are the suggestions offered to widen the range of experiences offered to students. Disappointingly, though, the examples of assessment procedures given to accompany these encouraging developments in the curriculum, in no way match the aims of the syllabus as stated in the sections on learning experiences and teaching approaches. What emerges are clear directives about changes in curriculum and classroom practice, with relatively little guidance on relevant forms of assessment; the why is there, the what is there but, the major aspect for teachers, the how, is omitted. Such situations must be remedied.

For some groups, there is also an investment in resisting change. The public generally are not confident about mathematics, so are often reassured when offered evidence of skills that they recognize from their own schooling. This can act as a retarding force to change and encourage a nostalgia for sometimes outmoded methods and skills or at least an unbalanced view of these.

We do not need to go back to basics, we do not need to go back to anything. We need to go forward and ensure that what we assess and how we assess matches the changes in what is taught and what will serve the best interests of students and society. We must be vigilant to ensure that short-term political expediency does not cloud important pedagogic innovation.

Changes in assessment should be reflected throughout the age range. It is not sufficient to change assessments for one age-group, or in one way only. Practical work is important for all students, whatever their year group; basic skills are needed in a variety of situations and problem solving strategies are essential if students are to be able to apply their knowledge. An adequate assessment programme requires that all these modes be used to evaluate achievement in all grades and at all levels.

We need to be bold in approaching change. Tradition and convention die hard, but doing things in one way because 'we've done it like this for 20 years' is not a good reason to avoid change. Some States have already implemented innovations; the Victorian Curriculum and Assessment Board's (VCAB) work on standard assessment tasks is an example.

In other places, there are groups of teachers who are already making great strides in alternative but complementary assessments. Indeed, some high school teachers in Western Australia (see Ganderton 1988) have gone a long way towards developing complex yet workable schedules for evaluating project work, which included examination of written work, practical outcomes where appropriate and interviews with students to gauge their understanding.

CONCLUSION

If assessment is to keep pace with the changing face of numeracy, it must reflect the continually changing needs of society. This requires a broader vision of assessment in which the range of techniques recognized as legitimate is extended as demands arise. Flexibility and adaptability should also be regarded as key aspects in ensuring that the system, once revised, does not ossify again. We do not want to create a new system, however good, that remains static. There has to be a genuine willingness on the part of educators, parents, students, employers and politicians, to accept that the outcomes of new assessments are valuable in themselves and not a poor version of 'proper' (that is, conventionally accepted) written tests. As long as a view prevails that 'this all seems like good stuff, but can they do their sums', changes will be marginal.

Changes in assessment, and indeed people's confidence in alternative forms of evaluation, are not likely to happen overnight. The least that can be hoped for is that those people who are retarding change by wanting to maintain the status quo or go back (usually to basics — whatever they are) will examine their motivations and perhaps risk a step into new territory.

Ultimately there is good assessment and poor assessment. Neither results solely from the means used nor the personnel involved. Both need constant reviewing and retraining, respectively, in the light of changes in educational practices and societal needs.

REFERENCES

ACER 1971–79, *ACER Mathematics Tests — Topic Tests AM Series, 1–6*. ACER Melbourne.

Australian Association of Mathematics Teachers 1988, Discussion document on assessment, Circulated for the Biennial Conference of Australian Association of Mathematics Teachers, Newcastle, January.

Booth, L. 1984, *Algebra: Children's Strategies and Errors*, NFER-Nelson, Windsor, England.

Booth, L. 1986, 'Difficulties in algebra', *The Australian Mathematics Teacher*, **42** (3), 2–4.

Carraher, T. N. 1988, 'Street mathematics and school mathematics', *Proceedings of the Twelfth Annual Conference of the International Group for the Psychology of Mathematics Education*, Vol. 1, Veszprem, OOK Printing House, pp. 1–23.

Cockcroft, W. (Chairman) 1982, *Mathematics Counts: Report of the Committee of Inquiry into the Teaching of Mathematics in Schools*, HMSO, London.

Cooper, T., Joffe, L. & Smith, R. 1988, Using groups to develop higher intellectual functioning in mathematical problem solving, Paper presented at ACER seminar on Intelligence, 24–26 Aug.

Cribb, P., Fenby, B., Newton, W., Snow, P. & Caughey, W. 1988, *The Mathematics Framework P-10*, Mathematics Centre of Curriculum Branch, Ministry of Education (Schools Division), Victoria.

Dawson, C. 1988, 'Degree value now in decline', *Australian*, 20 Jan., p. 16.

Department of Education and Science and the Welsh Office (DES/WO) 1989, *Mathematics in the National Curriculum*, HMSO, London.

Department of Education, Queensland 1987, *Syllabus, Sourcebook and Teaching, Curriculum and Assessment Guidelines*, Department of Education, Queensland.

Education Department of Western Australia 1986, *Baseline Mathematics Tests*, Primary Research Branch, Perth.

Foxman, D. 1987, *Assessing Practical Mathematics in Secondary Schools*, HMSO, London.

Foxman, D., Ruddock, G., Joffe, L., Mason, K., Mitchell, P. & Sexton, B. 1985, *Mathematical Development: A Review of Monitoring in Mathematics 1978 to 1982. Parts 1 and 2*, APU/Department of Education and Science, London.

Foxman, D., Hagues, N. & Ruddock, G. (in press), *Mathematics Test Series with Practical Elements*, NFER-Nelson, Windsor.

Ganderton, P. 1988, Mathematical process development and its measurement, Honours thesis, Murdoch University, Perth, Western Australia

Graham, B.1984, 'Finding meaning in maths: An introductory program for Aboriginal children', *Aboriginal Child*, **12** (4), 24–39.

Hart, K. M. 1980, *Secondary School Children's Understanding of Mathematics: A Report of the Mathematics Components of the Concepts in Secondary Mathematics and Science programme*, Centre for Science Education, Chelsea College, University of London, London.

Joffe, L. S. 1981, School mathematics and dyslexia: aspects of the interrelationship, PhD thesis, University of Aston, Birmingham.

Joffe, L. 1985a, *Practical Testing in Mathematics at Age 11* (videotape and handbook), APU/Department of Education and Science, London.

Joffe, L. 1985b, *Practical Testing in Mathematics at Age 15* (videotape and handbook), APU/Department of Education and Science, London.

Krutetskii, V. A. 1976, *The Psychology of Mathematical Abilities in School Children*, Chicago, University of Chicago.

Lowe, I. 1988, *Mathematics at Work: Modelling your world*, Australian Academy of Science, Canberra.

Mason, K. & Ruddock, G. 1986, *Decimals: Assessment at Age 11 and Age 15*, NFER-Nelson, Windsor.

Morrison, J. 1988, 'Coalition to revise emphasis on three Rs', *Australian*, 25 Feb., p. 8.

National Council of Teachers of Mathematics (NCTM) 1989, *Curriculum and Evaluation Standards for School Mathematics*, NCTM, Reston, Va.

National Council of Teachers of Mathematics (NCTM) 1987, *Overview of the Curriculum and Evaluation Standards*, Working Draft, NCTM, Reston, Va.

Ransley, W. 1980, ' "Numeracy", "Basic skills" and "Real-life" ', *Australian Mathematics Teacher*, **36** (2), 9–12.

Swan, M., Gillespie, J. & Binns, B. 1988/9, *Numeracy through Problem Solving*, Longman, Harlow.

Task Group on Assessment and Testing (TGAT) 1987, *Report*, Department of Education and Science and the Welsh Office, London.

Treilibs, V. (ed.), 1980/1, *Mathematics as Work* series, Australian Academy of Science, Canberra.

Ward, G. & Farish, S. (compilers) 1984, *Progressive Achievement Tests in Mathematics* ACER, Melbourne.

Reforming mathematics: supporting teachers to reshape their practice

DOUG CLARKE, CHARLES LOVITT AND MAX STEPHENS[1]

INTRODUCTION

Each of the previous chapters in this volume has contributed to the task of reconceptualizing what 'being numerate' means. Some have also considered the kinds of changes in classroom practice that may be necessary to reform the mathematics curricula in the ways envisaged herein. There have been many attempts in the past to reform the teaching and content of the mathematics curriculum which have not lived up to their promise. We believe that this is, in part, a result of our failure to address the professional role of the teacher in any serious way. Too often teachers have been seen as a passive conduit between policy-makers/curriculum-developers and pupils, and not as active creators and managers of the learning environment. Only relatively recently, perhaps since the mid-1970s, have we begun to take seriously the matter of how teachers, in ordinary classroom settings, can firstly, develop their own positions on necessary changes to classroom practice, and secondly, how they can be active partners in bringing about such changes.

In this chapter, we have assumed that a reconceptualization of numeracy is necessary. We argue that it is also necessary to reconceptualize teaching strategies which will bring about this new vision of numeracy. The chapter is mainly concerned with providing strategies for this. Critical to our argument is the belief that a very considerable body of understanding about numeracy and appropriate teaching strategies already exists in the hands of

---

[1]We would like to acknowledge the significant support of Professor Tom Romberg of the University of Wisconsin, Madison, in the development of this chapter.

our best teachers. As a teaching profession we have failed to identify and document such good teaching practice, and this has meant that the collective wisdom of our best teachers has not been available to support other teachers interested in reshaping their own practice.

RECENT MOVES TO REFORM MATHEMATICS TEACHING

The agenda for reform

Throughout the 1980s, an agenda for reform of school mathematics has been articulated with remarkable consistency around the world. In this section, we shall consider, briefly, the nature of these reforms in the United States of America, the United Kingdom and Australia before proceeding to discuss principles which the experiences of the 1980s suggest underlie successful professional development of teachers of mathematics and hence successful implementation of such reforms in classrooms.

Reform in the United States of America

The National Council of Teachers of Mathematics (NCTM) has been addressing the issue of reform throughout the 1980s. This is reflected in the 1989 NCTM document, *Curriculum and Evaluation Standards for School Mathematics* which, after strongly endorsing the 1980 emphasis on problem solving (NCTM 1989, p. 10), went on to say that the driving force for the development of curriculum and evaluation standards 'is a vision of the mathematics all students should have an opportunity to learn, and the way in which instruction should occur' (NCTM 1989, p. 1).

The Standards document advocates far more than merely changing the content of school mathematics. It calls for reform in the teaching of mathematics at all levels. The statement on curriculum standards for grades 9–12, for example, recommends that mathematics teachers should provide students with 'many opportunities to experiment with ideas, develop strategies, formulate and communicate conclusions, apply fundamental skills, and interact in groups' (NCTM 1989, p. 90), and similar recommendations are addressed to teachers of grades K–4 and 5–8.

Reform in the United Kingdom

The widely acclaimed British report *Mathematics Counts* (Cockcroft 1982) was the product of a committee charged with the task of investigating mathematics curricula 'with particular regard to the mathematics required in further and higher education, employment and adult life generally' (Cockcroft 1982, p. iii). As was the case in the NCTM report, Cockcroft emphasized changes to content as well as appropriate teaching strategies. With respect to content, the report provided a 'foundation list of mathematical topics which should form part of the mathematics syllabus for all pupils' (Cockcroft 1982, p. 134). The foundation list provided details of what all students should learn in the areas of number, money, percentages, the use of calculators, time, measurement, graphs and pictorial representation, spatial concepts, ratio and proportion, and statistics (Cockcroft 1982, pp. 135–40). With respect to the learning environment, paragraph 249 of the Report strongly recommended that problem solving be an important emphasis in both primary and secondary school mathematics, and that students should develop the ability to work with others in devising appropriate problem solving strategies.

Reform in Australia

In the late 1970s Australian mathematics educators made significant moves towards establishing a problem solving emphasis in school mathematics (Clements 1987). The publication of both *An Agenda for Action* (NCTM 1980) and the Cockcroft Report (1982) had a strong impact on the thinking of Australian mathematics educators (Blane, Maurer & Stephens 1983; Blane, 1984). In each of these reform documents, with their dual emphases on changed content and changed practices, the classroom teacher was seen as being the critical factor in achieving change in school mathematics. Lampert (1988) argues that the reform documents present a consistent picture of the ideal mathematics teacher as someone who:

1. Encourages and fields questions, while knowing enough mathematics to direct inquiry without giving answers to students.
2. Enacts a curriculum that both responds to students' questions and is true to the central ideas of the discipline.
3. Analyses problems with students by drawing out their hypotheses and challenging them to disprove or confirm them.
4. Takes advantage of the fact that students are building up their own representations of scientific and mathematical ideas, provides experiences from which those representations can be formulated, finds out what students' representations are, and diagnoses and challenges faulty or limited representations.
5. Takes responsibility not only for communicating the subject but also for garnering students' commitment to learning the subject.

(Lampert 1988, p. 163)

However, the mere publication of reform documents and agendas for change does not, of itself, bring about change in teaching practice. The overriding question is how Lampert's (1988) images of the ideal mathematics teacher can be translated into teaching practice in ordinary classroom settings.

This issue is the driving force behind this chapter. We shall attempt to describe how some mathematics teachers have been able to change their classroom practice in educationally significant ways. In particular, our focus will be to report on a successful programme which has made teachers partners in the process of reform, and has thereby enabled them to change their practice and their view of numeracy.

The Mathematics Curriculum and Teaching Program

This section describes and interprets the experiences of primary and secondary teachers of mathematics who participated in the Australian Mathematics Curriculum and Teaching Program (MCTP). From 1985 to 1988 the MCTP was funded by the national Curriculum Development Centre, in Canberra, and carried the endorsement of the ministries and departments of education in all Australian states and territories.

The MCTP is first and foremost a professional development programme for teachers. It could be described as a major vehicle by which the reform agendas can be explored and adopted by classroom teachers. Central to its style of operation is recognition of the vast store of knowledge about teaching that resides in our best classrooms. Gaining access to this wisdom, and documenting and sharing it effectively is the particular challenge taken up by the MCTP. The value of this current practice is expressed by the *Mathematics Framework: P–10*:

> Yet current practice is the base we all build on and it contains much that is worthwhile. It embodies our store of mathematical understandings, and our knowledge of students and how they learn. (Victorian Ministry of Education 1988, p. 15)

During the programme, MCTP has developed and published mathematics curriculum materials, including books and videotapes, as well as producing professional development manuals on alternative assessment procedures, and models for achieving change in school mathematics programmes. MCTP materials and manuals were developed after extensive trialling in primary and post-primary schools throughout Australia. By making use of well-documented, exemplary teaching materials, derived from successful classroom practice, MCTP followed a model established by the earlier Reality in Mathematics Education (RIME) project (Lowe & Lovitt 1984; Victorian Education Department 1984).

FOUR PRINCIPLES FOR SUCCESSFUL REFORM

There are four principles which are fundamental if reform of mathematics teaching and learning is to be achieved. They are:

1. Any program which seeks to enhance the quality of teaching and learning in mathematics must convey to teachers, in practical terms, a clear image of what these changes might mean in the classroom. It must lead to an instrumental understanding of numeracy, an understanding of the purpose of school mathematics, and an understanding of the characteristics of effective learning environments.
2. It is not easy for teachers of mathematics to change their teaching methods. Impediments to change are usually deeply embedded in established patterns of classroom behaviour, and these reflect deep-seated assumptions about the nature of school mathematics and how it is best taught and learned. Recognizing and overcoming these obstacles is the first and most painful step along the road to reform of mathematics teaching.
3. Exemplary curriculum materials can assist teachers to think about their current roles, and to modify the way they teach. Such materials are

'exemplary' because they build upon what Shulman (1987) called 'the wisdom of practice'.

4. Reshaping the teaching of mathematics requires that teachers have access to a sustaining and well-structured environment for their professional growth. This must entail a partnership with all interested parties, including parents, employers and community groups.

These principles have been incorporated in both the RIME and MCTP projects. In what follows we will examine each of these principles in detail.

Principle 1: Consider the effects on classroom practice

Any programme which seeks to enhance the quality of teaching and learning in mathematics should convey to teachers a clear vision of what any proposed changes might mean for classroom practice. Central to this first principle is the need for teachers not only to recognize *what* they do in classrooms, but also to reflect upon *why* they do what they do.

Each teacher's personal reflections on what he or she does in the classroom, and why, will be influenced by such background qualities as the teacher's experience and confidence. It seems axiomatic that the quality of the learning environments that a teacher is able to establish will depend critically on the quality and extent of the teacher's own background experiences.

Teachers relating to new ideas and practice

Many teachers are seeking to improve and expand the quality and range of their current practice. In order to achieve this, they will need to explore ideas and theories that are currently outside their confidence or comfort zone. For example, a changed view of what constitutes basic skills may initially generate a degree of discomfort. Central to the operation of MCTP is asking teachers to 'suspend judgement' while they step outside their comfort zone to explore new ideas.

When teachers attending MCTP seminars were asked to analyse their current practice and to suggest new practices they would like to explore, they generated many of the topics shown in figure 8.1. Often these are not part of the normal teaching repertoires of individual teachers, who believe that they lack the confidence, experience and resources to incorporate such matters into their normal teaching practice.

So, for many teachers, the issues and concerns surrounding 'current practice' in figure 8.1 represent new educational territory. MCTP sought to help teachers to explore this new territory in ways that gradually reshaped their current practice. The teachers were encouraged to try new ideas in their classrooms, and MCTP attempted to ensure that they would be assisted in the resolution of the tension which almost inevitably arose in teachers' minds.

It is not suggested that *all* of the issues and concerns listed in figure 8.1 represent new educational territory for *all* teachers. For many teachers, some of these issues and concerns already lie firmly within their current practice, and it was these teachers who provided the classroom vignettes illustrated within the *MCTP Activity Bank* (Lovitt & Clarke 1988, 1989).

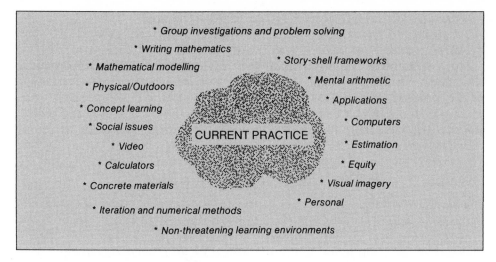

* Group investigations and problem solving
* Writing mathematics
* Mathematical modelling
* Story-shell frameworks
* Physical/Outdoors
* Mental arithmetic
* Concept learning
* Applications
* Social issues
CURRENT PRACTICE
* Computers
* Video
* Estimation
* Calculators
* Equity
* Concrete materials
* Visual imagery
* Personal
* Iteration and numerical methods
* Non-threatening learning environments

Figure 8.1 New practices, outside current practice, that teachers would like to explore.

Merely compiling a list of desirable features for classroom practice does not, however, necessarily provide a vision of quality teaching. MCTP sought to provide a greater clarity of vision by illustrating how these features had been successfully incorporated in classroom practice. These documented images of quality teaching form the greater part of the *MCTP Activity Bank*.

What constitutes good mathematics teaching?

By analysing the classroom activities to which teachers were willing to attach the label of 'quality', some general characteristics of good teaching were identified. (This means, of course, that the following list of features was generated retrospectively.) Teachers generally considered that quality mathematics teaching:

- starts from 'where the pupil is at';
- recognizes that pupils learn at different rates and in different ways;
- allows pupils time to reflect on their own thinking and learning;
- involves pupils physically in the learning process;
- encourages pupils to expand the modes by which they communicate mathematics;
- responds to the interests, concerns and personal worlds of pupils;
- conveys the wholeness of mathematics, rather than presenting it as a disjointed collection of topics;
- recognizes the importance of risk-taking for effective learning;
- encourages pupils to learn together in cooperative small groups;
- invokes the power of visual imagery;
- recognizes the power of story settings (story-shells) in which mathematical ideas are embodied;
- is non-threatening and encourages participation of all pupils;
- encourages a wide variety of strategies in problem solving and investigation;
- recognizes the key role parents play in the pupil's development;
- uses the full range of available and appropriate technology;

• recognizes the special needs of particular pupils; and
• uses a range of assessment procedures which reflect a changed view of what is valued knowledge and how it is taught.

It is the activities collected by MCTP, illustrative of the above features, which collectively can convey to teachers a vision of quality teaching. We feel it is essential that teachers explore such activities to develop insight into what is possible. Once a teacher or group of teachers has a vision of where she, he or they want to go, the process of getting there can be more coherently structured.

Principle 2: Start from where the teacher is now

Change in teaching practice does not start from a blank sheet. Established patterns of work by teachers and students in the mathematics classroom are difficult to change. Underpinning these classroom practices are beliefs held by teachers and students about mathematics and how it is taught and learned. These beliefs and practices are often impediments to change (Romberg & Price 1983). Helping teachers and students to recognize these impediments and to overcome them requires a sustained effort and a willingness on the part of teachers to become risk-takers.

Stephens & Romberg (1985) have documented how teachers who were using RIME materials not only recognized that their teaching roles were changing, but also saw that the introduction of the new materials had an impact on students' learning. Teachers also became aware of the difficulties arising out of the changes they were making in their teaching strategies.

Students' prior expectations

Teachers who were involved in MCTP professional development programmes often drew attention to the importance of gaining students' acceptance of what would take place during a mathematics activity: what the purpose of the activity was, what they would get out of it, and how it was different from what they had done before. Typical comments from teachers were:

> No matter how philosophically sound a lesson may be, if it doesn't meet students' expectations about what a regular maths lesson is going to be, they become suspicious of it. If there is a shift in the way mathematics is going to be taught, then there must be something built into the lesson which takes account of students' expectations, and how they might be changed.

> Not to do so is to sow the seeds of destruction . . . they will reject it because it is different.

> Sometimes a lesson turns out to be a disaster for a whole lot of little reasons. Not the least of these reasons is students' expectations of what a real mathematics lesson is supposed to be about.

Students have come to see mathematics as consisting largely of pencil-and-paper exercises, with a strong focus on the development of skills and obtaining the correct answer. When using RIME and MCTP materials, teachers recognized that they needed to change students' deeply embedded beliefs about school mathematics. Mathematical modelling, problem solving and open-ended investigations are strong features of RIME and MCTP activities, but many students feel threatened by such activities. One teacher reported, for example, that soon after she had introduced an MCTP activity to her class, a student asked: 'What are you asking us to do? You haven't shown us the method to use. How will we know whether we have got the right answer?' Such a comment reflects the fact that students have come to expect to be told exactly what to do in mathematics lessons, and how to do it.

Risk-taking

Teachers who have tried MCTP activities with their classes consistently report that, by so doing, they have come to recognize the importance of creating learning environments which encourage students to take 'risks' as they attempt to solve mathematical problems. As one teacher reported, 'There is a fair chance that someone will put forward an idea, or give an answer which you haven't anticipated. That puts teachers on edge'.

Some teachers, who described *themselves* as 'risk-takers', pointed to the uncertainty which they felt as they permitted the direction of the lesson to be influenced by students' questions and ideas. One teacher summed up his changed role by saying:

> It is necessary to convince the class that I really care what their answers are, and that I will respond to them. This approach casts me in the role of one who asks questions for which there may be no pre-determined answer. I have to convince the class that the problem we are working on is one where there may be no single correct answer. Their task is to ask their own questions, not to guess the answer I am supposed to have.

Teachers wishing to encourage students to take risks in their mathematics learning need to be warned, in advance, that initially many students will resent the new approach. Teachers will need to develop strategies aimed at helping students overcome such initial anxiety.

Group work

Another feature of RIME and MCTP activities which sometimes causes initial uncertainty among both teachers and students is the emphasis placed on group work. As one teacher commented: 'A lot of teachers, when they first think of breaking up the class into groups, think of potential chaos'. Nonetheless, a great number of RIME and MCTP activities involve group work.

The activities 'Outdoor Pythagoras', 'Volume of a room' (provided later in this chapter), and 'Fermi problems' (Lovitt & Clarke 1988, pp. 151, 225; 1989, p. 499) seek to involve students creatively in cooperative group work, but when a teacher who had used these activities with his class was asked to comment on them, he said that many students did not see them as real mathematics. They wanted to know why they were doing the activities, and were concerned that they were just playing games. They also wanted to know how they were going to be assessed.

All teachers interviewed agreed that it was important to convince students that working in groups is an important aspect of real mathematics. One teacher said:

> I would be disappointed if teachers saw group work as a diversion, and continued to use that kind of lesson on a wet Friday afternoon. If that is the case, then students will continue to see RIME as peripheral to 'real mathematics' . . . Of course, teachers say that group work and sharing ideas are valuable, but that has to carry over to assessment and reporting of mathematical achievement. Students' contributions to group work have to be recognized and incorporated into an assessment of their work in school mathematics. If not, then the message is very clear to students that what is done doesn't count in the final result.

It is clear from such examples that there is no easy way to reform the teaching of mathematics. Yet we know that some teachers are already skilled in, and comfortable with, cooperative group work and a problem-solving approach to mathematics teaching. However, others, although willing, lack the experience or confidence to step outside their accustomed roles. How can the profession tap into the wealth of accumulated knowledge and skills seen in our best teachers? Perhaps the most important feature of MCTP activities was that they grew out of the experiences and insights of good teachers of mathematics. The careful documentation of such activities has enabled other teachers to take their first steps towards changing their classroom practice.

Principle 3: Share the wisdom of practice

This third principle argues that teachers who wish to improve the quality and range of their teaching repertoire need access to the exemplary practice of the best teachers. However, capturing the spirit and substance of quality learning environments in a manner that others can reflect upon and learn from is not an easy task. One of the reasons for this is the difficulty in knowing what, and how, to document.

Shulman provides the following list of forms of knowledge needed for effective teaching:

> Content knowledge, general pedagogical knowledge, curriculum knowledge, pedagogical reasoning, knowledge about learners, knowledge about educational contexts, and knowledge of educational purposes and values. The informed application of this knowledge base leads to effective teaching practice. (Shulman 1987, p. 8)

Already there are well-established literatures on all of the forms of knowledge mentioned by Shulman, except for the form he called 'pedagogical reasoning' (the 'wisdom of practice') which is concerned with what able mathematics teachers do and why they do it. Arguably, this is the least codified component of all. Shulman makes the telling point that:

. . . one of the frustrations of teaching as an occupation is its extensive individual and collective amnesia, the consistency with which the best creations of its practitioners are lost to both contemporary practitioners and future peers. (Shulman 1987, pp. 11–12)

In order to document quality practice to provide models of good teaching for others it is necessary to help teachers, firstly, to become more conscious of what they do, why they do it, and why one teaching approach is likely to be more successful than another, and secondly, to document their activities in such a way that others will benefit from their knowledge and experiences.

One failed attempt to document specific illustrations of quality learning occurred early in the RIME project. Thirty-five teachers were invited to 'bring along their most proven, successful activity'. They were then challenged to write or document the activity so that others would be able to repeat the success in their own classrooms. The attempt failed, not because the activities were not educationally sound, but because the documentation failed to incorporate all the ingredients necessary for success, particularly the ingredient Shulman calls pedagogical reasoning. Teachers wrote down *what* they did, but not *why* they did it.

RIME activities, and now MCTP activities, reflect the accumulated wisdom and practice of good mathematics teachers, and the careful documentation of the activities has made possible the transfer of this wisdom to others. Results thus far indicate strongly that transfer does take place, that teachers are gaining access to the pedagogical reasoning of our best teachers, and in this manner are able to reshape and improve their own practice.

The classroom activities collected and documented by RIME and MCTP represent snapshot images of quality learning environments. The aggregation or collection of these images forms a gallery of the art of good mathematics teaching. Whether use of such a gallery begets shallow imitation or new conceptualizations in the learner depends upon the way the activities are used by teachers. The specific classroom activities which make up the *MCTP Activity Bank* can serve as vehicles which illustrate new understandings and reshaped practice. The activities are not meant to be seen as ends in themselves.

Principle 4: Provide structured environments

Teachers need to feel that they are working within a model of professional development which they themselves have chosen and which, in their view, will help them to achieve the types of changes they desire. Research literature on teacher change (e.g. Fullan 1985; Joyce & Showers 1980, 1987), and our own experience (Lovitt *et al.*, in press), suggest that for significant change to happen in classrooms professional development should:
- address issues of concern recognized by the participating teachers themselves;
- be as close as possible to the teachers' working environments;
- take place over an extended period of time;

- have the support of both teacher colleagues and the school administration;
- provide opportunities for reflection and feedback;
- enable participating teachers to feel a substantial degree of ownership of the professional development programme;
- involve a conscious commitment, by the teachers, to the programme;
- involve groups of teachers from a school, rather than individuals; and
- use the services of a consultant and/or a critical friend.

With these principles in mind, MCTP identified and documented eight models (see Owen *et al*. 1988) which have been found to be suitable, depending upon the circumstances, for effective professional development of teachers of mathematics. These models are: Structured Course, Sandwich, In-school Intensive, School Cluster Group, Postal, Pre-service Course, Peer Tutoring, and Activity Documentation. Two of these — the Sandwich and the Activity Documentation models — will be discussed in greater detail shortly, but first we will provide two examples of activities which illustrate the four principles.

TWO ILLUSTRATIONS OF PRINCIPLES 1 TO 4

The 'Volume of a room' activity

Example 8.1, drawn from the bank of activities collected and documented by MCTP, illustrates how the wisdom of practising teachers can be captured and shared with other teachers. It is included here to illustrate how the above four principles were embedded into the professional development activities of the MCTP.

The first principle expressed the need to provide teachers with vivid images of quality learning environments. The 'Volume of a room' activity portrays a classroom in which the features of visual imagery, estimation, problem solving, and cooperative group work have been deliberately added to an otherwise textbook treatment of the topic. The MCTP documentation style draws attention to the presence of these features within the instructional flow of the activity. In addition to the teaching features, the activity strongly affirms the concept of volume and appropriate units of measurement as valuable knowledge which should be part of any definition of numeracy.

It is intended that teachers should explore the potential of visual imagery early in the activity by encouraging pupils to generate mental pictures of a cubic metre. Traditionally, mathematics teachers do not have a conscious focus on the use of visual imagery (Bishop 1989); therefore, in the documentation of the activity a side annotation has been included which specifically calls for teachers to make sure that students do evoke visual images.

Another emphasis in this activity is problem solving. The teacher, having generated a list of students' estimates for the volume of their room, now wishes to proceed to the answer. This is a critical moment in the activity where a choice of two pathways is apparent. Should the teacher, the perceived expert, now say, 'This is how you solve the problem — you need to

Example 8.1 'Volume of a room' activity (Lovitt & Clarke 1988, pp. 151–2)

Volume of a room

The teacher uses visual imagery and estimation as strategies to focus on the number of cubic metres of volume in the classroom. This is followed by problem solving including construction of cubic metres, to find the correct answer.

Finally a discussion compares the answer with pupils' initial perceptions and focuses on the concept of filling space.

1. Which unit to measure the room?

> WE HAVE DONE A LITTLE BIT OF WORK ON VOLUME AND YOU'VE MET SOME OF THE UNITS OF VOLUME SUCH AS LITRE AND CUBIC CENTIMETRE.
> TODAY'S ACTIVITY IS ABOUT MEASURING THE VOLUME OF LARGER THINGS SUCH AS THIS ROOM...

> ...NOW WHICH UNIT SHALL WE USE — A CUBIC CENTIMETRE OR WHAT?

> A CUBIC CENTIMETRE IS TOO SMALL

> SO'S A LITRE

> A CUBIC METRE

The use of mental imagery is a deliberate attempt to access and start the activity from each pupil's current perceptions.

2. Mental imagery and estimation of the volume of the room

> YOU ALL KNOW HOW LONG A METRE IS, DON'T YOU?
> WELL, I WANT YOU TO IMAGINE A BOX OR CUBE WHERE EACH SIDE IS ONE METRE LONG.
> CAN YOU SEE IT IN YOUR MIND'S EYE?
> NOW LOOK AROUND THE ROOM.
> IMAGINE ALL THE FURNITURE GONE.
> THINK HOW MANY OF THESE ONE CUBIC METRE BOXES WOULD FILL THE ROOM

> ...WHEN YOU HAVE DECIDED ON A NUMBER, WRITE IT HERE ON THE CHALKBOARD

Encourage pupils to take care with, and pride in, their estimation skills, because later the correct answer will be worked out.

By writing their guesses on the chalkboard, children tend to take their guesses more seriously.

A major advantage for the teacher is that it produces a collective data base of the class's current understandings and perceptions.

3. Show the real cubic metre and let them guess again

> HERE IS A MODEL OF A CUBIC METRE. HOW DOES IT COMPARE WITH THE IMAGE YOU HAD IN YOUR HEAD?

> HAVE A LONG LOOK AT THE REAL CUBE AND HOW MANY OF THEM WOULD FIT IN HERE.
> IF YOU WOULD LIKE TO CHANGE YOUR ESTIMATE WRITE YOUR NEW ONE HERE

'At this stage the kids didn't know the formula, so their guesses were totally based on visual imagery.'

Being able to change guesses allows pupils a chance to review their thinking. Many significant insights occur at this stage. *'I'll have to rethink my ideas of size.' 'That table's about a cubic metre size.'*

4. A list of suggestions for solving the problem

Write them on the blackboard.

LOOK AT THE RANGE OF GUESSES WE HAVE, FROM 10 TO 350 CUBIC METRES

HOW CAN WE FIND OUT?

YOUR SUGGESTIONS

Find out how many cubes go over the front wall and how many faces rows of them there will be.

Find out how many cubes will cover the floor.

Rather than giving the formula (L x W x H), present the problem and hand it over to the pupils. Allow children to use their problem-solving abilities.

5. Work through the suggestions with the pupils

There will be a few ways. One advantageous method was to start in the middle of the room and four groups of pupils constructed cubes to radiate out from the four faces of the original cube. An extra cube can be built on top of the central cube to get an idea of height.

'I found the concrete approach allowed pupils to more easily visualise the filling of the room with rows and layers of cubes.'

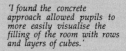

THAT'S NINE LONG AND EIGHT WIDE SO SEVENTY-TWO WOULD COVER THE FLOOR.

THEN YOU'D NEED ABOUT 3 LAYERS OF THAT SO THAT'S ABOUT 200 CUBIC METRES

By laying the stick cube flat pupils find a two-dimensional representation of a cube and other shapes.

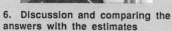

6. Discussion and comparing the answers with the estimates

WELL THE ANSWER IS ABOUT 200 CUBIC METRES

DID SEEING THE REAL CUBES HELP ANYONE?

ISN'T THAT INTERESTING. WHY DO YOU THINK SO MANY OF US UNDERESTIMATED?

GEE! THERE'S A LOT MORE THAN I FIRST THOUGHT THERE WAS

Many pupils underestimate, often by a wide margin. Do not disparage wide guesses *'we all make wrong guesses'*. Rather encourage pupils to appreciate how much power they will have as they acquire more accurate mental images.

Discussion should focus on whether pupils have a better appreciation of filling space and a knowledge of the cubic metre and its uses in measuring air, water, soil and rocks.

measure the length . . .' and proceed to present the formula in an expository manner, or should the teacher, for perhaps just five to ten minutes, hand the problem over to the pupils and let their problem solving abilities find expression? The documentation attempts to demonstrate why the teacher should choose the latter.

Whether the addition of these features, or the particular way they were combined, contributed to developing a quality learning environment is a judgement teachers have to make for themselves. However, the experience of teachers trialling the activity strongly suggests that 'Volume of a room' does just that. Having found that teachers greatly valued the activity, MCTP promoted this and other activities as images of particular teaching practices in order to generate recognition and debate about the characteristics of quality learning environments.

The second principle — accepting teachers for what they are now — suggests that change is more likely to be achieved by making small steps than by attempting large-scale reforms in a short amount of time. It has often been suggested that wars are ultimately won by engaging in, and winning, the battles along the way. This is also true of teacher change, where the local battles may inhibit large-scale change.

One example is the tendency of students to prefer traditional classroom environments, where well-defined sets of tasks are provided, to more open learning situations in which risk-taking and creative learning are called for. Students prefer traditional classroom situations because of the psychological safety they offer, and teachers wishing to move towards providing more active learning environments should ensure that any new approaches do not threaten students, that is to say, do not make them tense, anxious, and aggressive because of the fear of possible failure. Estimation tasks, if carefully introduced by teachers, are one way of breaking down students' fear of failure in mathematics. 'Volume of a room' can provide an excellent ice-breaker for this purpose. After generating mental images of a cubic metre, students are encouraged to use these images to estimate the number of cubic metres that would fill the room the students are in. Even apparently unimportant aspects of the activity, such as pupils being asked to record their estimates on the chalkboard, have been found to contribute to significantly greater student involvement and interest in the activity. It is important, too, that teachers know that students should be given the opportunity to change their initial guesses, for this will add strength to the 'participatory encouragement' factor. Finally, the teacher should not be concerned with arriving at *the* answer, but should deliberately focus on approximate answers (e.g. '*about* 200 cubic metres'). Estimation activities presented in this manner can provide teachers with a bridge from traditional to active mathematics learning situations, from lessons owned by the teacher and the textbook to activities owned by the students.

A common response from teachers who tried presenting estimation tasks in the manner suggested above was that all pupils became interested and involved, and the fear of failure was forgotten. The teachers appreciated being able to trial the new method, recognizing that since it had worked for other teachers it was likely to work for them. This desire to provide a supportive and structured introduction to change is a feature of the professional development models developed by MCTP (Owen *et al.* 1988).

This activity also illustrates the third professional development principle of creating conditions which facilitate sharing of successful classroom practices. Each MCTP activity is presented as an annotated summary of what has taken place in 'one teacher's classroom'. In reality, the activity as it is documented represents an amalgam of the contribution of many teachers. But MCTP has found that the 'wisdom of practice' can be shared among teachers provided that carefully documented statements which capture the spirit and substance of successful classroom activities are made available, and teachers are supported as they try these activities with their own students. In this way, teachers can learn from the experiences of other teachers.

The 'This goes with this' activity

The fourth MCTP professional development principle, which is concerned with the need to provide a structured supportive environment for teacher development, is illustrated in 'This goes with this' which is reproduced in example 8.2. The most important idea associated with this fourth principle is that teachers should be given support in preparing new learning environments, and they should be able to discuss with other teachers who have tried the same activities what worked for them, what did not work for them, and why. MCTP encouraged teachers to trial proven activities such as 'This goes with this', and assisted them to analyse and reflect upon the outcomes of the trials.

For teachers wishing to explore new ideas, this activity highlights several significant departures from the standard textbook treatment of the topics of fractions, percentages and graphs. The documentation of the activity conveys to teachers, in practical terms, how concrete aids can be used effectively, how the concept of percentages is developed without getting bogged down in the algorithm, how the teacher can assist students to evoke visual imagery, and how students can be encouraged to work in small groups. In addition, difficulties which may confront the teacher are discussed, and organizational hints for avoiding, or overcoming these are also featured in the documentation.

MCTP publications provide full documentation of over 100 activities like 'Volume of a room' and 'This goes with this' (Lovitt & Clarke 1988, 1989). A similar number of activities were documented in RIME publications (Victorian Education Department 1984). Great care was taken to provide full documentation because MCTP and RIME believed that this was an essential component of the structured and supportive learning environment which teachers needed if they were to be successful in changing the way they approached school mathematics, and the way in which what it means to be numerate can be defined and manifested in classrooms. Activities like these have been produced not as ends in themselves but as vehicles for discussion. Sample forms to facilitate such discussion are presented in the following section.

Example 8.2 'This goes with this' activity (Lovitt & Clarke 1988, pp. 144–7)

This goes with this

This activity is in three sections.

a. Demonstrating equivalence. The class is surveyed to find ice-cream preferences. A strip graph is made and bent to make a pie graph. 100 beads are put around it and there are the percentages.

b. Group work. Pupils generate their own data, make graphs and analyses, and present these findings back to the whole class.

Follow-up extensions. These activities are designed to reinforce the general concepts, imagery and concept of conversion from fractions to percentages.

SECTION A: DEMONSTRATING EQUIVALENCE

1. Collecting the data

Use information from a simple class survey such as 'favourite icecream flavour.'

> I WANT TO SHOW YOU DIFFERENT WAYS OF REPRESENTING THIS INFORMATION AND HOW THESE DIFFERENT METHODS ARE MATHEMATICALLY THE SAME AS EACH OTHER

> CHOCOLATE $\frac{8}{27}$
> STRAWBERRY $\frac{7}{27}$
> VANILLA $\frac{5}{27}$
> CARAMEL $\frac{3}{27}$
> OTHER $\frac{4}{27}$

The survey should generate no more than half a dozen categories.

Trials schools report the teacher should join the survey if needed to ensure that the class total is not an 'easy' number such as 20, 25 or 30.

'It seems better to express the results as numbers (e.g. 8 out of 27) rather than as fractions. (8 twenty-sevenths)'

Being personal, data collected from the pupils tends to increase their commitment and interest.

'I felt it worthwhile to allow discussion about the data itself. For example, "Strawberry is very popular but they don't sell it at our canteen. Why might that be?" This is preferable to using totally meaningless and artificial data.'

2. Fractions to strip graph

> ANOTHER WAY OF SHOWING THESE FRACTIONS IS ON A GRAPH

LEAVE ABOUT A CENTIMETRE OVERLAP AT ENDS. (SEE NEXT STEP)

CARDBOARD STRIP 'BLU-TAC' ED ON CHALKBOARD.

INVITE CHILDREN TO COME OUT AND MARK THIS INFORMATION ON THE STRIP.

COUNTING ON IS A FEATURE OF THIS TASK.

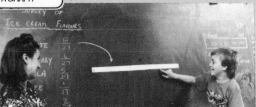

The 'heavy' paper needs to be about 80 cm — 100 cm long (to match the bead ring — see Section B step 3).

27 pupils would mean each division could be 3 cm.

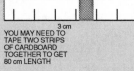

LEAVE A COUPLE OF CENTIMETRES OVERLAP AT ENDS FOR NEXT STEP

It is critical to use stiff paper to ensure the shape forms a circle.

'Every pupil could see that they were personally represented on, or "owned", a small segment of the strip graph.'

3 cm

YOU MAY NEED TO TAPE TWO STRIPS OF CARDBOARD TOGETHER TO GET 80 cm LENGTH

> THAT'S LIKE A NUMBER LINE

3. Strip graph to pie chart

Do this step slowly and demonstrably. The action from straight line to circle provides a visual image of the relationship.

JOIN WITH BLU
TAC USING
OVERLAP. LEAVE
THE MARKINGS
ON THE OUTSIDE

Place the cardboard ring onto butcher's paper and draw a circle by tracing along the inside edge. Join the segment lines to the centre.

Remove the cardboard ring, and complete the pie graph by labeling it.

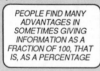

SO YOU CAN SEE, ALL 27 CLASS 'VOTES' HAVE BEEN TRANSFERRED ON TO THE PIE CHART

4. Pie chart to percentage

Place the 100-bead loop around the pie chart. The loop should be just a bit larger than the chart.

Convert the sections on the pie chart to percentages by inviting students to count the beads. Record these findings beside the graph and on a separate chart.

PEOPLE FIND MANY ADVANTAGES IN SOMETIMES GIVING INFORMATION AS A FRACTION OF 100, THAT IS, AS A PERCENTAGE

THAT'S 29 BEADS

I THINK IT IS CLOSER TO 30

'This section was a highlight for me as this conversion has always been difficult to get across.'

'The kids followed this easily — this equivalence was very real and concrete for them.'

One school reported a successful 'physical equivalent' pie chart. Pupils sitting in a circle display their votes on a card. (Use A4 size card and textas for visibility)

PUPILS SITTING IN CHAIRS

RULERS OR STRING TO SEPARATE SECTIONS

Several surveys can be quickly conducted and displayed this way.

Coloured beads are available in bulk from most pre-school or early-childhood supply centres.

'I was pleasantly surprised by the accuracy obtained from counting the beads.'

'The kids found it more natural and meaningful to verbalise their answer as '29 beads' rather than 29%.'

Interesting debate sometimes occurs about accuracy of counting or if someone notices the total is perhaps 98 rather than 100 due to rounding errors. However the major emphasis by far is the visual image generated of the equivalence of fractions to line graphs to percentages.

> The 'hi-tech' finish is impressive but it is important that the search for accuracy does not detract from, or confuse the concrete imagery from the earlier work.

5. Calculator accuracy

(Optional)

If pupils are able, or perhaps only for a few individuals interested in the challenge of precision, the calculator can resolve the dilemma of accuracy.

I TOLD YOU IT WAS 29.629 BEADS

SECTION B – GROUP WORK

1. Generating and collecting data for the group activity

Having demonstrated the various forms of presentation, this section details how pupils, working in groups, can have first hand experience of the conversions.

Every pupil individually fills out a questionnaire on about nine surveys (see worksheet). This allows for up to nine groups to undertake their own investigation.

> The prepared worksheet allows the survey to be completed in less than five miutes.

TV shows	Drinks
(Soapies)	Cola
Sport	Fanta
News	(Fruit juice)
Rock video	Pepsi
Films	Lemonade

YOU JUST HAVE TO CIRCLE YOUR CHOICE

> Trials found about four to seven choices in each category is effective and manageable.

All pupils then walk past collection boxes and 'snip off' their survey tickets into the relevant box. (e.g. ice-cream or margarine containers)

> *'I found this a very efficient way to collate data.'*

> By having say ten survey boxes, even though you have only six groups, adds flexibility and choice.

2. Pose the question

I WANT EACH GROUP TO PREPARE A REPORT TO BE PRESENTED TO THE WHOLE CLASS. YOUR PRESENTATION MUST INCLUDE THE INITIAL FRACTIONS, THE LINE GRAPH, PIE CHART AND PERCENTAGES

LET'S CHOOSE THE 'COUNTRIES WE WOULD LIKE TO VISIT'

OK! QUICK, BEFORE ANOTHER GROUP PICKS IT

The report should also include interpretation of the results and recommendations, for example, *'We should write a letter to the TV station to tell them that hardly anyone here watches the soapies.'*

3. Group work

Each group needs a piece of butcher's paper (or A3), a 100-bead ring, and a cardboard strip and sticky tape.

If there are 27 in the class, rule up a large piece of cardboard into 27 rows (plus extra for overlap) and then cut off one strip for each group.

> 'I felt it was very valuable for each group to physically handle the concrete aids — it seemed to help generate a lasting mental image.'

> 'I prepared some "100-bead rings" with the colours mixed at random. In others, for easy counting, I grouped the colours (in twos, fives or tens).'

The teacher moving around the groups can observe organisation, cooperation and initiative. Let groups organise themselves, but encourage all pupils to physically handle the material.

4. Reporting

> 9 OUT OF 27 WOULD LIKE TO HOLIDAY IN NEW ZEALAND

> THAT IS SHADED IN BLUE HERE ON THE STRIP GRAPH

> HERE IT IS ON THE PIE CHART

> IT'S A '33-BEAD' CHOICE. THAT IS, 33 OUT OF EVERY 100 PEOPLE

The completed graphs and charts could be displayed on a board (and used for reference in the future) or made into a class activity book.

There are enough tasks in the reporting to require every member of the group to participate in many ways.

> 'The groups were reporting back the class's own data.'

Listening to the language (not always formal) gives interesting insight into pupils' understandings.

Conclusion

Ask pupils their reactions to the use of the concrete aids.

One benefit of the repetition of the use of the 27 is that pupils nearly all realised that each vote was worth about 4 beads and saw relationships such as $10/27$ as about 10 lots of 4 beads — approximately 40%.

> 'I sent the project material home with pupils to show their families as a form of reporting.'

> 'I wanted to strengthen in pupils, the value of using concrete aids to get away from seeing maths as very abstract.'

TWO MCTP PROFESSIONAL DEVELOPMENT MODELS

The Sandwich model

The MCTP Sandwich model basically consisted of two seminar sessions, two to three weeks apart, with classroom trialling 'sandwiched' between these seminar sessions. Workshops at the first seminar session and the classroom trialling are usually only on one selected theme. At the second seminar, teachers who have now tried out the workshop activities in their own classrooms are encouraged to discuss freely what happened and to compare notes. Brainstorming sessions focusing on likely future developments are also provided.

The one-round sandwich is seen as the very minimum for effective professional development. Some consultants have used extended Sandwich models, with classroom trialling of ideas taking place between three or more seminar sessions. Another variant of the Sandwich model is when the seminars are replaced by less formal meetings of staff who will be involved in the intended change. For example, the mathematics teachers in a school, together with the school's curriculum coordinator, might be released from their normal teaching duties to meet with an outside consultant to discuss approaches which the mathematics department might choose to adopt. At such a meeting the consultant would be expected to indicate clearly what the new approach is likely to require of the teachers, and what additional resources, both material and human, would be needed. The teachers would then be engaged in workshops, possibly led by the consultant, or by a normal member of staff. Teachers would be encouraged to try the new approach in their classes, and to report back at a subsequent meeting (at which the consultant should probably be present, once again). At this next meeting, additional workshop experiences are provided, and the process of planning, trialling, and reflecting is continued, with further meetings being held whenever this is possible.

When teachers trial a new approach in their classrooms, it is sometimes helpful for them to complete a feedback/evaluation form, like the one shown in figure 8.2 (pp. 182–183), which was developed by MCTP. Throughout this trialling period, the consultant should be available either by telephone or in the school to support the teachers when this is necessary. Through trialling, teachers develop an informed view of the ideas and materials which will influence further decision-making. Sufficient time must be allowed for teachers to trial new approaches in normal school situations.

An example of how the Sandwich model was used by a group of teachers interested in becoming adept at making use of cooperative group activities in mathematics classes is shown in example 8.3 (p. 184).

With the Sandwich model it is preferable that the meetings be spaced so that teachers have adequate time to try the new approaches in their classrooms. In order to maintain momentum, and to ensure that teachers feel that they have not lost touch with the group, meetings should not be scheduled too far apart. Experience has shown that a period of about two or three weeks between meetings is satisfactory.

Appendix E — FEEDBACK SHEET ON MCTP ACTIVITY

SCHOOL.. TEACHER ....

PHONE NUMBER.............................. ACTIVITY..

These responses are extremely valuable to us and help greatly in the sharing of ideas. Please don't feel you have to comment in all sections — only those which are important to you. Please be honest!

1. Were you happy with the activity? ....
   (Yes/Maybe/No ....
   Please give reasons.) ....

2. How long did the activity take? ....
   Did you teach it in one session only ....
   or split it up? ....

3. Did you follow the plan exactly? ....
   If not, how did (or would) you ....
   modify the plan? How did the ....
   changes work? ....

4. Did you use extensions (or invent ....
   some)? ....
   Which ones? ....

5. In what grade level(s) did you use ....
   the activity? ....

6. What was the major value of this ....
   Unit to you personally? ....
   ....

7. The activity's major intent is to ....
   influence and broaden your ....
   teaching style. How could the ....
   printed plan be improved in this ....
   regard? ....

8. In teaching which topic is this ....
   activity most useful? ....
   ....
   ....
   ....
   ....

A joint project of the Commonwealth, States and Territories Curriculum Development Centre

9. How did you organise your room for this activity? e.g. conventional seating, seats arranged in groups, on the floor, multi-purpose room, outside.

10. How did the grade in general respond? Did any group of students respond differently from normal?

11. One main purpose of the activities is to have pupils develop the ability and confidence to think mathematically outside the classroom. Comment on the activity in the light of this goal.

12. Were the features listed on the front page of the plan evident in the actual class? Which ones?

13. Can you suggest appropriate student assessment techniques (if any) for this activity? How do we know if the children have gained from the activity what we hoped they might have?

15. General comments.

MANY THANKS FOR YOUR TROUBLE!
PLEASE MAIL THIS IMMEDIATELY TO ....

Figure 8.2 Trialling feedback/evaluation form (MCTP 1988)

Example 8.3 Using the Sandwich model to explore cooperative group work

A group of 30 teachers met after school on two occasions to explore the potential of cooperative group work in mathematics. During the first session of two hours, the group workshopped selected MCTP activities, such as 'Outdoor Pythagoras', 'This goes with this', 'Tell me a story' and 'Fermi problems'.

The activity, 'Fermi problems', is based on the article by J. & M. Ross in the NCTM 1986 Yearbook, *Estimation and Mental Computation*. In this activity, pupils are presented with seemingly insoluble, 'off-beat' problems like 'How many piano tuners are there in Melbourne?' Students typically surprise themselves when they pool their knowledge and use a series of approximations to arrive at quite reasonable estimates.

Teachers trying out 'Fermi problems' commented that students, after considerable initial doubts, were delighted with how much they in fact knew and how all members of the group had something to offer: 'Our piano gets tuned about every two years', 'I think they could tune about three each day', 'There are two pianos in our street, so I reckon that there must be one in every ten houses,' and so on.

All teachers completed the feedback sheet and returned to the second session, where in small groups they discussed their experiences, reflecting on both successes and impediments, and the features of group work that had emerged. They then took part in workshops at which other MCTP activities ('Money trails' and 'How many can stand in your classroom?') took place, and spent some time planning further actions.

We do not regard the Sandwich model as being necessarily the best model of professional development for teachers; it is nevertheless a vast improvement on the 'one-shot' curriculum day approach. It has become popular as a means of introducing an innovative idea to teachers. MCTP was involved in about 20 Sandwich Courses during the period 1985–88.

The Sandwich model of professional development yields courses that are easy to organize, are inexpensive to conduct, and make use of a methodology that is readily embraced by busy teachers. They are particularly helpful for introducing issues to teachers and for sensitizing teachers to the need to seek further professional development in a given area. Although full-day meetings are preferable, half-day or after-school meetings have also operated successfully.

The MCTP experience suggests that only one theme should be pursued in a professional development programme based on this model. Some of the most popular of these themes have been: assessment, problem solving, computers, applications of mathematics, and mathematical modelling.

The Activity Documentation model

With this model, teachers attending a seminar are invited to bring notes and equipment which will enable them to present activities that have been successfully used with classes in their schools. At the seminar, the teachers present the activities as workshops to small groups of participants. Teachers undertake to trial at least two of the workshop activities in their own classrooms. After the seminar, the teachers return to their schools, and trial the activities. Later, another seminar is held at which the teachers report on their trials. Groups are formed, with the members of each group concentrating on one particular activity. Full documentation of each activity is commenced at the seminar and, if necessary, this is completed by group members after the seminar. Finally, the complete set of fully documented activities is distributed to all seminar participants.

As the name implies, this model involves the documentation of successful innovative practice so that activities developed by one teacher, or a team of teachers, can be more widely circulated. There are many teachers working at the 'cutting edge' of innovative school mathematics, and these teachers have developed interesting activities which they know work well in their classes. Tapping into their knowledge and showing images or models of successful, quality practice is the purpose of activity documentation.

Through the Activity Documentation model, MCTP has collected working examples of good practice, and by thorough documentation and trial-ling, has assisted teachers to learn from each other. Curriculum leaders and pre-service teacher education institutions are now encouraged to establish networks of activity writers. A major benefit to those who become involved in documenting an activity is that it forces teachers to reflect on why the existing activity has been successful. This facilitates the recognition of important underlying principles of learning which otherwise might go unnoticed.

Trying to capture the spirit as well as the structure and the content of classroom activities is a complex and difficult task. The most usual form of documentation is the printed page, but other formats such as videotape are possible. The Activity Documentation model, as shown in example 8.4, provides a structured procedure which engages practising teachers of mathematics in the documentation of both their own and other teachers' successful classroom activities.

Example 8.4 Using the Activity Documentation model to explore the effective use of teaching aids in developing concepts

Three teachers from each of twelve primary schools were involved in the following example of the Activity Documentation model. A venue was booked for a one-and-a-half-day seminar, consisting of a full-day meeting (during school hours) and, a week later, a half-day meeting (also during school hours).

Day One
- Teachers from each of the schools came prepared to present, in small-group workshops, successful mathematics activities.
- After the activities had been presented, the teachers present were asked to select an activity which they would like to explore further. In this way, specific activity groups were formed, and the teachers in these groups discussed how the activity might be best documented.
- Each group began preliminary documentation of its activity.
- Teachers undertook to trial at least two of the twelve activities (the one on which they were concentrating, and another) during the following school week.

Day Two
One week later, a further half-day meeting took place. On this occasion:
- Teachers, working in the activity groups (formed on Day 1) shared their experiences in trialling the activities during the past week. There was an emphasis on recognising underlying learning principles.
- There followed a structured session, when the nature and purposes of documentation were detailed. Samples of documentation styles were presented, and discussed.
- Once again, teachers worked in their activity groups, with each group deciding how the documentation of its activity might be completed within the next fortnight. Group members were given specific responsibilities, and in each group a coordinator was appointed to oversee the completion of the documentation process.

Subsequently
Once all the groups had completed the activity documentation, materials produced were edited to ensure uniformity of style, and then sent to all seminar participants for further classroom trialling and comment.

Subsequently, after the detailed documentation had occurred, it was agreed that eight of these activities had great potential and should be more fully and carefully documented. The eight activities were collated, printed and distributed for formal trialling to all participants. Feedback continued over the following months. These activities now form part of the *MCTP Activity Bank* (Lovitt & Clarke 1988, 1989).

CONCLUSION

Any attempt to reform the mathematics curriculum depends for its success on a commitment to the support of professional development, and we believe that the four principles we have outlined in this chapter should form the basis of that support. While teacher growth and change is an individual process, teachers involved in change need to know where they have come from, where they are going, why they are going there, and should have access both to the best professional thinking of their colleagues, and to theoretically sound, supportive environments. All these features have been evident in the MCTP professional development programmes we have outlined.

In applying these four principles, MCTP demonstrated that well-planned professional development programmes can influence the way teachers behave in mathematics classrooms. In particular, it was found that the use of careful documentation of successful classroom activities, applied in the context of well-researched models of professional development, was likely to have a strong impact on the thinking and behaviour of teachers of mathematics.

The main purpose of this chapter has been to elaborate on principles that underpin effective growth opportunities for teachers, and to assist those planning professional development programmes for mathematics teachers to provide support for teachers seeking to reconceptualize their roles. The major message has been the need to identify, document, and share the considerable 'wisdom of practice' that already exists in mathematics classrooms.

REFERENCES

Bishop, A.J. 1989, 'Review of research on visualization in mathematics education', *Focus on Learning Problems in Mathematics*, **11** (1), 7–16.

Blane, D. 1984, 'Conflicts in mathematics education', in *Conflicts in Mathematics Education*, ed. A. Maurer, Mathematical Association of Victoria, Melbourne.

Blane, D., Maurer, A. & Stephens, M. 1983, The essentials of mathematics education, in *The Essentials of Mathematics Education*, ed. D. Blane, Mathematical Association of Victoria, Melbourne.

Clements, M.A. 1987, 'Victoria's positive contributions to the mathematical problem-solving movement', *Vinculum*, **24** (1), 23–6.

Cockcroft, W. H. (Chairman) 1982, *Mathematics Counts: Report of the Committee of Inquiry into the Teaching of Mathematics in Schools*, HMSO, London.

Fullan, M. 1985, 'Change processes and strategies at the local level', *Elementary School Journal*, **85** (3), 391–421.

Joyce, B. & Showers, B. 1980, 'Improving inservice training: The messages of research', *Educational Leadership*, **37**, 379–85.

Joyce, B. & Showers, B. 1987, *Student Achievement through Staff Development*, Longman, New York.

Lampert, M. 1988, 'What can research on teacher education tell us about improving quality in mathematics education?' *Teaching and Teacher Education*, **4** (2), 157–70.

Lovitt, C. & Clarke, D. 1988, *MCTP Activity Bank*, vol. 1, Curriculum Development Centre, Canberra.

Lovitt, C. & Clarke, D. 1989, *MCTP Activity Bank*, vol. 2, Curriculum Development Centre, Canberra.

Lovitt, C., Stephens, W. M., Clarke, D. & Romberg, T. A. (in press), 'Mathematics teachers reconceptualising their roles', in *Mathematics: Teaching and Learning in the 1990s*, National Council of Teachers of Mathematics 1990 Yearbook, ed. T. Cooney, NCTM, Reston, Va.

Lowe, I. & Lovitt, C. 1984, *Making Sum-think Happen*, Curriculum Branch of the Victorian Education Department, Melbourne.

National Council of Teachers of Mathematics 1980, *An Agenda for Action: Recommendations for school mathematics of the 1980s*, NCTM, Reston, Va.

National Council of Teachers of Mathematics 1989, *Curriculum and Evaluation Standards for School Mathematics*, NCTM, Reston, Va.

Owen, J., Johnson, N., Clarke, D., Lovitt, C. & Morony, W. 1988, *Professional Development in the Mathematics Curriculum and Teaching Program: Guidelines for consultants and advisors*, Curriculum Development Centre, Canberra.

Romberg, T. A. & Price, G. G. 1983, 'Curriculum implementation and staff development as cultural change', in *Staff development: Eighty-second yearbook of the National Society for the Study of Education*, ed. G. A. Griffin, University of Chicago Press, Chicago, Part II.

Ross, J. & Ross, M. 1986, 'Fermi problems', in *Estimation and Mental Computation*, National Council of Teachers of Mathematics, Year Book, NCTM, Reston, Va.

Shulman, L. S. 1987, 'Knowledge and teaching: Foundations of the new reform', *Harvard Educational Review*, **7** (1), 1–22.

Stephens, W. M. & Romberg, T. A. 1985, Reconceptualising the role of the mathematics teacher, Paper presented at the Annual Meeting of the American Educational Research association, Chicago.

Victorian Education Department 1984, *RIME Lesson Packs A and B*, Victorian Education Department (Schools Division), Melbourne.

Victorian Ministry of Education 1988, *The Mathematics Framework: P-10*, Victorian Ministry of Education (Schools Division), Melbourne.

Suggested further reading:
an annotated list

CHAPTER 1 NUMERACY AND SOCIETY: THE SHIFTING GROUND

Bishop, A. 1988, *Mathematical Enculturation: A cultural perspective on mathematics education*, Kluwer Academic Publishers, Dordrecht.
Alan Bishop argues that there are six kinds of mathematical thinking common to all cultures — counting, locating, measuring, designing, playing and explaining — and that they develop according to the processes of the culture and might form the basis of mathematics curricula. He further argues that accessibility must be an important criterion for the selection of curriculum content and that social usage of mathematical thinking should be incorporated alongside mathematical ideas. His view of social usage is, however, considerably richer than the techniques usually provided under the name of 'practical' mathematics. According to Bishop, we spend a great deal of time equipping children with skills that are rapidly being outmoded as calculators and computers become more readily available. A technique-oriented curriculum, he suggests, is generally not useful and cannot educate. This book challenges us to seriously rethink the mathematics curriculum.

Cockcroft, W. (Chairman) 1982, *Mathematics Counts: Report of the Committee of Inquiry into the Teaching of Mathematics in Schools*, HMSO, London, UK.
A comprehensive and thorough report on the teaching of mathematics. The Committee of Inquiry commissioned research studies to investigate the actual mathematics used in further and higher education, employment and daily life. The conclusions of these research studies were in many ways surprising and formed the basis of the rest of the Report which considers mathematics curriculum content and pedagogy in some detail. The Cockcroft Report has been influential internationally.

D'Ambrosio, U. 1985, 'Environmental influences', in *Studies in Mathematics Education: The education of secondary teachers of mathematics*, ed. R. Morris, Unesco, Paris.
D'Ambrosio has been extremely influential in bringing to the attention of the mathematics education community the nature of 'ethnomathematics' and its relationship to school mathematics. In this paper he considers a range of environmental influences on school mathematics. Of several points he makes, the three which are most relevant to the issues raised in *Being numerate* are, that for historical reasons practical mathematics has been largely absent from the academic curriculum of secondary schools, that the further up the educational ladder we go the stronger are the conservative pressures, and that 'learned' numeracy (as it happens in schools) actually eliminates the 'spontaneous numeracy' of children's daily lives. Many of his points are made in the context of school mathematics in Latin America. Nonetheless, the paper is interesting, the arguments powerful and the messages relevant to the Australian context.

Howson, G. & Kahane, J.-P. (series ed.) 1986, *School Mathematics in the 1990s*, Cambridge University Press, Cambridge.
A report of a symposium of the International Commission on Mathematics Instruction held in Kuwait in 1986. This book provides an excellent analysis of the issues and dilemmas facing school mathematics in the 1990s. Its concerns are wide ranging and

include the place of mathematics in education generally, the relationship of school mathematics to technological change, the concerns of both developed and developing countries, and the difficulties of effecting change on a significant scale.

CHAPTER 2 BECOMING NUMERATE: DEVELOPING NUMBER SENSE

Open University 1982, *Calculators in the Primary School*, The Open University Press, Milton Keynes, UK.
This publication provides a short course on the role of calculators in primary schools and is an excellent starting point from which to develop calculator policies and practices in primary schools. The authors focus on helping teachers to develop confidence in the use of calculators in the classroom in order to help children *learn* mathematical skills and concepts and also *use* these skills and concepts. The chapter headings 'About the calculator', 'Mastery and the mathematics curriculum', 'Skill and concept development', 'The calculator in mathematical problem solving', 'The calculator in everyday problem solving', 'Developing a calculator-aware curriculum' and 'Assessing calculator use' testify to the breadth of coverage of the publication. It is appropriate either as an in-service pack for groups of teachers or for use by individual teachers.

Open University 1986, *Calculators in the Secondary School*, The Open University Press, Milton Keynes, UK.
This later publication focuses on the use of calculators in mathematics in secondary education. The section headings are 'Getting to know your calculator', 'Helping pupils to use their calculator sensibly', 'The calculator and the secondary curriculum', 'The calculator in the classroom' and 'School calculator policy'. Like the primary publication, it provides an excellent basis for developing school calculator policies and practices and is appropriate either as an in-service pack for groups of teachers or for use by individual teachers. If used in the former way, a tutor pack is available comprising a video, booklet and BBC software which converts the BBC micro into a calculator for demonstration purposes.

Schoen, H. & Sweng, M. (ed.) 1987, *Estimation and Mental Computation*, National Council of Teachers of Mathematics, Reston, USA.
A collection of 27 articles on the topics indicated in the title. An underlying theme of the whole collection is that estimation is central to mathematics. The articles vary in quality, but the collection provides a very useful basis for consideration of the issues and practice related to estimation and computation. The first part, consisting of five chapters, raises the issues and gives an overview. The second and largest part is intended to help teachers develop new ways of thinking about estimating and mental arithmetic. Part 3 emphasizes the wide range of types of estimation and provides interesting examples of estimation activities. This is followed up in Part 4 with four chapters on estimation in measurement. The final part provides a review of research on teaching and learning estimation and a chapter on assessing computational estimation.

CHAPTER 3 BECOMING NUMERATE: DEVELOPING CONCEPTUAL STRUCTURES

Hart, K. M. (ed.) 1981, *Children's Understanding of Mathematics: 11–16*, John Murray, London, UK.
This book provides the results of an extensive research programme in the UK — 'Concepts in secondary mathematics and science' (CSMS) — which investigated children's understanding of mathematics in ten topic areas: measurement, number operations, place value and decimals, fractions, positive and negative numbers, ratio and proportion, algebra, graphs, reflections and rotations, and vectors and matrices. A chapter

is devoted to each of these topic areas, each describing the types of questions students in the 11–16 years age range can answer easily and the types they find difficult. Students' methods and errors are discussed in some detail and a heirarchy of levels of understanding is developed for each topic.

Booth, L. 1984, *Algebra: Children's strategies and errors*, NFER-Nelson, Windsor.
Hart, K. M. 1984, *Ratio: Children's strategies and errors*, NFER-Nelson, Windsor.
Kerslake, D. 1986, *Fractions: Children's strategies and errors*, NFER-Nelson, Windsor.
These three publications are an outcome of the 'Strategies and errors in secondary mathematics' (SESM) project in the United Kingdom which was a follow-up of the CSMS study and investigated in depth some of the problems commonly experienced by students in mathematics, aged 11–16 years. The research involved large numbers of interviews with students and the results are extremely illuminating. In each case, teaching experiments were developed to try to alleviate the problems students experienced and these books document the strategies. Two overall conclusions of the research programme were, firstly, that understanding students' attitudes and views about the nature of mathematics is central to understanding their errors and strategies, and secondly, that 'child methods' of dealing with mathematical situations often are not altered by traditional teaching strategies. Indeed, school methods and child methods can exist alongside each other.

Swan, M. 1983, *The Meaning and Use of Decimals*, Shell Centre for Mathematical Education, University of Nottingham.
This excellent set of materials is appropriate for use in primary and secondary schools and aims to correct misconceptions concerning the nature of decimal number. It provides calculator-based diagnostic tests and teaching materials to this end. Probably its real power lies in the model of conflict learning it adopts and in the way the use of calculators is embedded throughout.

CHAPTER 4   RECONTEXTUALIZING MATHEMATICS: NUMERACY AS PROBLEM SOLVING

Shell Centre for Mathematical Education/Joint Matriculation Board 1987, *Numeracy Through Problem Solving*, Longman, England.
These materials provide a series of teaching modules developed as part of a project on the assessment of numeracy and were designed to encourage a new approach to the teaching and learning of numeracy. The materials assume that students need to learn to apply mathematical skills in practical contexts and that this demands that they develop not only mathematical techniques but also strategic and tactical skills. The materials also provide an excellent assessment resource. Modules have been produced on the following topics: Design a board game, Produce a quiz show, Plan a trip, Be a paper engineer, and Be a shrewd chooser.

Mason, J., Burton, L. & Stacey, K. 1982, *Thinking Mathematically*, Addison Wesley, London.
Thinking Mathematically unfolds the processes which lie at the heart of mathematics. It analyses the processes of mathematical problem solving and fosters them in the reader. Intensely practical, it demands the reader participate in each question posed so that the subsequent discussion speaks to immediate experience. In this way, a deep-seated awareness of the nature of mathematical thinking can grow. Emphasis is placed on following leads, getting stuck, pondering, and provocation and insight, rather than on polished textbook solutions.

Newton, W. 1983, *Real Maths — School Maths* (video), Victorian Ministry of Education, Melbourne.
This video demonstrates some of the discrepancies between the mathematics that students meet at school and the mathematics that is used in simple shopping tasks. The

methods of calculation that people use in the street are contrasted with the algorithms that are presented in school. The video shows interviews with children who are able to succeed at the former but not the latter.

Campbell-Jones, S. (producer) 1985, *'Twice Five Plus the Wings of a Bird'* (video), BBC Panorama, Horizon Series.

This programme addresses some of the major concerns in mathematics education today and surveys some of the insights and answers that are emerging from current research. The relationship between school mathematics, everyday 'street' mathematics and mathematics at work are explored. Difficulties arising both from symbolism and from misunderstanding concepts are illustrated. The place of algorithms in a calculator-rich environment is discussed, and methods of teaching which develop number sense and an adequate method of computation are illustrated. Suitable for in-service education and for parent education.

Stacey, K. & Groves, S. 1985, *Strategies for Problem Solving*, Victoria College Press, Melbourne.

This book provides a thoroughly trialled programme for developing mathematical thinking in junior secondary classes. It provides teachers with a practical synthesis of problems, strategies and classroom techniques for encouraging students to reflect on their experience. The underlying teaching strategy is to involve students in intriguing mathematical activities, specifically chosen to demonstrate particular problem solving skills. The sample lesson plans contain a wealth of information including detailed aims, suggestions for classroom organization, explicit teaching strategies, extracts from children's work and a discussion of common errors, mathematical notes and copyright-released worksheets.

CHAPTER 5 BEYOND THE MATHEMATICS CLASSROOM: NUMERACY FOR LEARNING

Paulos, J. A. 1989, *Innumeracy: Mathematical illiteracy and its consequences*, Hill and Wang.

Both readable and provocative, this book defines innumeracy as an inability to deal comfortably with the basic ideas of number and chance. John Paulos focuses on the interaction of people in their daily lives with the results of mathematical thinking or, more precisely, a lack of mathematical thinking, and in particular, 'a lack of numerical perspective, an exaggerated appreciation for meaningless coincidence, a credulous acceptance of pseudosciences, an inability to recognize social trade-offs' (p.5). He is particularly critical of the lack of emphasis in education on such things as estimation, inductive reasoning, and the nature of chance processes, all of which permeate our lives. While one could readily argue that some of the misconceptions or logical fallacies he details may be addressed in fields other than mathematics, his essential point is compelling.

Open University 1980, *Mathematics Across the Curriculum*, The Open University Press, Milton Keynes, UK.

This is a fully developed Open University course for practicing teachers at the primary and secondary levels. The course defines the 'basics' in terms of adult needs for using mathematics. Sets of case studies provide a wide range of examples of uses of mathematics in 'adult contexts' and 'school contexts'. These, together with 14 units addressing topics such as planning, measuring, getting started, making sense of space, and representing for understanding, provide an excellent basis for considering numeracy demands across and beyond the mathematics classroom. The authors focus particularly on what they call 'informed numeracy', and on the differences between skill-getting and skill-choosing and -using.

CHAPTER 6 BEYOND THE MATHEMATICS CLASSROOM: NUMERACY ON THE JOB

Austwick, K., Richards, P. & Livingston, K. 1985, *Maths at Work*, Cambridge University Press, Cambridge. (Student Booklets and Teacher's Guide)

This project had its origins in research commissioned by the Cockcroft Committee. The research investigated the mathematics involved in the employment undertaken by young school-leavers in the 16–18 years age bracket. A series of thirteen student booklets (with titles such as 'Recording figures', 'Checking procedures', 'Statistical methods' and 'Drawings and related calculations') profile the actual work of young employees and the mathematics they do, and provide a variety of learning experiences for students between 14 and 17 years of age. The materials are an excellent resource and the teacher's guide is clear and comprehensive. Although the materials are based on young workers in England and Wales, they have considerable relevance for Australian students.

Foyster, J. 1988, *Mathematics Beyond the Classroom*, Curriculum Development Centre, Canberra.

An illuminating and interesting book which reports on a small investigation of the mathematics required by young workers in the electrical, hospitality, and metal trades, horticulture and business studies. The publication asks the question 'What improves on-the-job mathematics?' and considers the contradictions and conflicts involved in balancing educational and vocational concerns. It also provides a review of earlier Australian research on the same issue.

Howson, G. & McLone, R. (ed.), 1983, *Maths at Work*, Heinemann Educational Books, London.

A collection of articles each of which discusses the mathematics used in a particular field. The topics range from safety in the chemical industry, to mimicry, to traffic flows in roundabouts and carbon dating in archaeology. Written particularly with teachers in mind, the readings have much wider appeal. The articles provide the history of a problem, discuss how practical problems become mathematical, and how insights about a situation may be gained by the mathematical study of it. While the applications are not those of the 'average worker', they do indicate the versatility of mathematics and its applicability to a wide range of problems and fields often not regarded as particularly mathematical.

CHAPTER 7 EVALUATING ASSESSMENT: EXAMINING ALTERNATIVES

Clarke, David 1988, *MCTP Assessment Kit*, Curriculum Development Centre, Canberra.

This professional development package provides a rationale for altering assessment strategies in mathematics and documents alternatives in some detail. It includes linked lessons which indicate how assessment can be part of the ongoing learning and teaching processes, and blackline masters to be used in professional development programmes. The kit is extremely practical and makes a significant contribution to the debate on assessment in mathematics and can be used either for professional development programmes or by teachers working individually or in groups.

CHAPTER 8 REFORMING MATHEMATICS: SUPPORTING TEACHERS TO RESHAPE THEIR PRACTICE

Lovitt, C. & Clarke, Doug 1988, *MCTP Activity Bank* (Vol. 1), Curriculum Development Centre, Canberra.

Lovitt, C. & Clarke, Doug 1989, *MCTP Activity Bank* (Vol. 2), Curriculum Development Centre, Canberra.

These two activity banks are part of the material outcome of a professional development programme for primary and secondary teachers of mathematics. Chapters include Mental arithmetic, Concept learning, Social issues, Mathematical modelling, Estimation, and Visual imagery. Each chapter documents lessons and highlights what it is about these lessons that make them 'work'. It is an excellent and highly successful programme which provides detailed advice on teaching practice, communicating in very powerful ways the thinking of the teachers who developed the activities.

Notes on the authors

Anne Chapman has taught mathematics at secondary school, TAFE and university levels. She was tutor in numeracy at Murdoch University assisting students to develop their numeracy skills across the curriculum. She is currently engaged in doctoral studies in the area of the construction and communication of meaning in the mathematics classroom.

Doug Clarke is lecturer in mathematics education at the Institute of Catholic Education, Oakleigh, Victoria. From 1985 to 1987 he was the National Facilitator of the Mathematics Curriculum and Teaching Program (MCTP), a Curriculum Development Centre (CDC) professional development programme for teachers of mathematics K–10. In the past he has taught secondary mathematics, worked as a mathematics consultant in both primary and secondary schools, and worked with pre-service students at Monash University. One of his major interests is strategies of support for teachers as they seek to explore 'new territory' in mathematics education.

John Foyster is the author of *Mathematics Beyond the Classroom* (CDC, Canberra, 1988). He is coordinator of Evaluation and Curriculum Development for the Senior Secondary Assessment Board of South Australia and is currently working on a book about the Schools Commission's Innovation programme.

Lynn Joffe is currently an independent consultant, mathematics educator and psychologist. She works in both primary and high schools and in tertiary institutions and is involved in developing curricula and assessments. She was formerly a Senior Research Officer at the National Foundation for Educational Research (NFER) in Britain, where she was part of the Assessment of Performance Unit (APU) team, concerned with national assessment of performance in and attitudes towards mathematics. In recent years, she has spent considerable time working in Australia at Monash University and at Brisbane College of Advanced Education.

Marian Kemp has taught mathematics in the United Kingdom, Jamaica, Bahamas, Nigeria and Australia for sixteen years. She is now a lecturer in mathematics education at Murdoch University, involved with the pre-service and in-service education of teachers at the primary and secondary levels. Her research interest is in numeracy across the curriculum.

Barry Kissane is a lecturer in mathematics curriculum studies at Murdoch University. He has taught high school mathematics and mathematics education for nineteen years. Recently he has worked in curriculum development in the United States and teacher education in Indonesia. His current interests include numeracy, technology, mathematical thinking and gender issues in mathematics education.

Charles Lovitt has been involved in many state and national mathematics activities. He has been co-author of the Victorian RIME (Reality in Mathematics Education) and, more recently, coordinator of the national Mathematics Curriculum and Teaching Program (MCTP). He currently works within the Victorian Ministry of Education coordinating a statewide in-service programme for mathematics and science teachers.

Alistair McIntosh is senior lecturer in education in the Department of Mathematics and Computer Education at the Western Australian College of Advanced Education. He was previously mathematics advisor with the Leicestershire Local Education Authority, during which time he was a member of the Cockcroft Committee of Inquiry into the Teaching of Mathematics in Schools and Chairman of the Association of Teachers of Mathematics (UK). He has also been President of the Mathematical Association of Western Australia. His interests are in primary mathematics education generally but particularly in the changing face of computation.

Kaye Stacey is a senior lecturer in the School of Education at the University of Melbourne where she is involved in the preparation of secondary teachers. Previously she has worked at Victoria College in pre-service primary teacher education and at the Universities of Sydney and Melbourne teaching mathematics. Her current interests are in problem solving and mathematical thinking at all ages, and in the processes of curriculum change.

Max Stephens works for the Victorian Ministry of Education in its School Programs Branch. His responsibilities there include the coordination of professional development programmes for literacy and numeracy in primary schools, and the introduction of VCE Mathematics courses in Years 11 and 12. He is currently the President-elect of the Australian Association of Mathematics Teachers and past-President of the Mathematical Association of Victoria.

Malcolm Swan is a lecturer at the Shell Centre for Mathematical Education, Nottingham University, England, where for the past 10 years he has been conducting research into children's understanding of mathematical concepts. A teacher still at heart, he is particularly interested in developing methods and materials which encourage children to use mathematics in their everyday lives.

Sue Willis is a senior lecturer in mathematics education at Murdoch University where she is involved in the education of primary and secondary teachers. For the period 1988–90, she is seconded to the Commonwealth's Curriculum Policy Unit in Canberra, where she coordinated the Commonwealth programme, The Education of Girls in Mathematics and Science, and is part of the writing team for the national mathematics curriculum statement. Her interests lie with equity issues in education, particularly gender equity, and the development of numeracy.

Index